E RM

250 293

BA /JC

The Strides of Vishnu

The Strides of Vishnu

Hindu Culture in Historical Perspective

ARIEL GLUCKLICH

OXFORD
UNIVERSITY PRESS

2008

OXFORD
UNIVERSITY PRESS

Oxford University Press, Inc., publishes works that further
Oxford University's objective of excellence
in research, scholarship, and education.

Oxford   New York
Auckland   Cape Town   Dar es Salaam   Hong Kong   Karachi
Kuala Lumpur   Madrid   Melbourne   Mexico City   Nairobi
New Delhi   Shanghai   Taipei   Toronto

With offices in
Argentina   Austria   Brazil   Chile   Czech Republic   France   Greece
Guatemala   Hungary   Italy   Japan   Poland   Portugal   Singapore
South Korea   Switzerland   Thailand   Turkey   Ukraine   Vietnam

Published by Oxford University Press, Inc.
198 Madison Avenue, New York, New York 10016

www.oup.com

Oxford is a registered trademark of Oxford University Press

Library of Congress Cataloging-in-Publication Data
Glucklich, Ariel.
The strides of Vishnu : Hindu culture in historical perspective /
Ariel Glucklich.
    p. cm.
Includes bibliographical references and index.
ISBN 978-0-19-531405-2
1. Hinduism and culture—History.   2. India—Civilization.
I. Title.
BL1215.C76G58 2007
294.5'16—dc22   2007009300

1 3 5 7 9 8 6 4 2

Printed in the United States of America
on acid-free paper

For Natalie, Elon, and Avi

For Natalie, Elon, and Avi

Acknowledgments

I wrote this book with my students in mind—before my very eyes in fact—and with feedback from many of them. I wish to acknowledge the following in particular: Ketan Bhalla, Samir Bhatiani, Colin Burke, Tim Casey, Prajakta Chitre, Aneesh Deshpande, Elizabeth Fossett, Sunder Jambunathan, Anuj Jayakar, Shaan Kataria, Amit Krishnan, Parsa Ludhi, Robert Macina, Ravi Magia, Lauren McGaughy, Emma Miller, Sameer Mittal, Anisha Modi, John Moellering, Runit Mungale, Emily Robbins, Hemal Sampat, Samit Shah, Mira Shastry, Amaan Siddiqi, Shelly Singh, Mithuna Sivaraman, Simi Sonecha. I owe a special debt of gratitude to William Elison and thanks also to Wendy Doniger for recommending him. I am grateful to Cynthia Read as always, to the generously critical readers she recruited, and, of course, to Jennifer Hansen.

Contents

Chronology

BCE

2800–1700	Indus Valley Civilization; Urban centers (Mohenjodaro, Harappa).
1400–900	Early Vedic period. Indo-Aryans settle Punjab and further east.
900–500	Late Vedic period. Continued Indo-Aryan settlement in Ganges plain. Rise of Mahajanapadas.
800–400	Spreading deforestation, urbanization (wood construction). Painted Grey Ware. Kaushambi is earliest major city.
500	Rise of Magadha east of Kaushambi.
400	Approximate date of Buddha's death.
364	Nanda dynasty.
327–25	Alexander the Great in Taxila region.
320	Rise of Maurya dynasty founded by Chandragupta.
268–233	Rule of Ashoka (third Maurya ruler).
185	Sunga dynasty begins under Pushyamitra.
175	Rise of Indo-Greek empire in northwest India.
155–130	Menander (Milinda) rules Indo-Greek kingdom.
57–35	Azes I; beginning of Vikrama era.
100–0	Rise of southern and eastern kingdoms (Shatavahana, Kalinga).

CE

30	Rise of Kushana empire.
78	Rule of Kanishka begins; start of Shaka era.
250	Decline of Shatavahana.
320	Chandragupta I; rise of Gupta empire.
335–75	Rule of Samudragupta.
375–413	Chandragupta II and peak of Gupta empire; Kalidasa.
405–11	Fa-hsien visits India.
415–97	Kumaragupta, Skandagupta, Budhagupta; decline of Gupta empire.
500–27	Hun rule in northern India.
606–47	King Harsha of Kanauj.
630–43	Hsuan-tsang visits India.
770–821	Pala dynasty in East India.
788–820	Shankra.
985–1014	Rise of Chola empire in South India.
1000–27	Mahmud of Ghazni invades India.
1137	Death of Vaishnava theologian Ramanuja.
1192	Mahmud of Ghur defeats Rajputs; Muslim hegemony.
1206	Delhi sultanate begins with Aibak.
1297–1311	Sultanate wars with Mongols; conquest of South India.
1320–88	Tughluq dynasty in Delhi.
1451–1526	Lodi dynasty (Sultanate) in Delhi.
1526	First of the Mughals, Baber, defeats last Delhi sultan.
1556	The Mughal Akbar becomes ruler in Delhi.
1605–27	Rule of Jahangir and his wife Nur Jahan.
1627–58	Shah Jahan builds Red Fort and Taj Mahal.
1658–1707	Rule of the Mughal Aurangzeb.
1757	Battle of Plassey; Robert Clive defeats the nawab of Bengal.
1765	Clive becomes governor of Bengal.
1793	British Permanent Settlement changes revenue collection in Bengal.
1843–48	British rule consolidated.
1857–8	Sepoy mutiny; East India Company rule ends; India under the Crown.
1877	Queen Victoria becomes empress of India.
1885	First Indian National Congress.
1905	Partition of Bengal; swadeshi campaign begins (against English products).
1906	Muslim League founded.

1919   Rowlatt Acts; Amritsar (Jallianwala Bagh) massacre.
1930   Gandhi's most successful campaign—the salt march.
1940   Muslim League adopts Pakistan Resolution.
1947   Indian independence; partition.
1948   Assassination of Gandhi.

The Strides of Vishnu

FIGURE I.I. Map of Ancient India.

Introduction

Sixty-five miles south of Patna in the state of Bihar is the ancient sacred city of Gaya. Situated on a tributary of the Ganges River—the Falgu—Gaya has been a pilgrimage center, a *tirtha*, for nearly three millennia. Buddhist scriptures claim that Siddhartha Gautama (Buddha) meditated and attained enlightenment under the Bodhi tree in Bodhgaya, just a few miles away. Every year, thousands of Buddhist pilgrims arrive from all over the world to see the place where their religion was born.

In the old center of Gaya stands an impressive Hindu temple, which the Buddhist pilgrims ignore. Queen Ahilya Bai of Indore built it in 1787, following a visit to this sacred place. She was not interested in Buddha's enlightenment; she had other reasons for visiting Gaya. The first was a footprint-like indentation in the rock measuring about 40 centimeters, and the second was an adjacent banyan tree called Akshyabat, or Immortal Banyan. The temple courtyard she commissioned enclosed both the tree and the footprint, and the temple is now called Vishnupad Temple (Temple of Vishnu's Footstep; *pad* means step).

The "footprint" attracts pilgrims, followers of Vishnu who wish to see a mythical event recorded in stone, while the Akshyabat draws a different crowd of visitors. These come to perform—with the help of priests—elaborate rituals, in which rice balls are offered to deceased male relatives on the first anniversary of their death. Many of these visitors—though by no means all—believe that performing these ancient rituals (called *pinda-pradana* or *shraddha*) under Akshyabat guarantees their relatives a happy afterlife.

These are just the most prominent attractions of Gaya. The town and surrounding countryside make up, in fact, a whole constellation of sacred objects. The river itself is sacred, and a number of bathing tanks near it are especially purifying. There are several other banyan and pipal trees besides Akshyabat, along with sacred *tulasi* plants, which are reminders of the god Vishnu and his consort Lakshmi. Nearby hills (Ramshila, Brahmayoni, Murali) are sacred, and in addition to the Vishnupad Temple, pilgrims attend several others.

Hundreds of places like Gaya can be found throughout India, even a few other temples called Vishnupad. The Akshyabat and its memorial rituals too, are not unique. Near Asi Ghat in Varanasi, a majestic *nim* tree like the Akshyabat towers above the rice ball rituals. Casual visitors to Gaya and other such places rarely fail to note what they call the "colorfulness" and intensity of the place. They see *puja* offerings of water, flowers, leaves, fruits, along with the burning of camphor flames, verbal offerings of mantras (*japa*), storytellings, group recitations (*sankirtana*), music performances, gift giving, and other, less ritualized activities. An aura of saturated religious meaning pervades Gaya, but it seems just beyond the reach of the visitor's grasp. The temple architecture impresses visually, of course; the suggestion of a revered myth—the three strides of Vishnu—adds another dimension, ancient and timeless at the same time. The rituals for the ancestors, the priestly chants, obsequies under a large tree: How does it all fit together? Must you multiply it by one thousand to get a sense of Hinduism as a whole or is this one place a perfect nutshell?

Because I have named this book after the myth, it is only fitting that I should begin with a brief summary of its plot, at least one version that appears in a medieval text, the *Vayu Purana*. During a certain cosmic age, the king of the demons, whose name was Bali, controlled all the worlds. Vishnu became incarnated as a dwarf and approached the demons as they were performing their sacrifice. The dwarf asked Bali, on behalf of the other gods, for as much space as he could cover in three strides. The demon readily agreed, and Vishnu took three steps: the first covered the entire earth, the second covered the atmosphere, and the third measured heaven in its entirety. Revealing himself in his own brilliant light, Vishnu then sent the demons to hell, and he himself became master of the three worlds.

One of those steps has left its trace on the ground in Gaya, pilgrims to Vishnupad Temple say. The myth itself has been told in countless versions dating back to India's oldest text—the *Rig-Veda* (1.22.17–21). Each telling of the story differs from the others in some way, however trivial, and each change brings with it a new meaning. In some versions, the dwarf explicitly represents the sacrifice (the altar) by means of which all the worlds are won. Other versions could be, more implicitly, about time (overcoming space), about the journey of the sun across the firmament, or perhaps about the conquest of the entire universe by the spaceless (and immeasurable) soul. The story can even be about ritual food, as Laurie L. Patton has recently demonstrated.

None of that has much to do with Buddha's enlightenment or even directly with the ritual actions beneath the Akshyabat. In all likelihood, the tree had been venerated long before Buddha meditated nearby, perhaps before the *Rig-Veda* was composed. Sacred trees grow everywhere in India, and the practice of revering them dates back to ancient autochthonous cults in which phenomena of nature—certainly enormous banyan trees—were regarded as seats of spiritual presences. The Buddhist and Hindu customs came later.

What we see in Gaya is a highly textured interlocking of multiple traditions comfortably coexisting in a single location. Other places throughout India function in the same way, often adding elements from Jainism, classical Greek cultures, Islam, tribal customs, or other sources. The full collage of India's cultural map includes them all.

One of my professors at Harvard, David Eckel, once compared India to a pan of lasagna. Several layers of culture can be identified in any location you wish to explore. Layering can be found in Europe and the Near East, too, of course: the difference is the sauce, if you will. In India, rising civilizations have tended to embrace or encompass existing ones instead of annihilating them. The result is a single multiflavored dish. You can see this inclusiveness in Gaya and everywhere in India—a huge pan of lasagna indeed: measured from its northern edge in what is today Afghanistan down to its southern tip in Kanyakumari, the historic Land of Bharata (Bharatavarsha), spanning over 2,000 miles. Walking or riding an ox-cart from end to end is a six-month journey! And with their stunningly diverse natural and human ecologies, the two geographical extremes are worlds apart. Perhaps a better metaphor than the lasagna pan would be the whole kitchen. This diversity raises questions of definition in regard to Hinduism: Is it a single religion or is "Hinduism" a convenient (and imported) term that masks and does not fully unify a whole range of Indian cultures and traditions? Most scholars opt for the second option, as do I, but this book will revisit this question in a number of places.

I grew up in a country that lies at precisely the opposite end of the cultural and geographical scale—Israel. During my school years in the sixties, it was common practice to journey by foot in the paths of historic figures and events. We trekked the pilgrimage routes to Jerusalem, explored the landscape of the Maccabean wars, and followed the rebels against the Romans up the path to

Masada. The history of Israel is ancient—its distances minuscule. You could jog from the hometown of Jesus (Nazareth) to the place where Salah al-Din defeated the crusaders (Karnei Hittim) in less time than it would take you to run the New York marathon.

This is a tiny pan. The layers, too, are nearly devoid of sauce. Like India, Israel is the birthplace of many religions, but its history is a story of displacement and rejection, not encompassment. The many Canaanite peoples, the Israelites, Persians, Greeks, Syrians, Romans, Christians, Arabs, Ottomans—successive layers insisted on different, better ideas. The Jewish narrative, which Christians have misleadingly called Judeo-Christian (there is no true synthesis there), became the dominant one, as we know: a single creation, a troubled but exclusive relationship to God, tests, failures, redemption, a final ending. Many of my readers will have come from a similar cultural world: one story, one (albeit contested) meaning. So how can one write a short book about a civilization like India's, where vast spaces encompass so many cultures without ever imposing a single or even central narrative?

That is why I have chosen Vishnu's strides as the metaphor for conveying the type of effort required. A dwarf who covers all of existence with a mere three strides—the presumption (I don't know the Sanskrit word for chutzpah) of "covering" Hinduism—a vast conglomeration of traditions—in one small book. The myth of Vishnu suggests that some things can stand for other things, either as metonymy or as ritual symbols. The ancient ritual altar is both a symbol for God (Prajapati) and a part of God. Similarly, these twelve chapters represent a tiny fraction of what could be (and has been) said about Hinduism. Nonetheless, they capture something essential.

Here is a different metaphor: Imagine taking a visitor from Europe, who wants to "see America," on a cross-country drive. You only have two weeks to get from Rehoboth Beach, Delaware, to San Francisco, so you will not be zigzagging much. You may choose a single road, say Highway 50, and stick with it. Your visitor will get the Appalachians, Mississippi River, the Great Plains, and the Rocky Mountains. He will miss the Great Lakes, New Orleans, Glacier Park, and all the rest. My twelve chapters are the functional equivalent of taking the single road in this way. Your friend will "see America"; in some sense, he can talk about it intelligently. But he will have to come back and take other routes if he wishes to see and know more.

Properly speaking, this is not a book about Hinduism at all. It neither surveys nor summarizes its vast subject; other books do this exceptionally well, . As this book follows its single track, it leaves out landscapes that some might consider the best parts of Hinduism. The reader will find virtually nothing from Tamil (South Indian) literature, miserably few details about yoga, not one single word about the *Kama Sutra!* I have chosen one narrative within Hinduism that interests me, and I think it provides a good way to explore my subject, but it must be remembered that it is only one narrative among myriad.

The subject of this book is, in a word, thought. What did some Indians, usually leading intellectuals, think about ultimate reality (God, Brahman, the world beyond the senses)? What did they think about the world? And how did they relate the two domains?

When we ourselves investigate India's past, we find these three braided strands of human living at work—ultimate reality; the world; the relation of the two. At different moments in India's long history, priests, scientists, encyclopedia writers, and other scholars have expressed their visions of ultimate reality with great eloquence. At the same moments, other people have been busy building things: cities, roads, bridges, altars, temples, theaters, social and political institutions. Texts reveal some of the intellectual riches, and archeological excavations many of the material achievements. But it cuts the other way, too: the texts often tell us about world-building, while the physical objects reflect planning and thinking. At no point in India's history did a significant number of leading thinkers believe that the world was irrelevant or that the domains of the spirit and matter could not be mediated.

Consider, for instance, the ancient sacrifice and the altar on which it took place. Priests ran the sacrifice, men who were experts in the domain of divine mysteries. Meanwhile, lowly workmen—bricklayers—had to shape, bake, and place bricks into the physical structure that made the sacrifice possible, the altar. The two types of workers (priest and bricklayer) required a third, someone who would mediate between the physical and the spiritual tasks. This was the mathematician, who planned the geometrical design for the altar and worked out the best way to execute the plans. The altars, as I will show in chapter 3, were remarkably complex structures, often shaped like animals and birds and requiring significant geometrical calculations. Here we see the three strands: the religious idea, the material work, and the mediating science—the transcendent, the worldly, and the scientific technique.

The second strand, and the thinking that went into it, fascinates me beyond the other two; in a sense, it encompasses both. This is where human reason joins the material world with ultimate concerns. It may not be as exotic or colorful as India's expansive theologies, but it is not as mundane as India's sociology and political economies.

Naturally, the second, mediating strand is far from simple. I shall be looking at two major types of "rationality" (to use a term from Western sociology of knowledge) that it embraces: symbolic (or representational) and participatory (indexical). Symbolic rationality includes, for example, Sanskrit grammar, or the science of iconography, with which temple images were designed to symbolize abstract ideas. In contrast, participatory rationality can be seen in such sciences as Ayurvedic medicine or medieval alchemy, or in practices such as women's vows. The two rationalities are the dominant methods pragmatic Hindus have used throughout history to reason about religion. A third type of rationality also emerged in India, best exemplified in the philosophy of Shankara (eighth century CE). Here the distinction between the two realms of matter and spirit is regarded as false; there is only one reality (Brahman), and it is not accessible to reason at all. It constitutes a unique way of knowing—"insight" may be the best term. This philosophy, Advaita Vedanta, has been very prestigious in India, but it remains the exception to the norm of participatory practices and symbolic thought.

This book's story of reason's work in bringing together God and world in India unfolds historically though several major stations. As the historical narrative proceeds, we should remain aware of the contexts in which Indians have worked within the world, both to build things and to create meaning. The fascination with ultimate reality has always gone hand in hand with the desire to build, rule, fight, and perform on stage. This book gives a small sample of the contexts in which this story of God and world unfolds.

Summary of the Chapters

The first chapter briefly discusses the arrival of scientific archeology in India under the supervision of Mortimer Wheeler. In the excavation of Taxila, he used new methods for uncovering, dating, and interpreting the succession of cultures in a given location. I contrast this type of excavation with the early medieval digging that took place in Ellora and resulted in the chiseling of the Mt. Kailas temple there out of sheer rock. These two types of excavation, used as metaphors, raise the question of knowledge: How should we come to know other cultures in a postcolonial age and how should we think about the history of knowledge that combines religion with science?

Most books about a religion in its historical context start at the beginning. This is a narrative-based choice: a good story starts at the time and place where things began, like the Genesis of the Hebrew Bible. Often, a religion begins with its founding figure (Moses, Jesus, Buddha) and grows from that base like a tree. For Hinduism, which does not have a distinct historic founder, the beginning was the Indus River civilization, the Rigvedic culture of the Indo-Aryans, or both of these. But Hinduism is decisively not a single narrative: the metaphor of one tree with one root system simply does not work. It is a constellation of religions only some of which look back to a primordial past for their origins. But more troubling yet, the beginnings of Hinduism have been notoriously difficult to document and therefore subject to heated disagreements. Chapter 2 briefly looks at these arguments but focuses primarily on some of the major intellectual accomplishments of India's oldest literary body: the Vedas. The chapter examines the esoteric knowledge of the oldest text, the *Rig-Veda*, with special emphasis on its ritual application to the construction of the sacrificial altar.

Chapter 3 follows the archeological work of G. R. Sharma in Kaushambi, near Allahabad, where the Yamuna and Ganges rivers join. The chapter looks at this important urban center during the first historically documented period in Indian history, that of the Maurya Empire, or more specifically, the third century BCE. The discussion is anchored in the type of evidence that allows contemporary students to understand both the material and intellectual cultures of a major urban center in ancient northern India.

Chapter 4 looks at the latest books in the Vedic corpus, the Upanishads. The oldest of these continued the tradition of ritual speculation but moved to explore the homology between the human and the cosmic. The esoteric knowledge of the *Rig-Veda* thus gave way to psychological introspection, which yielded revolutionary insights into the nature of reality. The chapter looks at King Janaka of Videha, who sponsored a contest among the experts of his day on these subjects. The contest in the royal court provides the framework for exploring the philosophy of Yajnavalkya—a central figure in the Upanishads and one of the most creative minds in ancient India.

Chapter 5 returns to the historic period of Kaushambi during the Mauryan years—our point of departure in chapter 2. With the Vedic period over, the economic, political, and religious picture becomes increasingly complex. The centuries between the third century BCE and fourth century CE are the most formative in the emergence of Hinduism. This chapter looks at many of the material and intellectual contributions of this age, including the two great epics (*Mahabharata, Ramayana*) and the flowering of the Vedic sciences. Geometry, grammar, political science, and the legal and social sciences (dharma) will receive special attention because of the way they express the efforts to link ideas about transcendent reality with pragmatic needs.

Chapter 6 moves forward through the centuries between the Mauryan empire and the next great Indian empire, the Gupta. During these centuries, a succession of numerous rulers, including several foreign dynasties, dominated in North India. This chapter focuses on the important city of Mathura and on the Kushana ruler Kanishka as one example of the challenges of political unrest and cultural diversity that confronted the Brahmins. A number of traditions and literary masterpieces emerged as the definitive foundations of Hindu political and religious legitimacy. The most famous is the *Bhagavad Gita*, although an earlier precedent will also be examined: the *Shvetashvatara Upanishad*. The *Manu Smriti* was also a work of intellectual synthesis, but the most important response to the centrifugal forces of rampant pluralism in Mathura was Krishna devotional religion, as one sees in such texts as the *Harivamsa* and the tenth book of the *Bhagavata Purana*.

The years ushered in by the Gupta dynasty are often described as the golden era of Hindu civilization. Chapter 7 will focus on a number of narrower themes that run through those creative years. The rise of the Guptas, particularly Samudragupta, demonstrates the maturing understanding of what makes a legitimate king, both as the sponsor of religious events such as the horse sacrifice—a very old institution by that time—and as the very embodiment of Vishnu. The chapter will look at the creative genius of the Gupta years—the theater of Kalidasa and the drama theory of Bharatamuni, the new temples and iconography, the science of architecture, the enormous encyclopedia the *Brihat Samhita* of Varahamihira, and other cultural achievements. I will argue that the intellectual and artistic accomplishments of the cultural elite are ultimately products of symbolic sciences, indications of a refined sensitivity to the gap between God and world and to the bridging of arts and sciences.

The book up to this point has tilted in favor of elite masterpieces, the work largely of Brahmin men. Certainly the vast literary corpus of India lends itself to this. Chapter 8 tries to move in the direction of popular thought, the intellectual products of women, villagers, craftsmen, doctors, and magicians. Unfortunately, because the literary record does not reflect the work of these social groups, we are still limited to the literature of the elite. However, some works—the *Atharvaveda, Kaushika Sutra, Rig Vidhana, Charaka Samhita, Devi Mahatmya,* and others—reflect the more pragmatic rationality of those who did not produce the religious and philosophical masterpieces. The chapter will examine the more popular, less metaphysically inclined rationality, which aimed at control over the world and recognized its intrinsic powers.

Chapter 9 examines the texts most closely associated with medieval Hinduism—the Puranas. I focus on a limited number of themes in order to clarify these often difficult texts. Prayaga and Kashi were two of the most important centers of pilgrimage in northern India, as they are today. By means of documents called *mahatmyas,* the two places vied for supremacy as the most sacred and purifying for pilgrims. Sacred geography and sacred history as well—Puranic cosmography and cosmology—are important ways the Puranas mapped the world. The chapter looks at such mythical conceptions as types of rationality—ways of understanding reality and creating a meaningful ethos.

I examine two familiar myths, with an emphasis on Vishnu: the flood myth and the myth of the churning of the ocean. Mythical interpretation is a politically saturated activity, and chapter 9 points out some of its pitfalls but highlights the rewards of understanding these immensely influential texts.

Chapter 10 returns to the intellectual traditions of the Brahminical elite, specifically philosophers. The topic of Indian philosophy is immense, with the six major schools and their subsidiary branches, the Buddhist and Jain philosophers, and other intellectual traditions such as the Carvakas, which have been gaining increasing attention in recent years. Out of sheer necessity, the chapter focuses primarily on two schools: the two Mimamsas—the early (Purva) Mimamsa and the later (Uttara) Mimamsa, better known as Advaita Vedanta. Specifically, I shall focus on Kumarila Bhatta and Shankara, the eighth-century philosophers who, had they met, might have carried out a debate on the nature of ultimate reality, the conditions and methods for knowing that reality, and the value of scriptural interpretation.

Chapter 11 briefly surveys key religious developments during the centuries of Islamic rule in northern India. These are framed by Alberuni's scientific survey of medieval India and by Jacob Needham's monumental and empathetic efforts to evaluate the scientific histories of Asia. The chapter will show that traditional forms of knowledge—the theology and popular devotion of men like Chaitanya, Tulsidas, and Kabir—demonstrate that Hindu thought was not intrinsically aversive to an understanding of the world. In fact, although hardly scientific by Needham's standards, popular and mystical devotion (bhakti) undermined both conservative dharma and pure philosophical speculation in favor of a reformed and practical social outlook.

The last chapter briefly looks at key intellectual developments in response to British colonialism in modern India, focusing on Rammohun Roy, Mohandas K. Gandhi, and Sri Aurobindo Ghosh. I examine Aurobindo's concept of *sanatana-dharma*, the eternal dharma, as the imposition of unity on a pluralistic and multivocal tradition.

Although this book is not an apologetic work, it is not a survey or an objective study either. It assumes that over the centuries Indian thinkers and actors have reasoned about the world they have encountered and have discovered meaning in it with the best tools at their disposal. Although some of their work may be subject to criticism, this can only follow a serious effort to understand the creative and intellectual impetus behind Hindu world-building. And as Indian communities grow larger and more influential in the West, the study of Hinduism will become increasingly implicated in our own evolving worldview.

I

The Dig and the Temple

One evening in early August 1943, Brigadier General Mortimer
Wheeler was resting in his tent after a long day of poring over
maps, drawing up plans for the invasion of Sicily. Wheeler was a tall,
rugged-looking man who sported a bushy moustache in the fashion
of English officers of his time. Through the open flap of his tent, he
spotted the corps commander, General Sir Brian Horrock, hurry-
ing across the encampment, waving a telegram in his hand. Barely
concealing his excitement, Horrock handed the telegram to Wheeler
and exclaimed: "I say, have you seen this—they want you as [reading]
'Director General of archaeology in India!'—Why, you must be rather
a king-pin at this sort of thing! You know, I thought you were a reg-
ular soldier!"

Thus in the hot Algerian evening, with his eyes cast across the
Mediterranian on the historic battle ahead, Mortimer Wheeler begins his heroic autobiographical narrative about archeology in India.
The moment in the desert reads as both trivial and momentous: the
redirected career of one British officer ushers in a new era for Indian archeology. Of course, the general noted, he could not leave his
post before the invasion. He finally boarded his ship—the *City of
Exeter*—to join a convoy of allied ships headed east in February 1944.

Mortimer Wheeler had been invited to become the director general of archaeology by the India Office of the British government in
its last years of rule in South Asia, and by the viceroy of India (Lord
Wavell), who governed on behalf of the Crown in Delhi. Summoning

a general from the battlefields of Europe was an extraordinary measure, an admission both of the desperate condition of Indian archeology and an acknowledgment of its vital importance. By the 1940s, India had distinguished itself as one of the great archeological locations in the world, along with Greece, Egypt, and Mesopotamia. A succession of eminent archeologists preceded Wheeler at the directorship of Indian archeology, even before its official founding in 1871, when Alexander Cunningham became its first official director. The renowned scientists who followed Cunningham at the post included James Burgess, John Marshall, N. G. Majumdar, and K. N. Dikshit. These men—and many others—had supervised some of the most remarkable discoveries in archeological science and brought India its prestige as a storehouse of great historical treasures.

Cunningham's colleague James Prinsep not only discovered the famous rock edict of King Ashoka at Dhauli, Orissa, he was the man who between 1834 and 1837 deciphered the Brahmi and Kharoshthi scripts in which the Indian king had his pronouncements written down. This achievement was critical in establishing a firm toehold for dating in India's history, which had been notoriously lacking in datable evidence. Decades later, it was John Marshall who excavated the Indus River cities of Harappa and Mohenjodaro and pushed back the age of Indian civilizations to the early centuries of the third millennium BCE—contemporary with the Nile and Mesopotamian civilizations and far earlier than Greece. It was Marshall, too, who excavated Taxila—the great Indian-Hellenistic center in northwest India and the first place on Mortimer Wheeler's itinerary as he set out to survey his vast new realm.

The new director took the Frontier Mail train from Bombay to Delhi and from there to Rawalpindi—the British military base in what was then called the North-west Frontier, the northern region of Punjab and Kashmir. Taxila, or Takshasila, was a further 20 miles from the city, in a valley bounded by the massive Himalaya range. Wheeler described a valley covered with yellow mustard seed and flooded with sunlight as he arrived. As he surveyed the beautiful scene and the long-neglected archeological dig at the four sites of Taxila, Wheeler knew that it was time to fix Indian archeology and that Taxila was the perfect place to launch his campaign. After all, it was here that the young Macedonian king, Alexander, had begun his own conquest of the lands of the Indus River and its six tributaries in 327 BCE—the anchor date for Indian historiography. But it was Taxila, too, that made Wheeler conscious of what exactly ailed Indian archeology and what had to be done.

Despite impressive early discoveries, Indian archeology suffered from a number of serious flaws. Too much work was invested in uncovering spectacular objects, "treasures of the past," which then found their way into museums. Monuments—especially religious objects such as Buddhist stupas, Hindu temples, statues, and artwork—were highly prized, drawing both attention and money for exploration and preservation. Though valuable and inspiring, such archeological work contributed far too little to the scientific reconstruction of past cultures in their contemporary and sequential settings. Worse, Marshall, who had focused on a small number of prestigious digs, failed to apply the principle of stratification to his work, opting instead for what Wheeler contemptuously called the bench-level method. The cure for this, Wheeler insisted, was stratigraphy.

General Augustus Pitt-Rivers had adapted stratification, from the science of geology, to archeology. The method involved vertical slices (trenches) at strategic locations around the dig—each section revealing the layers that accumulated with the succession of destruction and rebuilding of the site by generations of inhabitants. Archeologists who ignored this method would fail to map the correct sequence of cultures in any given location. This was Marshall's great failing. And because Marshall also tended to ignore less glamorous sites throughout India, he remained unable to map out a connected history of cultural sequence for all of India. Both vertical and horizontal knowledge of India's past thus remained a patchwork of impressions bounded by vast empty spaces. Text-based historiography had undoubtedly revealed the immensity of human effort and productivity in India, but archeology was failing in its mission of placing historical knowledge on solid scientific grounds. Marshall and his followers at the Archeological Survey were gifted men, but the institutional science of archeology in India, as of 1944, was in a sorry state.

Taxila

Taxila was renowned in Indian literature, primarily as one of the two important Buddhist centers of learning, along with Nalanda. It was here that Kumaralabdha founded the major philosophical school of Sautrantika, and apparently the great Hindu grammarians Panini and Patanjali had also worked here centuries earlier. Taxila marked the extreme northwest edge of King Ashoka's vast Mauryan empire in the third century BCE and was the city where, indeed, his grandfather, Chandragupta Maurya, had perhaps been educated. The city served as the launching point for Alexander of Macedonia's march on the Indus valley. According to several ancient traditions, the poet Vyasa composed the revered Sanskrit epic the *Mahabharata* here, and even earlier, the Upanishadic philosopher Uddalaka Aruni taught a stunningly innovative monistic philosophy.

The physical location seems ideally suited for a city of such great distinction. The valley lies in the so-called Sind-Sagar Doab, the stretch of land between the Indus and Jhelum rivers. The valley is fed by several minor streams; it is fertile and enjoys generous annual rainfall. The region is also situated at the intersection of three busy trade routes connecting India to central and western Asia. By means either of caravan or river transport, this luxurious valley also connects the northern Punjab and Kashmir regions to the Persian Gulf and from there to the Red Sea. The city, in ancient times, sat on a virtual highway for trade, cultural exchange, and political or military explorations among the leading civilizations of the world.

However, in the middle of the nineteenth century, the group of mounds known as Dheri Shahan (mound of kings), across the hills from Rawalpindi, stood mute. In 1863, Alexander Cunningham identified the mounds with ancient Takshashila. Half a century later, John Marshall, driven by his keen interest in Greek history and antiquities, came to excavate the site, and remained there for twenty-one years. His extended digging unearthed enormous quantities of objects, including city fortifications, architectural structures designed in distinct Hellenistic styles, numerous Buddhist stupas and monasteries, along with hordes of smaller treasures: art objects, sculptures, jewelry, coins, tools, and seals. Marshall's apparently exhaustive excavations confirmed the profound influence of Hellenistic cultures (Greek, Bactrian, Parthian, and others), along with a strong Buddhist presence and, to a lesser extent, Hindu and Jain influences. Marshall managed to shed a bright light on an ancient urban civilization that had prospered between the sixth century BCE and the fifth century CE.

Marshall confirmed the stature of a prominent ancient city—his revelations supplemented and extended existing textual information on Taxila. And the Taxila museum was stocked with unearthed treasures—kept under glass for historians, art critics, and the general public to see. However, Marshall's work struck Wheeler as unscientific, impressionistic, and glamour seeking. The failure to follow a basic stratification procedure and record the precise location (horizontal and vertical) of identified objects could only distort the value of the objects in the museum. Prized objects removed from their context reveal either a partial or an altogether false picture of their function in the cultural world from which they have descended. The hunt for treasures needed to be replaced with a sweep for knowledge, a mapping of human effort in time and space, which is the true goal of historical research in the ground. The new techniques Wheeler intended to bring to the reexcavation of Taxila would determine the course of modern Indian archeology and contribute to the emerging scientific knowledge of India's past in a postcolonial age.

The New Digging Method

Wheeler imagined archaeological work both as a military campaign and as the management of a rail system. It required a well-trained team, disciplined and organized, who set clear objectives and followed a rigorous schedule. The site had to be scouted, surveyed, photographed; a camp would be set up, and the entire campaign would be administered by a leader with the aid of his officers. Wheeler's team, which became known as the Taxila School, produced some of India's most distinguished archeologists in the second half of the twentieth century. Wheeler began to apply vertical "stratigraphy" (a term borrowed from geology) and grid planning, along with the extensive use of comparative materials (such as Roman coins) for precise dating.

As a general rule, digging begins with the laying of trenches: at the highest point of the mound, across the fortification, and at other strategic locations. These "slices" reveal the layers of the site in the same way the Colorado River exposes the geological strata of the northern Arizona mountains through which it cuts. The layers represent sedimentation, of course, or the work of time in a given spot. At the same time, the horizontal excavation (in any given stratum) exposes the traces of human action at a given moment in time.

The second feature of this method is the grid. At a small distance away from the actual excavation, the team lays out a two-dimensional grid made of stones. Each square measures a yard or meter across, and the entire grid is a scaled model of a given horizontal layer (a cultural slice) of the site. This map— sometimes called the pottery yard—is the place where unearthed objects are placed before cleaning and processing. They are labeled according to their location in the grid, so by the time they arrive for analysis by the archeologists, their location in time and space in the dig is familiar. The combined vertical and horizontal mapping of the excavation site reveals both the timetable of the train and the train itself, in Wheeler's metaphor. The train, in an urban dig, is the "general layout and shape of the streets and shrines, its palaces, its houses and its shops" (Srivastava 1982, p. 37). We may find a single trace of the Parthian culture in Taxila in the vertical cut, but only the horizontal grid tells us what the Parthians were like and what they achieved in Taxila during the time allotted to them by history.

And indeed, the new techinques showed the full scope of historical knowledge, demonstrating that Taxila was far more than Marshall had imagined. In fact, at the time of its flowering in the fourth century BCE (when Alexander of Macedonia arrived) it was already the oldest city in South Asia. Under its vibrant surface lay additional layers going back to Neolithic times in the fourth millennium BCE, proceeding to later Bronze Age cultures, and even to the much more recent culture known today as the Gandhara Grave Culture of around 1000 BCE, which was the trace, mostly in the form of graves, of the arrival in this area of the Aryan or Indo-European-speaking people who would gradually come to dominate northern India. A succession of cultures would also follow in the city of Taxila after its early years, and these were carefully measured and recorded by the Taxila school: Achaemenians, Macedonians, Mauryas, Indus Greeks, Scythians, Parthians, Kushans, Sassanians, Kidara Kushans, White Huns. Only systematic excavations and scientific recording and publication could show that this city at the extreme northwest edge of the subcontinent might serve as a scientifically reliable exploration of northern India's history. The dig reveals what an immensely deep "lasagna pan" of succeeding cultures—some indigenous, others indigenized—India truly is.

The story of Taxila, then—the excavated city—is the story of how we have come to know India in recent decades. The Romantic and colonial yearnings for treasures of the past—art objects and intellectual exotica—gave way to a hard-nosed pursuit of clarity and systematic knowledge.

Kailasa

A thousand miles south of Taxila, in the western state of Maharashtra, digging has been taking place for centuries—and little of it has been archeological. Fifteen miles outside of Aurangabad is a small village called Verul. It is a pilgrimage center (*tirtha*) of minor renown in a vast country that boasts far more prestigious religious attractions than this dusty place. The village houses an eighteenth-century temple, financed by a wealthy princess called Ahilyadevi. The temple—Ghrishnewar—is a shrine for Shiva, as it is said to hold one of only twelve *jyotirlingas* (iconic emblems of the god, possessing a rich mytho-logical and ritual significance) in all of India. But it is not the village that draws the largest crowds to this temperate and hilly region.

The northwestern parts of Maharashtra are known for the Sahyadri hills, a range of basalt traprock marked with deep canyons and streams. Along the arching canyon, cut by the Waghora River in nearby Ajanta, a large number of caves were carved into the stone over the course of several centuries during the first millennium CE. Artists and craftsmen who worked on behalf of Buddhist patrons chiseled out most of these caves, and Mahayana Buddhist monks used them as places of meditation and residence. The breathtaking view along the crescent-shaped canyon and the details of many of these rock masterpieces draw thousands of awed visitors annually.

By comparison, the village of Verul is unimpressive, and Ellora is only the second stop on the tour of the rock monuments. However, less than one mile outside the village stands one of the greatest achievements in India's distinguished history of art. The full depth of its significance is perhaps belied by its initial appearance. The Kailasa temple, technically known as Ellora Cave XVI, stands snuggled against an unimpressive hill of the same basalt rock that pervades the landscape. Kailasa, of course, is the name of Shiva's abode, the mountain that marks the center of the cosmos in Shaivite theology. The structure, then, is a temple to Shiva—Kailasa, his residence.

The temple is an accurate copy of another—the Virupaksha temple, which is located in Palladkal, Karnataka (in South India). As such, it is also modeled on the Kailasanatha temple in Kanchipuram—one of the most impressive and sacred temples in South India. The temple here, outlined by the hill, is thus South Indian—Dravidian—in style, but is twice the size of the temple it replicates. Its dimensions, about the same of those of the Parthenon in Athens, cannot fail to impress the visitor. The tower, known as the Shikhara, stands about 100 feet high. The entire structure, sitting on a very high plinth, is over 200 feet long and 100 feet wide. The temple is surrounded by a huge courtyard, measuring 280 by 160 feet. Enormous lions and elephants carved in stone flank the main structure, and the courtyard is approached through a high *gopura* (gateway), with niches in which huge sculptures are carved, depicting various gods of the Hindu pantheon: Shiva Nataraja, Vishnu in several of his incarnations, Brahma, Garuda, and others. The entrance door, with the two rivergoddesses Ganga and Yamuna on either side, leads the visitor into the temple court. The temple itself consists of several inner halls, some spacious enough for the whole congregation, others—such as the innermost, the *garbha-griha* ("womb house," or inner sanctum)— far smaller. Outlining and upholding the inner spaces are huge pillars, reaching up to the carved ceilings about 50 feet above the floor. Like other South Indian temples of great wealth, this one has a central place of worship surrounded by subsidiary shrines, all of them filling out vast spaces with detailed stone work—both large scale and miniscule.

The sponsor was clearly trying to impress someone, perhaps the Buddhists and their patrons, who had their own stone monuments spread throughout the region. Indeed, the evidence of a sponsor's wealth and devotion is everywhere. Historians know who this ambitious man was: Krishna I, the second ruler in the Rashtrakuta dynasty, who ruled during the second half of the eighth century CE. That information comes from an inscription on a copper plate installed by another king, referring to a grant and self-dated at around 813 CE. However, a temple of this magnitude could not possibly have been fully completed during the fifteen years of King Krishna I's rule—though the main features were.

Historians and art experts agree that the monument shows evidence of several styles, indicating eight or ten historical phases. These observations apply to various aspects of the temple structure, the carving and stone work around it, and various features of the surrounding shrines and courtyard.

This draws attention to the most astounding feature of Kailasa—and the reason for comparing it with Taxila. For while archeologists normally dig into the earth, layer after layer, to arrive at the oldest age of the city or structure buried at the very bottom, at Kailasa the opposite holds true. The further down one looks at the temple, the newer it is.

When King Krishna I commissioned a temple at this site, all that existed was the naked hill, about 200 feet above the surrounding countryside and made of solid basalt. The temple was not "built"; not a single block of stone or any other material was brought to the spot. Instead, the temple was literally excavated from the hill, carved and chiseled by expert artists from the top down. The Kailasa temple, in other words, is the greatest temple-monolith ever created—a huge sculpture carved out of the rock and hollowed out and decorated with nothing besides what was already there.

The work probably began with two parallel trenches dug into the hill at the shoulder. By the time the two trenches were finished, each measured roughly 90 by 17 by 33 meters, or about 200 feet long and 50 feet wide. The depth of each would correspond to the height of the temple, or about 100 feet. Connecting the two trenches at the higher end of the slope was a third trench measuring more than the width of the temple (150 feet) and as deep as the others. That trench was 30 feet across. The trenches marked the edges of Kailasa and provided the working space for both the diggers and for the sculptors. No scaffolding was ever required, because the chiseling of the temple contours—top first and on downward—was synchronized with the digging of the trench.

The artwork was formed by large groups of rock carvers based on existing plans, which were modeled after the two South Indian temples already mentioned. The overall structure, with the main features of the temple complex, probably took about twenty years to complete. But experts now believe that the entire monument was fully completed during the rule of Krishna III, the last ruler of the Rashtrakuta dynasty. If this is correct, Kailasa took roughly two centuries from first strike to the last (c. 967 CE).

Taxila and Kailasa as Metaphors

Today as always, Taxila and Kailasa have very little in common. Taxila is still an active archeological dig, just outside the suburbs of Islamabad in Pakistan.

Kailasa is a tourist attraction—second fiddle to the Ajanta Buddhist caves nearby—just north of Auruangabad in Maharashtra. Never before have the two places shared pages in a single chapter as they do here. But there is a strong and instructive intellectual juxtaposition to be made when two modes of digging— archeology and temple building—are used as metaphors. The metaphors are extended and complex, but worth following for what they show us about studying India. As a matter of fact, the twin metaphors represent the first and most basic lesson to be learned about India.

Two modes of archeological digging can be said to dominate the way we think about India's past. For the sake of convenience I will call them, somewhat simplistically, romantic and scientific. Cunningham and Marshall are two examples of romantic scholarship, the Taxila School of the scientific. Both types of exploration seek historical certainties, first and foremost in the matter of dating. The scientific agenda in archeology aspires to uncover the succession of cultures in time and give a full account of each culture's way of life. At its best, scientific archeology also looks at cultural process, the dynamic transformations and comparative influences of uncovered cultures.

Scientific archeology in Taxila, and throughout South Asia, has provided a three-dimensional map of India's past, based on "nuclear" areas: central locations that dominated regions at different moments in history (page 2). Naturally, the earliest urban centers clustered around rivers, the great source of economic lifeblood.

When collated with information gleaned from written sources, rock and pillar inscriptions, coins, grants, scriptures, epics, and folk literature, the picture of India's past begins to fill out—although a tremendous amount of work remains to be done. The notion of regional historic centers—in fact, of multiple Indian histories—resonates well with the multiplicity of calendars in India. Dating traditionally was not based on a universal system like the Roman, Jewish, or Muslim calendars. Each region or city had its own method of measuring the present against the past by reckoning time. The most frequently used method, naturally, was to count the years of a specific king's reign in a particular area. Each new dynasty brought a new calendar with a new starting date, as follows.

MAJOR CALENDARS IN INDIA AND THEIR STARTING DATES

Kaliyuga (3101 BCE)
Buddha Nirvana (544 BCE)
Mahavira Nirvana (528 BCE)
Gupta (320 BCE)
Vikram Samvat (58 BCE)
Shaka (78 CE)

Harsha (606 CE)

Islamic Hijri (622 CE)

Persian (622 CE)

Christian (0)

Scientific archeology and historiography in India, despite their great influence, have been flawed by a number of major misconceptions. The first is the confusion between cultures and ethnic groups. The presence in Taxila, for instance, of the traces of numerous cultures does not necessarily indicate the arrival and then departure (or annihilation) of distinct "peoples" or ethnic groups. Even for the dominant culture of northern India—the Indo-Aryans—most scholars today prefer to use language as the characteristic identifying marker, not any geographical or ethnic criterion. Furthermore, the clear-cut succession of cultural stages that the strata of a dig seem to represent is too rigid. The dynamic flow of cultural life, the past-present-future of any city in India's history, is an organic and flowing process. Objects from the past are stored for the future, and the present is rich with concerns and projections to an anticipated future. For true cultural development—the life of human minds—a more flexible archeological science was necessary.

"New archeology" arrived on the scene in India during the 1960s, and it added this more humanistic dimension to the goals of scientific archeology. Brought by scholars such as H. D. Sankalia and K. Paddayya, the new discipline was more finely attuned to symbolic interpretation of historic objects. It recognized that objects are not just sedimented deposits; they also represent what the French scholar Bourdieu called social praxis. For instance, fragments of pottery encode conceptual categories—they are not just old tools (or clues for dating) but snapshots of the imaginations (and social practices) of their makers and users. The design, shape, size, and patterns reveal how potters thought and what conceptual categories guided their work. Similarly, the temple is not merely a structure to house the deities or a symbol of the cosmos; it is also a meeting place, theater, school. The goals of new archeology now included the uncovering of the symbols and ideologies of those people who lived and acted in the sites being excavated. In other words, digging was wed to anthropology and to cultural studies.

The flip side of this so-called interpretive archeology, particularly after the 1970s and the emergence of postcolonial theory, has been that the digger has become aware not only of the ideology of those people who lived in Taxila (or Mathura or Vijayanagar) but the politics of contemporary Indians and his or her own as well. His, or her own work—the act of digging—came to be recognized as a form of social praxis. It was no longer privileged as a vantage point.

John Marshall and the other Victorian archeologists could never have known this. They could not see that stocking museums with treasures from India's glorious past (or that of Greece) was a form of trophy hunting, a triumphalist display of exotica from a worthy but supposedly inferior past. Now we have become hyper-self-conscious; we see ourselves reflected in every type of work—even science. We have discovered that knowing others is also knowing ourselves, and this knowledge becomes one measure of the way we live in our own world. In discovering what is in our world we are also discovering our own "being in the world." Here the metaphor of Taxila recedes, and we can turn again to Kailasa.

While the diggers in Taxila have uncovered the soil in order to remove objects and label them with precision, the diggers in Kailasa were digging as a way of being. They were not removing objects imbued with the value of information out of the meaningless background (soil) but were shaping the substance of that background—in this case basalt rock—into meaning and value: the temple. The diggers of the temple were, in a sense, looking for something in the mountain. The mountain was the "womb" (*garbha*) of the future temple, in which a dark cavity would be the *garbha-griha*. As I will show in chapter 7, in most temples the *garbha-griha* is an artful reproduction of an idea of a mountain, while here it was the real place. This ought to be the model for how we study India's past (or that of any civilization) and India's religions. Two lessons stand out in particular: (1) India and its past is continuous with our own. In studying India we come to understand our own world. (2) There is no separate domain called the religion of Hinduism. Ancient Indians made and occupied a world in which action—technology, science, and commerce— embodied imaginative and intellectual impulses. The construction of a temple (planning, measuring, chiseling, cooperating) is as expressive of "religion" as are the rituals for the god who will come to occupy the structure.

In some sense, a book about India must resemble a temple. It cannot pretend to be a detached map of an objective world. Instead such a book is an extension of the world it studies, another form of self-reflection that contains only those elements of India's past that the author uses for constructing the book's own discursive universe.

2

Sacred Knowledge and Indian Origins

The academic study of religion mimics sacred scriptures in at least one significant way: It overvalues the beginning. The typical textbook about Hinduism, for example, begins with the Indus Valley cities or perhaps with the Vedas, both representing the earliest known strata of Indian civilization. The Hebrew Bible begins with the book of Genesis, which was hardly the first composed. The Gospel of John begins with Logos, and many Vedic hymns—not to mention the monumentally influential epic the *Mahabharata*—lead us directly to the origin of things. This is both a sensible and satisfying way to organize the way we know the world: What matters in contemporary times depends in some ways, whether by continuity or fracture, on how it first came to be. For a long time, even the tone of textbooks resembled that of scripture. Origins were narrated with the assured voice of the all-knowing narrator who may have sounded like this: "The beginnings of Hinduism trace back to a race of militaristic nomads who invaded the Indian subcontinent . . ."

Recent trends in cultural and literary studies, particularly postmodern and postcolonial theories, have done away with the narrator who holds the God's-eye view of the world. But the question of origins has retained its supreme importance. We should hardly be surprised, then, that the most hotly contested and politically charged question within Indian studies is the following: What is the origin of the civilization that has dominated India for millennia and often goes by the name Hinduism? To be more specific, did this civilization arrive with the migrating Indo-Aryans or did it emerge in India itself, where no such migrations actually took place? These questions, representing the so-called Indo-Aryan controversy, exercise some of the best minds in a significant number of sciences and academic disciplines (Bryant and Patton 2005), ranging from anthropology to zoology. Included are archeology, biology (human genetics and genomics), botany, paleontology, linguistics, geography, historiography, astronomy, geology, and many other subdisciplines. The question, to repeat, is simple: Did the civilization that has been known to Westerners as Hinduism come with migrating non-Indians into the subcontinent or did it take birth in India?

While the majority of scholars today believe that migrating Indo-Aryans brought the earliest Hindu scripture (the *Rig-Veda*) with them in the form of oral literature, a significant and perhaps growing number of scholars, primarily within India, dispute this. This book shares the former view but calls attention to the secondary but also interesting issue with which this chapter opened. The dispute over Indian origins closely mirrors the disputes over sacred knowledge in which the writers of the *Rig-Veda* themselves engaged. The driving agenda is this: What is the nature of knowledge and how does knowledge contribute to or detract from what we hold most sacred?

In the case of the Indo-Aryan controversy, the competing values are, at least implicitly, those of objective truth sought by scientific inquiry versus politically and culturally driven knowledge. Both sides support the former, and both accuse the other of engaging in the latter; one hears of nationalistic agendas from the "into India" side and of colonialism from the "out of India" side. In either case, knowledge—the many sciences listed earlier—is a tool: not just for dispassionately understanding our history and world but also for advocating a deeply prized position. Knowledge is contested today, as always, although what it reveals as "sacred" (most highly valued) has shifted over the millennia.

The Indo-Aryans

The subjects of the Indo-Aryan controversy were energetic and rambunctious people who probably arrived gradually from central and western Asia. They have been called Aryans (from *arya*, "hospitable one"), but this should not be taken as an ethnic term. "Indo-Aryans" is the somewhat more precise linguistic category that most scholars today prefer to use. As noted, the majority of scholars today, largely on the basis of linguistic evidence (for example, the absence of South Asian linguistic characteristics such as retroflection west of India), do support the migration hypothesis. The arrival of the Indo-Aryans probably took several centuries and was mostly peaceful, and evidence indicates that a genuine cultural exchange took place as they encountered indigenous populations, including the late phases of Harappa culture. Few archeological remains attest to the material culture of the mobile population or to the events of those centuries, between 1750 and 850 BCE. The major exception may be the Gandhara Grave Culture in Swat Valley, known in the *Rig-Veda* as Suvastu (8.19.37), where some remains have been discovered that are consistent with Vedic culture (a three-fire ritual site, horse furnishings and a chariot, pottery, and food remnants).

Virtually everything we know about these extraordinary people derives from their prolific literary output—primarily the *Rig-Veda*, which they composed, memorized, and recited with astounding precision. The 10 books and 1,028 hymns of this the most sacred among India's scriptures correspond in time to the early migratory phases of the Indo-Aryans in western Punjab (Land of Seven Rivers) and further east to the Gangetic plain. These phases span roughly one thousand years (1750—850 BCE), corresponding to books 1–9 for the earlier periods and book 10 for the last. Taken literally—a risky business with all the poetic Vedic texts—the hymns in these books unfold an impressively detailed if spotty canvas. They describe the Indo-Aryans' economic and social life, the physical and natural geography of their journey across northern India, and some political consequences of the historic cultural encounter with the indigenous people. Numerous hymns offer glimpses of a pastoral migratory life with several types of domesticated animals. The horse was a novelty in India and is an indication of the Asian origin of the Indo-Aryans. The text refers to chariots and to metal (*ayas*), both of which—along with the horse—accounted for the powerful impact of the migrations. There are further descriptions of local trees and plants, mountains and rivers, forts and cities, local tribes, imported and indigenous foods, medicines, clothing, and many other aspects of life.

Cows and horses were especially prestigious and expensive: "You gods who are all here and who belong to all men, give far-reaching shelter to us and our cows and horses" (8.30.4; O'Flaherty) Similarly, Vedic culture prized the bull, though not merely for economic reasons: "The bull with the powerful neck, increasing in size and strength, will drive together the possessions of the enemy without opposition" (5.2.12; O'Flaherty). Of course, the Indo-Aryans described dozens of wild animal species, from the antelope—a revered animal—to lions, jackals, eagles, and geese, and down to frogs and even ants. Careful mining of Rigvedic attention to detail in every area of life can be extremely rewarding. And in the absence of material remains, this evidence has often had to suffice among researchers, even those hard-nosed Marxist historians who, like D. D. Kosambi, have insisted that material history is foremost. But, to repeat, this is tricky work.

While the poets of the *Rig-Veda* observed nature with a keen eye, they also cautioned each other, and us as well, that they were not merely describing the world as it was; theirs was not an empirical-scientific agenda. As soon as animals, birds, trees, or the lightning made their way into Vedic poetry, they became symbols: containers of secrets. A goat was not necessarily just a goat, and a buffalo could be something other than the animal itself: "The buffaloes bursting with seed, veiling themselves, have united with the mares in the same stable. The poets hide the path of the Truth; they keep secret their highest names" (10.5.2; O'Flaherty). What are the poet's buffaloes and how can they possibly mate with mares? If the suggestion seems both full of meaning and absurd, you have been cautioned by the poet himself. How else could the poet say *trope* or *metonym*?

The poets of the *Rig-Veda*, the *rishis*, were crafting verbal tools, and they were conscious of being extraordinarily skillful with esoterica: "Inspired with poetry I have fashioned this hymn of praise for you [Agni, god of fire] whose very nature is power, as the skilled artist fashions a chariot" (5.2.11; O'Flaherty). The poets of the *Rig-Veda*, then, by its own account, aspired to formulate masterpieces of concealment. Although some linguists (Karen Thomson and Jonathan Slocum) do not believe that the text is intentionally obscure, scholars of Vedic religion, with the Dutch Indologist Jan Gonda as a preeminent example, argue that the language of the text is performing religious work that is so sacred that it must remain concealed. That work, which Laurie L. Patton calls *viniyoga*, is the manipulation of hidden connections for ritual purposes, or more broadly, actively interpreting the universe. In our own insatiable thirst for transparent historical facts, we must bear this in mind when we use the *Rig-Veda* to reconstruct what we call the "Vedic world."

The Vedic Worldview

Because of its sheer size and the many centuries of work it took to compose and assemble, the *Rig-Veda* could not possibly present a single cosmology. But some uniform threads run through it; an especially bold one is what appears to be the authors' impetus to classify the universe—to identify the basic patterns within all forms of complexity.

Time moved in cycles: the year died at its conclusion, to be reborn with the help of a ritual at the start of the new year. Three seasons made up the year: spring, rains, and autumn. But multiples of that number played an important role when the year was reckoned as having six seasons or twelve months. These would later make their way into ritual instructions, for example, the number of bulls assigned to the plow during the Agnichayana (laying of the bricks for the fire altar), which symbolically reconstituted time. Space, too, consisted of three parts: the three worlds were earth (*bhuh* or *bhur*), the atmosphere (*bhuvah*), and the sky (*svah*). These three Sanskrit words—or sounds—have become extremely familiar to all Hindus both in the myth of Vishnu's strides and as the apogee of Vedic ritual cosmology. In their vowels and consonants, they hold the secret power of the Vedic ritual as a whole—a concept that would later be called Brahman. For example, the three worlds are invoked at the opening of the great Gayatri Mantra ("May we attain that excellent glory of Savitar the God so he may stimulate our prayers," Rig-Veda 3.62.10; T. H. Griffith):

> Om bhur bhuvah svah
> Tat Savitar varenyam
> Bhargo devasya dhimahi
> Dhiyo yo nah pracodayat

The three worlds were governed by gods, or *devas*. No one could say precisely how many *devas* there were, not even the Vedic and Upanishadic thinkers, who speculated that the number could exceed three thousand, or three hundred, or perhaps it was only thirty-three, or two, or perhaps one. And like everything else in the Vedic universe, the gods were classified in a number of ways, but primarily according to the three social classifications (*varnas*) of Brahmins, Kshatriyas, and Vaishyas/Shudras. Due to the size and longevity of the Rigvedic literature, each god came to embody a number of meanings or values. Among the Brahmin gods, for example, Agni represents both the ritual fire and an abstract concept such as radiance. Vach represents speech, Mitra truth. Among the Kshatriyas, Indra is strength, majesty, violence; Varuna is justice as well as royalty; Rudra ("the howler") is the procreative. Among the remaining two *varnas*, the Maruts embody prosperity and abuncance, Sarasvati nourishment and wealth, and Surya (the sun) life-giving energy. It is important to bear in mind, as Brian K. Smith indicates, that the classification is not formal, nor are the boundaries between the classes fixed. Many of the gods find a place in more than one social category.

In a manner of speaking, the *Rig-Veda* was an immense encyclopedia of gods, goddesses, demons (*asuras*), spirits, and other celestial and ethereal beings. But if one gauges the importance of a god by the number of hymns in which he or she is addressed, Agni, Soma, and Indra will seem to have occupied the minds of the Vedic poets more persistently than the others, at least in later Rigvedic times. There may be no stronger proof of the value of the Vedic sacrifice than the prominence of Agni and Soma or of the awareness of tribal power than the many hymns to Indra. But Vedic religion was far from simple.

Many of the hymns to specific gods balance a deep reverence for natural phenomena with an intuitive and even philosophical curiosity about underlying principles—abstract powers. For example, Indra is both god of the storm (bearing his *vajra*, weapon), a Kshatriya king, and then royalty itself. Vayu, too, is both the wind that blows through the trees and the god who purifies humans of their sins. The books of the *Rig-Veda* undoubtedly reflect an evolving and deepening religious sensibility, in which nature continued to matter to Vedic poets even after they had begun to identify and discuss more abstract ideas.

The Indo-Aryans performed Vedic rituals, predominantly sacrifices, on behalf of the gods, and timed them to mark key moments in the passage of time. There were the new year sacrifices, the four-month sacrifices that ushered in the seasons, the first fruit offerings, and most important of all, the fire sacrifice (Agnihotra)—the paradigm or perfect model of all sacrifices. Needless to say, the ritual fires, too, were classed into types, usually three: the householder's fire, the southern fire, and the offering fire—each with its distinct ritual location and purpose. And, three (later four) types of priests rose to prominence, specializing in distinct functions: the *hotri* priest recited the mantras, the *adavaryu* performed the many detailed actions, and the *udgatri* sang *samans* (songs). Each was accompanied by assistants, whose numbers varied according to the importance of the sacrifice and the wealth of the sacrificial patron.

Although the early Indo-Aryans worshiped nature and slaughtered animals to feed specific gods with specific goals in mind (prosperity, health, children), there was always a speculative dimension to this natural and pragmatic religion. In its inceptual form, the theorizing seems to have taken hold by means of numbers and categories. One can only be amazed at the elaborate numbering and classifying that accompanied poetic speculations and ritual instructions. If philosophers today claim that reality consists of both substance and form, their Vedic counterparts intuited a universe that consisted of concrete individual substances squeezed into fundamental categories (form) by means of numbers. Vedic numbers acted as the philosopher's stone—the key to understanding the underlying structure of reality. The sacrifice, in turn, was not just the site of ritual offerings but also the locus of numerical speculation: the occasion for asking questions about numbers and their meaning. One of the best examples of this is the following passage on the riddle of the sacrifice:

> This beloved grey priest has a middle brother who is hungry and
> a third brother with butter on his back. In him I saw the Lord of All
> Tribes with his seven sons.

Seven yoke the one-wheeled chariot drawn by one horse with seven names. All these creatures rest on the ageless and unstoppable wheel of three naves.

Seven horses draw the seven who ride this seven wheeled chariot. Seven sisters call out to the place where the seven names of the cows are hidden. (1.164.1–3; O'Flaherty)

The entire hymn is a lengthy and elaborate meditation that brilliantly weaves together a religion of nature with abstract speculations about meaning, general principles, and the search for unity within diversity. Two features dominate: persistent riddle-making and the manipulation of numbers. There is the number three: brothers, naves of the wheel, sticks for the sacrifice, long-haired ones, hidden parts of speech. There are sixes, which are pairs of three: realms of space, spokes of the wheel, shapes of the father, twins. Other things come in groups of five, seven (sons, horses, wheels), or yet other numbers. Two and one clearly mattered a great deal; the two birds are particularly intriguing, and the "One" remained unspecified and seemingly supreme.

The hymn was about the world surrounding the poet, of course: birds, cows, horses, chariots, wheels, sacrifices, and speech. But the poet asked his listeners to ponder what else these natural and physical objects could possibly be. What did the cow stand for and what did the chariot represent, especially if it had but one wheel? Scholars today agree that Vedic sacrifices were preceded by races and various types of contests. Brahmin specialists often traveled long distances to show what they could do in competition and established reputations as masters of the sacrificial riddles. It seemed that the sacrifice itself—not just the hymn—was speculative to the core.

But speculation took on a distinct quality in the Vedas. The ritual sacrifice was a mystery of hidden connections (*bandhu*), where numbered objects were compared and equated across classification systems. One natural object would be identified with another, or a natural object could be elevated to an abstraction, a principle. The seven horses could be the seven priests, or perhaps the seven offerings. The naves of the wheel were the seasons, the wheel was the year, the chariot was the sacrifice, and the sacrificial fire was the sun. Of course, these identities may have applied in one ritual but not in another; the game of discovering connections was context-sensitive and fluid.

The successful competitor was able to solve such riddles quickly and imaginatively: the more hidden connections he recognized for each object, the better his performance. But underpinning mere virtuosity was an earnest search for that core of unity that permeated the dazzling multiplicity all around. Such a task could be excruciatingly difficult, as this passage demonstrates:

> O Agni, who makes things clear, who am I, that upon me when I have broken no commandments you have boldly placed like a heavy burden thought so high and deep, this fresh question with seven meanings for the offerings? (4.5.6; O'Flaherty)

The sacrifice as a whole was replicated in the hymn itself. Both acted as offerings to the gods, both matched symbols with real objects, and both intentionally obscured their central ideas in similar ways. In other words, the Vedic hymn, like the sacrifice, identified and manipulated several levels of existence at once: mythological, cosmological, and syntactical. Another example (10.130.1; Elizarenkova):

> The sacrifice that is drawn through with its threads on all sides
> is offered with a hundred and one acts, serving the gods.
> These fathers are weaving (it), (these) who have arrived.
> They sit by the spread out (sacrifice, saying): "Weave forward!
>   Weave backward!"

Some scholars today regard the search for unity as the defining characteristic of Vedic religion. The visible aspects of nature and its powers, the diversity of gods and human communities, even levels of thought are all interconnected by means of a hypothetical universal order, a hidden principle of order. The term poets gave to that principle was *rita*. The word may have originated from a word in an ancient Near Eastern language (Mitanni), *arta*, truth or law. The poets connected this to the cyclic pattern that governed the universe, human society, and thought. The planets moved in conformity with *rita*, and even the gods who controlled nature ultimately obeyed it. The word is etymologically related to "rite"; and indeed, the correct ritual procedure conformed to cosmic order and reinforced the unifying harmony that *rita* has eternally imposed on the universe.

Speculation

As Vedic poets increasingly reflected on underlying ideas, their curiosity increased, and their questions deepened. Is *rita* entirely abstract or is it embodied in a single God? Who is he? Why does the universe exist, and how did creation take place? The answers were sophisticated and diverse. Apparently no one edited the *Rig-Veda* to reduce all the answers to a unified doctrine, as the

Buddhists tried centuries later with the teachings of the Buddha. Instead, all 1,028 hymns must be read to see the full range of answers. However, some theologies and cosmogonies gained greater prominence, even renown, among the traditions that would later emerge in India. The following was one of the later Rigvedic hymns, and at the time of its composition, the god Prajapati—Lord of Creatures—was only beginning to ascend to the rank that would make him the highest god in the Brahmanas (texts that came after the *Rig-Veda*).

> In the beginning the Golden Embryo [Hiranyagarbha] arose. Once he was born, he was the one lord of creation. He held in place the earth and this sky. Who is the god whom we should worship with this oblation?
>
> He who gives life, who gives strength, whose command all the gods, his own, obey; his shadow is immortality—and death. Who is the god whom we should worship with the oblation?
>
> Let him not harm us, he who fathered the earth and created the sky, whose laws are true, who created the high, shining waters. Who is the god whom we should worship with the oblation?
>
> O Prajapati, lord of progeny, no one but you embraces all these creatures. Grant us the desires for which we offer you oblation. Let us be lords of riches. (10.121.1–3, 9–10; O'Flaherty)

In this hymn, the figure of Prajapati combines the mythical personality of the earlier creator gods with far more abstract qualities. The earliest creation hymns had been far more mythical, of course. Indra, for instance, whose stature diminished with the rise of Prajapati, brought forth the world in a primordial act of violence against an immense snake (for some translators a dragon) called Vritra:

> Let me now sing the heroic deeds of Indra, the first that the thunderbolt-wielder performed. He killed the dragon and pierced an opening for the waters; he split open the bellies of mountains.
>
> Indra, when you killed the first-born of dragons and overcame by your own magic the magic of the magicians, at that very moment you brought forth the sun, the sky, and dawn. Since then you have found no enemy to conquer you. (1.32.1,4; O'Flaherty)

The hymn reads almost like a legend or a nature myth: a heroic god slays the enemy of life with the thunderbolt as his weapon. However, like so many others, this hymn conceals an idea of impressive originality: the power of the god (his *maya*) was magical. But where precisely was the magic? The act of creation, after all, seemed so violent, without any hint of supernatural causality. Why did the poet boast on behalf of Indra, who destroyed with his own magic "the magic of the magician?" The suggestion here that God possesses a deceptive power in addition to his brute force not only was seminal but also would be influential for millennia, especially in the theology of Vishnu.

But the same primordial and mythical waters were still important for the poet who spoke later of Prajapati (or Hiranyagarbha, the Golden Germ). One god began to dominate, but the water was still pregnant with both fecundity and meaning. Prajapati knew all the other gods and embraced them as their creator, too—the father of the gods (and the demons, siblings of the gods).

While the relatively new theology of Prajapati still retained mythical images that swirled around sacrificial symbolism, other ideas tugged at the endless curiosity of the more philosophically minded poets. These poets speculated about creation without any personal god whatsoever:

> There was neither non-existence nor existence then; there was neither the realm of space nor the sky which is beyond. What stirred? Where? In whose protection? Was there water, bottomlessly deep?
>
> There was neither death nor immortality then. There was no distinguishing sign of night nor of day. That one breathed, windless, by its own impulse. Other than that there was nothing beyond....
>
> Who really knows? Who will here proclaim it? Whence was it produced? Whence is this creation? The gods came afterwards, with the creation of this universe. Who then knows whence it has arisen?
>
> Whence this creation has arisen—perhaps it formed itself, or perhaps it did not—the one who looks down on it, in the highest heaven, only he knows—or perhaps he does not know. (10.129.1, 2, 6, 7; O'Flaherty)

Such was the mystery that an answer, any answer, would surely distort the problem. The point was to ask. For who indeed truly knew? The question resonated so deeply that Who (Ka) became the name of the creator, Indra's name for Prajapati. Centuries later, Ka became identified with the name of the creator god Brahma in the mythological texts of the Puranas (see chapter 9). But for now, the poets astutely wondered how, after all, could something that exists (the entire universe) come about from the complete absence of existence? How could something emerge from nothing? To the poet, the question itself defied logic, and perhaps that was the heart of the matter—that the mystery of creation was something that transcended thought, and demanded a new language.

Philosophical agnosticism was just one of many strands of thought the Vedic poets weaved. The dominant insight remained focused on the sacrifice, with its combination of technical detail and hidden connections. Most prestigious of all the hymns that speculated about creation and the meaning of the sacrifice was the Purusha Sukta, the Hymn of Man. In time, this hymn would capture the imagination of Indian legislators and theologians looking for ways to conceptualize their intuitions about morality and authority. The entire fabric of Indian society (dharma) would become identified with the ideology this hymn so majestically articulated.

> The Man has a thousand heads, a thousand eyes, a thousand feet. He pervaded the earth on all sides and extended beyond it as far as ten fingers.
>
> It is the Man who is all this, whatever has been and whatever is to be. He is the ruler of immortality, when he grows beyond everything through food....
>
> When the gods spread the sacrifice with the Man as the offering, spring was the clarified butter, summer the fuel, autumn the oblation....
>
> From that sacrifice in which everything was offered, the verses and chants were born, the metres were born from it, and from it the formulas were born.
>
> Horses were born from it, and those other animals that have two rows of teeth; cows were born from it, and from it goats and sheep were born....
>
> His mouth became the Brahmin; his arms were made into the Warrior, his thighs the People, and from his feet the Servants were born. (Rig-Veda 10.90.1, 2, 6, 9, 10, 12; O'Flaherty)

Looking at the *Rig-Veda* with the help of hindsight, we can see that the ritual of the sacrifice and the theories that centered on it had the longest-lasting impact. This becomes easier to understand when taking into account the nature of the science—both theoretical and practical—of the *Rig-Veda*. On the theoretical level, the ancient poets seemed to be searching for an understanding of a diverse world in terms of consistent principles. The most significant of these may have been the idea of correspondence between seemingly unrelated phenomena. Because the *Rig-Veda* text is highly poetical, it would be easy to regard this agenda as essentially poetic and even mystical. But the text gives evidence that the recognition of correspondences brings together both empirical observation and symbolic, even mathematical acuity. This means that the intellectuals of the Vedic period engaged in astronomy, mathematics (including geometry), logic, grammar, taxonomy, and more pragmatic fields such as medicine.

If one wishes to learn more about these areas of Vedic knowledge, the place to look is not the speculative hymns. Indeed, the fulcrum of Vedic scientific thought was the sacrifice, particularly as it came to be described in the later Vedic texts.

The Hawk Altar

Scholars in recent years have become very interested in the ancient Indian sacrifice as something far more elaborate than the mere taking of a life. Although at the core of the sacrificial ritual was a violent act, which the Dutch Indologist Jan Heesterman has called "a riddle of life and death," the sacrifice was far more. The riddle itself was never solved, only acted out, and the act, the play, was like a soccer game played by just one team: the actions had to be carefully choreographed, and the suspense that might have once been present was gone. What remained of the violent action was a ritual staging of elaborate rules, an applied sacred science of mathematical logical precision. The preparatory ritual for the sacrifice—the laying of the bricks for the sacrificial altar (Agnichayana)—is a perfect illustration of this.

Before undertaking any major sacrifice in ancient India, one had to construct the sacrificial altar. The building of the fire altar—the Agnichayana—stood out, in fact, as the most complex of all the public rituals. These were known collectively as *shrauta* because they conformed to revealed authority—*shruti*. The rules for the altar-building ritual, like the entire body of sacred knowledge in the eighth century BCE, were available only in memorized texts (table 2.1). Among the most prominent was the *Shatapatha Brahmana*, but equally detailed instructions figured in the Shrauta Sutras (aphoristic texts about shrauta rituals). These texts bore the names of the two distinguished families of Brahmins who composed and memorized them: Apastamba and Katyayana.

Early Western scholars, accustomed to Protestant minimalism in matters of religion, regarded such Vedic rituals as infuriatingly recondite, as though

TABLE 2.1. Vedic Literature

	Rig-Veda	Samaveda	Yajurveda (Black, White)	Atharvaveda
Samhita	Shakala	Jaiminiya	Taittiriya (B) Vajasaneyi (W)	Shaunaka
Brahmana + Aranyaka	Aitareya	Jaiminiya	Taittiriya (B) Shatapatha (W)	Gopatha
Upanishad	Chandogya	Katha Shvetashvatara	Brihadaranyaka	Mandukya

there were something truly important to which Brahmin priests failed to attend while they minded the minutiae. Of course, the details were the main thing, just as those thousands of drops of paint on Jackson Pollock's canvas do, in fact, make up the work of art. The following description represents less than 1 percent of the actual procedure, barely enough to give readers a whiff of the extraordinary attention to detail.

Several preparatory rites preceded the laying of the fire altar, including the sacrifice of five victims: man, horse, bull, ram, and he-goat. Priests had the heads of the victims built into the altar, while the bodies were immersed in the water tank where the clay was mixed from which the bricks of the altar were molded. The victims, in other words, literally became part of the physical altar. In later times, incidentally, ritual performers could substitute, most commonly, golden images for the living victims, especially the man. The precious metal not only demonstrated wealth but embodied a central idea of the theology that motivated the ritual. As I will show, this theology involved the Hiranyagarbha "(Golden Germ)," fire, the sun, and a creator god as interlocking symbolic concepts that could be evoked by means of objects forged from gold.

Brick-making extended beyond simple masonry to a complex ritual that manipulated additional animals, antelope skin, sacred grass (*munja*), and other symbolic items. The sacrificer's wife, often a queen or a wealthy woman of high caste, measured the first brick to match the size of her husband's foot. She then scratched three lines on the top of the brick. Other bricks did not receive as much attention, but each was made in a slightly different manner and took its own unique name, which the texts explained with puns or vague allusions to myths.

The altar consisted of five layers of brick. The odd layers pointed in one direction, the even layers in another. The altar did not always take the shape of a hawk or falcon (fig. 2.1); it could be a chariot wheel, a heron, an eagle, a tortoise, or a more abstract figure. Because the outline of the altar was highly irregular, while the number of bricks remained fixed, and because the bricks often varied

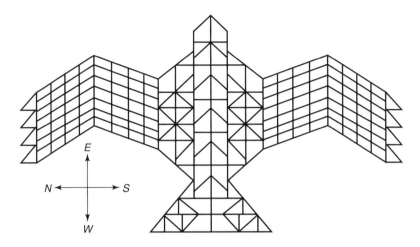

FIGURE 2.1. Falcon Altar. From *Geometry in Ancient and Medieval India* by Dr. T.A. Sarasvati Amma copyright 1979. Reprinted by permission from Motilal Banarsidass, Delhi, India.

in size and shape (rectangles, triangles, oblongs, and various combinations), the builders had to have a solid grasp of geometrical principles. These specialists enjoyed no freedom with the craft of altar-building: They could neither break off the bricks nor improvise their size just in order to achieve a smooth surface. Solid craftsmanship met precise calculation, but freedom played no role in either. This was a sacred task, after all. In fact, as the builders placed each individual brick in its proper place, the priests chanted mantras such as this: "Growing up joint by joint, knot by knot" (*Shatapatha Brahmana* 7.4.2.14; Eggeling) The obscurity of the phrase should not be confused with its sanctity; by the end of this chapter, the strange statement will make sense.

The first time a sacrificer performed the Agnichayana, each of the five layers consisted of two hundred bricks, for a total of one thousand. For the second performance, the number increased by one thousand for the entire altar, and it kept growing by that increment with each performance. The tenth performance—a feat of leisure and wealth— involved five layers of two thousand bricks, each brick individually named and put on the altar with its own mantra! The duration allotted for this ritual varied from one day per layer to a whole year for the entire rite. However, before the altar's first brick took its correct place, the ground had to be prepared.

The sacrificer plowed the sacrificial area with a plow made of *udumbara* wood (a tree associated with the power of the Kshatriya, the member of the warrior caste). Six, twelve, or twenty-four oxen pulled the plow. At the correct location—roughly where the torso of the hawk would be—the central sacrificial space (*vedi*) was outlined, measured by means of a rope to precisely twice the sacrificer's height. The priests then sowed an exact number of kernels from a specified type of corn into the furrow the plow had cut.

Only after the ground was symbolically impregnated could the builders place the first brick, named Svayammatrina, precisely at the center of the sacrificial space, after a Brahmin priest had blown on it. Other priests stretched a creeper across the brick as the second one (called Dviyajus) was placed at a specific distance to the east of the first. After completing the first layer, one brick at a time and mantra by mantra, the priests placed upon the bricks a live tortoise, which they had anointed with ghee (clarified butter), honey, and curds and covered in moss. The higher layers were built around the creature. Of course, as the ritual proceeded and actions accumulated, the priests continued to chant additional mantras and *samans* in an ongoing flow of sound.

With the altar fully built, but before ending the Agnichayana ritual, the sacrificer took his seat to the north of the hawk's tail. As a matter of strict ritual precaution, the sacrificer had been required to abstain from several types of behavior. This rule of abstention, called *vrata*, increased in severity as the sacrificer performed more Agnichayanas and focused mainly on sexual and eating prohibitions. An *udumbara*-wood bench covered with antelope skin provided the sacrificer with comfort while priests sprinkled him with the butter remains of one of the many subsidiary rites taking place. The main rituals that depended on the laying of the altar could now be performed.

Some scholars believe that the Agnichayana began as an independent ritual, divorced from those that would hinge on it. The sacrifices (*yajna*) during the Brahmana (late Vedic) period, in which the Agnichayana became prominent (c. 800 BCE), consisted of three major categories: the minor sacrifices (*ishti*), animal sacrifices (*pashu*), and soma sacrifices. The elaborate fire altar served the latter two categories. These were major rituals with a deep theological meaning and strong public interest. What that meaning was and why the public had a stake in obscure rituals remains part of the mystery.

The Meaning of the Agnichayana

What did the construction of the altar mean to the priests and to the sacrificer? And how did the thousands of minute details contribute to the religious agenda built into the altar? On one level, these are not difficult questions at all: just listen to what the priests said when they chanted mantras, sang songs, or studied the instructions provided in the (memorized) manuals—the *Yajurveda*, the Brahmanas, and other texts:

> He who desires heaven should build a falcon-shaped altar because the
> falcon is the fastest among all the birds. Having become a falcon
> himself, the sacrificer flies up to the heavenly world. (*Taittiriya
> Samhita* 5.4.11)

But on a deeper level, such explicit theologies only raise further questions,
requiring that we dig beyond the words to that level where secrets, puzzles, and
concealment become coherent.

Still, the mantras did reveal some meaning. The simplest ones resonated
with the actions: As the priest did X he may have chanted "I am doing X" or "I
command you to do X." But many mantras provided more information. For
instance, as part of the plowing ceremony, priests made the following statement: "Yoke the ploughs and stretch across the yokes." Then, while planting
the corn seeds, the priests continued with the following: "Into the ready womb
here cast ye the seed" (*Shatapatha Brahmana* 7.2.2.5; Eggeling). In the mind of
some participants, the furrow, clearly, played the role of a symbolic womb,
perhaps because the altar that would be built on it was itself taking birth, or
because the rituals performed on that altar were expected to give birth to specific results. The erudite priest undoubtedly knew other reasons for imagining
the furrow as a womb, and it would not have occurred to him that he needed to
reduce them all to one.

As the priests anointed the tortoise with honey prior to entombing it in the
altar, they chanted: "Honey the winds pour forth for the righteous, honey the
rivers; full of honey may the plants be for us" (*Shatapatha Brahmana* 7.5.1.4;
Eggeling). Clearly, the symbolism of fecundity, prosperity, and wealth dominated key aspects of priestly thought—after all, they often worked to enhance
economic interests. The ritual, in fact, integrated mundane considerations with
occult practice as symbolic objects were literally embodied in the sacrificial
altar. Thousands of similar details, some partially hidden and others exceedingly obscure, resonated through the minds of the performers with the constant flow of action, chanting, and singing.

But the priests, who carefully followed the ritual manuals, knew much
more. The tortoise was not just an animal that symbolized farming or germi-
nation. On a deeper level it was also the creator god himself, Prajapati, who had
assumed the shape of a lowly animal. The priests knew this through a theology
built on hidden connections (*bandhu*) that could be revealed in a number of
ways; in this case it was a pun: the creator was the one who had created (*kar*) a
world, and the tortoise was *kurma*, hence they were one and the same (*Shatapatha Brahmana* 7.5.1.5)!

Similarly, the heads of the sacrificial animals went into the fire pan because the fire pan, too, was the womb—one of many, as it turns out (*Shatapatha Brahmana* 7.5.2.2). Thus, although those specific animals had been destroyed in the sacrifice, they found their place in the womb that would regenerate them in the form of wealth for the sacrificer. Again, the texts informed the priests that the sacrificer had to take the three steps of Vishnu in order to achieve the prized unity with the sun, who strode across the three worlds on its daily journey (*Shatapatha Brahmana* 6.7.2.10). So Vishnu was, in fact, the sacrifice, which was also Agni (the god of the sacrificial fire)—and that was precisely what the sacrificer aspired to become during the ritual. The theology of hidden connections affirmed that the sacrifice was not just about multiplying wealth; it transformed the identity of the sacrificer by establishing a set of surprising cosmic relationships.

Clearly, behind the rich display of symbolic manipulations, a carefully concealed but increasingly coherent theology began to emerge. Pragmatic economic considerations enframed within a magic rationality gave way to a more abstract cosmological agenda. Modern readers may actually look up the ritual in full in the *Shatapatha Brahmana* or, better yet, view the documentary film (*Altar of Fire*) that recorded the last detailed performance of the Agnichayana. The experience is bound to confuse and perhaps benumb us, unless the central religious message is allowed to stand out clearly in the sea of detail:

> In the first place that Agni (the Fire-altar), the year, is built; thereafter the Great Litany is recited. When Prajapati became relaxed, the vital fluid flowed upwards. Now, that Prajapati who became relaxed is the year; and those joints of his which became relaxed are the days and nights. And that Prajapati who became relaxed is this very Fire-altar which here is built; and those joints of his, the days and nights, which became relaxed are no other than the bricks. (*Shatapatha Brahmana* 10.1.1.1; Eggeling)

The meaning begins to take shape; we start to understand what the ritual was doing: the complex and mathematically elaborate construction that resulted in the sacrificial altar was a symbolic replenishing of time itself (the joints of Prajapati). In other words, time was sanctified, because time was the body of the creator, mediated through the altar. The rituals that would later take place on the altar—time or god embodied—would continually replenish both and would allow the sacrificer to mystically identify with these cosmic levels of experience. The sacrifice, in sum, was not just a barter exchange with God: "Here is my best goat, now give me one hundred." It established instead that life with its farming and health and progeny were all part of a divine order. The ritual made it so.

This is the theology of the Agnichayana in a nutshell. We can see it for ourselves by looking at the texts of the Brahmanas. But are the ideas of feeding and identifying with God hopelessly archaic and irreparably magical? Or, rather, does a hidden rationality somehow persist through the ages, such that we may actually recognize a grain of truth in the Agnichayana? Can we make sense of the fundamental identity: Prajapati is Vishnu is Agni is the sun; the sacrificer is all of them and the ritual feeds and restores time itself? Those who wish to skip directly to the answers, in the form of the Vedic sciences, may read chapter 5 next.

3

A City Where the Rivers Meet

The Yamuna River leaves the Himalaya range and runs for nearly a thousand miles before dissolving into its greater sister, the Ganges. It strings together some of India's most prominent religious centers, from Mathura to Prayag, and on to Varanasi after its convergence with the Ganges. A leisurely boat cruise downstream would ideally take place between September and December: The water still flows briskly, thanks to the summer's monsoon, but no longer as the churning brown rush that immediately follows the rains. By early spring, the Yamuna has become a vigorless and shallow stream. Departing from Mathura (one could start in Delhi, not far from Raj Ghat, where Mohandas K. Gandhi was cremated after his assassination in 1947), the boat will carry you easily through a broad plain of fertile farmland, villages, and small towns on either side of the river. The yellow flowers of the mustard planted in straight lines across the fertile brown soil dominate the view, but there are fields of cotton, too, as well as sugar cane, rice, and vegetables, and small clusters of fruit trees.

Life along the river is leisurely and quiet; the Yamuna is no highway. Bathers wade into the stream, praying early in the morning with their palms cupping the water, or briskly working up lather after the sun has turned hot later in the day. In Agra, beneath the rear wall of the Taj Mahal, dozens of men and women slap fabric against rocks at the edge of the river, washing clothes as though in anger, and laying them to dry in the sun. These are the washed-out saris of the not-so-wealthy customers who have hired *dhobis*—members of the caste that specializes in doing the laundry of others. Long strips of faded cotton—saris can be over 12 feet long—mark the edge of the river behind India's main tourist attraction.

Hundreds of miles downstream—you can't be in a hurry to do this—at the city of Allahabad, the stream silently flows into the greater one, the Ganges. The river bank here is unusually broad and sandy—like a popular beach—and the waters of the two rivers meet in whirling vortices and eddies. This is known as the *sangam*, the "coming together," of the rivers, and for religious bathers it is one of the holiest places in all India. According to tradition, a third river, the Sarasvati, rises up from its subterranean course and joins its two sisters at precisely this spot. Every 12 years, when Jupiter enters Aquarius and the sun enters Aries, tens of millions of Hindus, including hundreds of revered holy men (*sadhus*) and teachers (gurus), make the pilgrimage (*yatra*) to this place. The occasion is known as the Maha Kumbha Mela, the Great Pot Festival. It marks the periodical enjoyment of the nectar of immortality, a drop of which fell on this spot when the gods and demons fought over it shortly after creation.

Another 70 or 80 miles downstream—the Yamuna at this point has completely disappeared into the Ganges—is Varanasi (or Banaras or Kashi), India's holiest city. The river here makes a surprising turn to the north before it continues in a southeasterly direction, watering the flat-country regions of eastern Uttar Pradesh and then Bihar. It finally releases it holy waters into the Bay of Bengal, having unobtrusively taken you through a renowned ancient kingdom, Magadha, with its capital, Pataliputra. You can't tell by looking at the villagers and bathers or the bicyclists running errands among the villages and small towns, but this was once the seat of India's greatest ancient kingdom and home to its greatest historic figure, King Ashoka. The countryside is like that: immersed in its busy agricultural seasons. Unlike those of Kashi (or Rome or Jerusalem) the river banks here give away nothing of the region's glorious past. All you can see from the boat is a busy yet slow-moving rural present. If you like history—and the Ganges river system runs through more history than any other river in India—you have to know where to look.

Backtrack to the *sangam* at Allahabad (going upstream requires a lot of muscle; it is more work than touring). Keep going for about 30 miles. Now look to your right, on the northern bank of the Yamuma. Several mounds stand out above the plain, green with overgrown grass, marked with paths where local villagers walk on their daily business among the three area villages. It is all so ordinary, just like the other hundreds of miles of village life along the river, with nothing to attract the eye of a casual tourist. But this place is different. One of the villages here is known as Kosam—an extraordinary name that shows that the countryside does have a memory. Alexander Cunningham, alerted to the name by E. D. Vaylay and B. Shiva Prasad, visited this place in 1861. Intuitively, or perhaps on a lucky hunch, he identified this sleepy area and the green mounds with the ancient city of Kosambi or Kaushambi. If true, this would prove an exciting discovery for students of India's history.

Ancient Kaushambi was a major urban center on a key trading route—the Yamuna. Almost exactly halfway between Mathura and Pataliputra, it never attained the religious distinction of the one or the political power of the other, but it was, after all, right in between the two. Numerous texts, Hindu, Buddhist, and Jain, mention the city, indicating that it existed longer than any other Gangetic city except Kashi. Some of the oldest literary references to Kaushambi include the *Aitareya Brahmana* (c. 800 BCE), the *Shatapatha Brahmana,* and the *Kaushitaki Upanishad* (c. 700 BCE). Numerous Buddhist texts discuss Kaushambi as an important city that Buddha visited on several occasions. Over a millennium later, the renowned Chinese Buddhist pilgrim Hsuan Tsang toured Kaushambi (630–46 CE), and Fa-Hsien described it in the early fifth century CE. The latest mention of the city, toward the end of its distinguished history, is in a copper-plate inscription (dated to the eleventh century) that records a grant by a king called Trilocanapala (king of Kanauj). In sum, although the city was certainly not very important by the time it made its last historic appearance, the span of the records demonstrates that in one form or another Kaushambi existed from Vedic times until premodern India: about two millennia.

Cunningham knew much of this, but the Archeological Survey of India lacked resources for less-than-glamorous sites like this one. Higher profile locations and monuments receive attention earlier—cities like Mithila, Taxila, the Indus Valley cities (Harappa, Mohenjodaro), Hastinapura, Rajgir, the Buddhist stupas (Sanchi, Bodhgaya). Not until 1937–38 did the Archeological Survey get around to excavating at Kaushambi. Unfortunately, the excavation was imprecise and unlayered. It did, however, confirm Cunningham's hunch: this was indeed the historic capital city of the Vatsa people and seat of the famous ancient king Udayana, whom several texts identified as a contemporary of Buddha (sixth century BCE). However, because the excavators proceeded in a horizontal manner rather than using the humbler but more precise vertical trenching, this effort was virtually useless for dating and for measuring the sequence of cultures that inhabited Kaushambi over time. That work would have to wait for a decade or two, until G. R. Sharma from Allahabad University did it properly.

G. R. Sharma was one of the young students in the Taxila School, set up by Mortimer Wheeler in the 1940s. Following in the footsteps of the old master, Sharma insisted on seeing more archeological work carried out by university teams such as his own at Allahabad. He committed himself to Wheeler's new methodology, with its military order and discipline at the site of the dig. The excavation itself would be limited to a narrow space, exposed by trenching in order to reveal all the layers accumulated over the centuries. The work had to be methodically recorded and promptly published: Sharma's two expeditions in Kaushambi (1949 and 1959–60) came out in two volumes; the second dig was reported first.

The Allahabad Museum already had "treasures" from the earlier excavations in Kaushambi: numerous female figures in bronze and terra-cotta, goddesses, seals and coins. But apart from stocking museums with antiquities, Sharma saw more compelling reasons for funding an expensive dig in the mounds of Kosam. A pillar identified as dating to King Ashoka's reign (268–24 BCE), with several edicts inscribed on the stone, attested to the importance of the place at the time of the Mauryan empire. Ashoka had placed such pillars— royal bulletin boards—throughout his large empire, but mainly in centers of political influence where they would be most effective. And indeed, even the covered remains of Kaushambi suggested to Sharma a city of distinction.

The circumference of the area encompassing the mounds was about 4 miles. The bulging contours of the landscape marked a rampart of about 30 feet high, with huge towers (70 feet) at the corners and what appeared to be a deep moat surrounding the entire fortification. Only a major city would be so well fortified, gated, and defended. The position of the mounds indicated that the city was approached by major roads from the cardinal directions, each road flanked by watchtowers as it neared the city gates. This seemed consistent with an urban center that sat at a key geographical intersection of major trade routes connecting some of the most important regions in India for a whole millennium after 500 BCE.

Sharma knew that a stratified uncovering of a city that had endured for so long, at the very heart of the Gangetic civilization, would reveal the sequence of the cultures that occupied this area and would provide an exhaustive temporal map of central Gangetic cultures. Correlated with other such maps— Mathura on the same river system or Taxila on the upper Indus River system— Kaushambi could help historians locate major pieces of the hugely complex historical jigsaw puzzle that is north India's history.

Sharma chose the location of the trench with care. It was near the exposed section of the 1937–38 excavation, which had uncovered a tremendous quantity of cultural remains in a nonsystematic manner. The vertical cut would thus complement the horizontal exposure. The site was near the Ashoka pillar, which had been erected at a central location, at a junction of busy roads. The workers dug all the way down to the natural alluvial soil, beneath all the layers of human construction and accumulated debri. They dug about 30 feet and counted 27 distinct layers at that specific spot. Other locations might have revealed a different number of layers; budget constraints limited each expedition to one or two trenches—a mere porthole view into the past of a huge city. Furthermore, as of 1949–50, carbon 14 dating was not yet available to Sharma, so the layers had to be dated by other means. However, before the final report of the Kaushambi excavations was published in 1969, carbon dating became available and was used to fine-tune the existing estimates.

The earlier dating methods included primarily the collection and analysis of pottery from the excavated layers, along with coins, seals, terra-cotta figurines, and various artistic and religious objects. Pottery was a well-established but general tool, with Northern Black Polished Ware, Gray Ware, and Red Ware known to correspond with distinct historic periods in north India. Coins were more precise. The inscribed ones indicated the identity of the ruler who had them minted; for instance, the early Kaushambi coins inscribed by King Brihaspatimitra have been dated to around 230 BCE, slightly later than the reign of King Ashoka. But even the uninscribed coins (such as those with an elephant on one side and an arched hill on the other, or the so-called Lanky Bull coin), copper or bronze (later silver), cast or uncast, provided useful dating information. Seals, where adequately preserved, also provided names—for instance, the Dutukasa seal was inscribed in the Mauryan period—while other objects from the dig often contained stylistic information that indicated their general period, if not a precise date. Some of the terra-cotta human figurines, for example, revealed a certain aesthetic style (hair arrangement, ornamentation) that was distinctly associated with the art of the Shaka-Parthians (Bactrian invaders of northern India) rather than of India. These figurines were evidence of a foreign rule at the time (c. 150 CE) when the Shaka-Parthians were known—from other locations (Mathura) and written sources—to have ruled in northern India.

Gathering all the material his team dug up, which he later tested with the greater precision of carbon dating, Sharma proposed major periods for Kaushambi's long history (table 3.1). Other historians, including B. B. Lal, have provided alternative analyses of the same archeological finds, though Sharma's work has remained the point of reference for discussions of Kaushambi.

The archeological layers in Kaushambi confirm what we know about the major political "eras" (a term that in India is not precisely apt) of North Indian history in the region of the Gangetic river system. Chief among these was the period of the great Maurya empire (321–185 BCE), represented in layers 12 to 19. An abundance of physical evidence attests to this era; the most significant was found above ground: the famous pillar (now in Allahabad). Interestingly, on

TABLE 3.1. The Periods of Kaushambi

Period	Dates	Layers	Findings
I	1100–800	27–24	Grey Ware (pottery)
II	800–600	23–17	Barren (rotted wood?)
III	600–150	16–9	Northern Black Polished Ware; uninscribed coins; Lanky Bull
IV	150 (BCE)– 350 (CE)	8–1	Brick structures; later wares; Kushana and other coins

Source: G. R. Sharma, *Excavations at Kausambi 1949–50.* Delhi: Manager of Publications, 1969.

that same pillar, Samudragupta—the second ruler of the second great Indian empire (the Gupta, fourth to sixth century CE)—chose to publish a long eulogy to his father, Chandragupta I, and to his own accomplishments. With new words carved onto an old pillar, he established a heritage—a declaration of cultural continuity—between the two vast empires. Six hundred years had passed since the Mauryas, but the royal bulletin board for this region of the empire, the Ashoka pillar, remained the same. Thus, despite the fact that there are comparably few physical remains in Kaushambi that directly link it to the second empire (the Gupta), the pillar indicates that the city was important to the two foremost Indian dynasties.

Sandwiched between the two political powerhouses were lesser kingdoms, not all of them Indian in origin. In Kaushambi alone, these included the Mitras, the Kushanas, and the Magahas, along with the Bactrians. One must bear in mind that the area of North India that included the two river systems (Ganges and Indus) and the huge watershed region between them (*doab*) was dotted with well over five hundred cities and dozens of states and kingdoms during the fifth century BCE alone. No single time line, Kaushambi's or any other, can possibly reflect the wealth of cultures, political rivalries, and sheer human energy that pulsated through the vast region. The historical time line Sharma proposed for Kaushambi is the bare outline for just one city, however prominent it may have been.

The deepest layers, those that predate the Mauryas, are vague. In an archeological sense they are prehistoric: lacking clear data that can be collated with specific textual information. These fifteen layers represent about seven hundred years of habitation in the city. At the very bottom, the oldest layers of Kaushambi's existence (c. 1000–800 BCE), the major finding consisted of Grey Ware pottery in shards, some with painted black rims. At the top of these archeological layers, diggers found regular-looking circular holes in the ground that may indicate the use of posts, probably made of wood. It is possible, Sharma has argued, that the next two hundred years of the city (800–600 BCE) were characterized by an extensive use of wood for construction—the entire region was still dense with forests of *ashvattha, udumbara, bilva,* teak, *amra, nim, pippali, nyagrodha, khadira,* and other trees. Little of the wooden construction material could be expected to survive the hot and humid climate of the region, even in the soil. Indeed, the excavation revealed nothing other than featureless deposit in the layers that represent this so-called late Vedic period.

The following periods, from about 600 BCE (late Vedic and early Buddhist and Jain periods) until the Maurya rule (c. 300 BCE) are some of the most formative centuries of ancient Indian history. Old tribal communities dissolved and regrouped into political units called *janapada,* states. Many were ruled by kings who controlled increasingly powerful cities such as Ujjain, Kosala, Mithila, Mathura, and indeed Kaushambi. The shifting landscape of political and economic realities triggered profound cultural changes, including the emergence of Buddhism and Jainism. The excavation in Kaushambi revealed numerous layers of accumulation (layers 12–16) with Northern Black Polished Ware, along with a number of architectural remains, including walls built of clay blocks. The diggers uncovered several pits, ring (reinforced) wells, and other parts of a drainage system, probably for sewage. They also uncovered sections of a street, beads and charcoal fragments, and a number of terra-cotta figurines of an apparently religious nature. The end of this period, high in the dirt layers, yielded an uninscribed square cast coin showing a tree surrounded by a railing, with an arched hill and perhaps an elephant on the flip side. Comparing this important find with the numismatic analysis of John Allan, the renowned English coin expert, Sharma dated this coin to the period immediately before the rise of the Mauryas, when the Anga dynasty ruled Kaushambi (fourth century BCE).

Kaushambi and History

If Kaushambi represents one slit through which to view ancient North Indian history, then, as expected, the view is both narrow and multilayered. In order to zoom in for a closer view of the early formative centuries, one needs a firm toehold on just one moment in Kaushambi's past. From that perspective, looking backward to the first seven centuries of Indo-Aryan civilization in India, one may begin to imagine the history of the cultures we today call Hinduism. To some readers, this may seem like an odd suggestion. Why not simply follow the history of Indian cultures from A to Z, beginning with the earliest known material and move in chronological order? Why set up an arbitrary "moment," a historic present time, from which to survey the "past?" The answer is that history, to a large extent, is a subjective category, a narrative. And far more interesting than our "history of India" is the lived experience and self-understanding of Indians at important points within the flow of their own time. This is especially important to keep in mind when studying the thoughts and intentions that motivated past generations, not just the wars they fought or the objects they built. This has been the emphasis of new archeology, and increasingly historiography, in India. How did ancient Indians regard their own past, and what kind of a history (narrative) did they construct? In the light of this, how did their perceived past shape their present and future?

Assuming, then, that there are good reasons to choose a historic moment and view the centuries that came before from the perspective of that point in time, what period should we choose? The obvious choice is the period termed by Sharma subperiod 1B, which corresponds to the third century BCE (c. 260–230 BCE). These are the peak decades of the Mauryan dynasty, which was headquartered in the Magadha capital city, Pataliputra, just after Ashoka converted to Buddhism. At that time, Kaushambi was the regional seat of the governor (*mahamatra*) who served under Ashoka.

From an archeological perspective, this period offers plenty of material, and a relatively detailed view of the city emerges in its oldest known form. And as noted previously, the early years of the Mauryan empire and the arrival of Alexander of Macedonia have served as the anchor dates for Indian historiography. But most important, during the Mauryan decades an intellectual revolution reintroduced a new tool that had not been seen in India for over a thousand years: writing. Although a few literary references (in the *Ramayana*) hint that writing did prevail among Brahmins, no hard evidence supports this. The pillar Ashoka placed at Kaushambi, with its inscribed edict in the language called Magadhi (a version of Sanskrit), is written in a script called Brahmi, which James Prinsep deciphered in 1837. The edicts represented an enormous cultural innovation for third-century Indians and an indispensable leverage mechanism for Indian historiography.

Writing in India

Over a thousand years earlier, on the banks of the Indus River in northwest India (now in Pakistan), several urban centers were nearing the final stages of a long period of prosperity. Mohenjodaro and Harappa had been the most highly developed and influential among these river cities. At their peak, around 2500 BCE, these cities matched the cities of Egypt and Mesopotamia in cultural sophistication and technological development. Mohenjodaro and Harappa are widely known for their urban planning and the design of their elaborate baths and sewage systems. Even more intriguing, among the vast quantities of archeological material dug up at the Indus River sites were several seals inscribed with elaborate writing, which remains undeciphered. The pictographic writing, more than the physical cities, conveys the level of cultural sophistication these civilizations had achieved. However, over the course of centuries, as the cities declined and disappeared, the enormous Indus-Gangetic region saw the arrival of Indo-Aryan peoples who did not write but spoke an apparently foreign language. As noted, the topic of the Indo-Aryan arrival has recently become politically charged, but most scholars today agree that the Indo-Aryans migrated from Central Asia, via the regions later known as Persia and Afghanistan, into South Asia. The evidence for this theory is almost exclusively linguistic but looks solid. In the course of time, by the fifth century BCE, the language spoken by these people came to be known as Sanskrit. However, it still retained many of the ancient features that tied it linguistically to European languages, and set it apart from South Asian ones.

Sanskrit was a dynamic and flexible language, and it was put to use in a variety of contexts, including religious poetry and speculation, philosophy, sciences, law, medicine, and grammar. As one might expect, Sanskrit was particularly well cultivated by the class of intellectuals known as Brahmins, but it was the dominant language among all the Indo-Aryans, until regional variations (known as Prakrits) began to emerge around the fifth century BCE.

One of the most interesting facts about the immense literary culture that sprang up with the use of Sanskrit was its predominantly oral nature. During the early formative centuries of Indo-Aryan cultures, all the "texts" existed only in the minds of those relatively few members of families (*gotras*) who had committed them to memory. Chief among the memorized texts were the revealed scriptures, the Vedas with their many subsidiary genres (for instance, Brahmanas and Upanishads), the sutras (scientific texts) that expanded Vedic learning, and more popular narratives such as the *Mahabharata* and *Ramayana*. A king who wished to consult a Brahmin on a matter of public concern, say a ritual or a legal issue, was literally using a living text, or even library. At the same time, a Buddhist monk who wished to "look up" something Buddha may have said in one of his sermons or check on a point of monastic ethics would also consult a living text in the shape of a learned scholar, perhaps another monk in his own monastary. If any of the numerous works that existed at that time was actually written down—highly unlikely, according to historians—none has survived.

An oral culture, however sophisticated, is bound by distinct limitations. It tilts heavily toward the top: those who know the texts and agree to share their knowledge tend to dominate. Social hierarchies, revolving around sacred knowledge, became virtually inescapable. When writing did emerge, it changed this social and political fact by opening up information in an unprecedented fashion. Naturally, the dissemination of knowledge in written form, for the first time since the Indus Valley civilization of India, was bound to produce profound cultural consequences. This turning point came when the royal edicts of Ashoka (c. 260 BCE) were inscribed on pillars that were erected throughout the empire for all to see. These may represent the earliest examples of written Sanskrit we have today. The inscriptions were written in Magadhi, the local vernacular dialect of the Sanksrit of the period (known by linguists as Middle Indo-Aryan). Most of the edicts were carved in scripts called Brahmi and Kharoshti, which scholars argue may have arrived from West Asia. Some of the inscriptions in the western regions included translations into Greek and Aramaic.

The third century was thus an exciting time, and Kaushambi was a dynamic place to be, close to the heart of the Mauryan empire and important enough to draw the great emperor's attention.

The City under Ashoka

The Mauryas rose to preeminence at some point between 324 and 313 BCE, when Chandragupta Maurya removed the last of the Nandas and established imperial rule in Pataliputra. This was also roughly the time of his encounter with Alexander of Macedonia. Within half a century, through successful military campaigns, the Mauryan empire covered virtually the entire subcontinent. Ashoka, who was Chandragupta's grandson, inherited the throne in 269 and continued the vigorous expansion of the empire, before he decided to renounce violence and convert to Buddhism.

The archeological period in Kaushambi for the reign of Ashoka (subperiods 1A and 1B) shows a very large city built in a neat pattern. A major road, about 16 feet wide and paved with a thick layer of brick fragments and lime, cut through the center of the city. Primary lanes ran off from the main street at right angles, and lesser alleys off of these. Many of the streets were lined with shops, and the road was busy with traffic, including heavy vehicles that left deep ruts. Stone posts protected some corner buildings from the damage of turning carts. The houses, built with burned bricks, were carefully planned in relation to the direction of the streets. Many of the houses had two stories, but, because the second floors (and roofs) were made of wood, little has survived of the upper structures. Virtually all the homes, including the modest ones, were designed around an inner courtyard, with separate rooms for men and women. A sophisticated system of waste and water drainage ran throughout the city, including terra-cotta ring wells, soakage jars, drains, and tanks. In addition to private homes, there were several large buildings, probably public. Literary sources suggest that these may have been Buddhist monasteries and government buildings. One of the large Buddhist monasteries, named Ghoshitarama after a wealthy banker, was identified on the basis of an inscription dated to the first century CE. But the Buddhist scriptures name it as a place visited both by Buddha and his disciples, including Sariputra and Ananda. Apparently, the structure was four-sided with a central courtyard, pillared veranda, and numerous surrounding cells for meetings.

Cutting-edge archeology today demonstrates that a great deal of social and cultural information can be gleaned from the raw material of archeological digs. Information about family size and gender roles, social hierarchy, professional specialization, practices relating to purity and pollution, and beliefs about danger, luck, and the significance of directions are all embodied in the planning of ancient cities, the construction of houses, and the design of smaller objects. But even simple inference can lead to reasonable conjectures about the life of Kaushambi in the third century BCE. The city population had to have been large, consisting of dozens of professions, from food producers, transporters, and sellers to builders and planners, carpenters, carvers, administrators, law enforcement personnel, educators, religious professionals, and many others. The city was a regional hub and a major commerce center, and the river alone probably generated several professional and social groups, including boat builders, fishermen, operators of ferries, boat navigators and captains, and the religious professionals one sees near rivers (cremators, priests, exorcists and healers, astrologers).

This economic and social picture hangs on a few textual citations and a wealth of concrete archeological evidence for the period when Ashoka ruled over Kaushambi. A detailed analysis of hundreds of specific objects would further enrich this historic view of an important regional center. But only up to a point. What did the residents of Kaushambi believe or imagine? Can the city's archeology help us reconstruct the mental life—the culture—of its citizens over two millennia ago?

However, religion does not grow in a vacuum—there is a direct link between the physical city and the imagination of the people who live there. This is an elusive but critical point. The science that went into the construction of buildings or the design of minute objects—the geometry, chemistry, engineering, and other sciences—is as much a part of Kaushambi's religious worldviews as the rituals and beliefs that objects were made to serve. The genius of a place is often expressed in the way ideas combine with raw matter, and the way the past is integrated into the present as scientific knowledge.

According to economic historians of India—Marxists, including D. D. Kosambi, and others, among them K. V. Sundara Rajan—it is the material context that leads to cultural achievments. The complex economy of Kaushambi, with its diverse means of production, monetary system, transportation, accumulated and stored wealth, and taxation system, supported a dynamic intellectual elite. Priests, monks, and other experts created both the physical and cultural superstructures of a lofty culture. Among their accomplishments was a mythology that glorified the king and the Brahmins, a seasonal and annual calendar, a and legal system anchored in relgious values. Due to the value of cultural objects Indian archeology has an important role to play alongside textual and religious studies in reconstructing ancient worldviews. And ranking high among the archeological products of the new urban civilizations—the archives for the civilization of Kaushambi, so to speak—were the objects that reveal an emerging sense of history: a perceived past.

Kaushambi's Past

As noted, in 260 BCE, during the rule of Ashoka, hundreds of men in Kaushambi acted as living libraries with the aid of their prodigious memories. We still have these texts today; anyone can look up what these experts acquired patiently during the course of a lifetime. The following chapters will look at many of these works. However, none of these "books" were, properly speaking, works of history. There is no indication that third-century Kaushambi had history, even in the sense of the Greek Herodotus or the Jewish Yoseph ben Matityahu (Josephus). Instead, it had a "living past"—the investment of prestige in memorizing ancient scriptures and the vesting of authority in objects and institutions that drew on the past. Among the hundreds of objects uncovered in the remains of the city, three stand out as eloquent testament to the ways its residents situated their present in relationship to their past. Two of these archeological discoveries are impressive in their magnitude; the third seems enigmatic and may raise some questions but is also very suggestive.

The Edict

The first object, often bundled up with the very existence of Kaushambi, is Ashoka's pillar inscribed with what is known as its "schism edict." The emperor posted the following message, which was addressed to the regional governor (*mahamatra*) but was meant for all the residents: "The beloved of the gods commands the *mahamatra* of Kaushambi: No member of the Buddhist *sangha* [monastic movement], which I have united, should get the chance to sow division. Any monk or nun who splits the *sangha* shall be expelled from the monastery and shall be made to wear white [nonmonastic] robes."

The text, reconstructed and translated from the legible portions of the inscription, became familiar throughout the huge empire. Kaushambi received one of several versions of the schism edict. The words of the royal pronouncement reinforce textual evidence that Kaushambi was an important institutional center for Buddhism. And like early Christians but unlike Hindus, Buddhists sought to define a universal and uncontested doctrine that could be traced back to the teachings of a single founder—Buddha. Clearly, then, an awareness of continuity, even what might be called a tradition, emerged in Kaushambi in the form of reverence toward the correct teachings of a historic figure, the founder of a Dhamma (Pali for *dharma*, here meaning "tradition" or "Buddhism"), namely, Buddha. This backward-looking perspective may have prevailed among the Buddhist (and Jain) residents of the city, but it was known to everyone as a privileged ideology. After all, the king guarded it with words he had inscribed on stone.

Among the Hindu residents of the city, such a traditionalist approach to the past existed in the reverence toward the Vedas. However, these revealed scriptures remained largely obscured by the oral and Brahminical nature of their transmission.

The Clay Figurine

The second archeological object, a figurine made of clay, embodied a more distinctly local sense of history, one that supported the city's view of itself. This figurine was shaped in a preexisting mould consisting of two parts that had to be pressed together by hand while wet clay was poured in through a hole. The finger marks of the craftsman remain on the figurine, which may have been a common object in Kaushambi during the first few centuries BCE. The figurine is an elephant with two riders, male and female. The female is seated behind, leaning against the male, who drives the elephant, and she is holding a purse in her hand. G. R. Sharma and other scholars have interpreted the figurine as a representation of King Udayana's escape from Avanti with his second wife, Vasula-datta. The story of the escape is a romantic one, and it has made its way in several versions into some of the most distinguished Indian texts, including the *Dhammapada* (a Buddhist text disseminated in a number of Middle Indo-Aryan languages), the *Meghaduta*, a Sanskrit poem, and the *Kathasaritsagara*, a much later collection of stories.

Udayana was not the first king of Kaushambi and the Vatsa state—he was seventeenth in his line. But he was the most famous, reaching a level of stature and prestige that only a few other ancient kings have surpassed in the popular Indian imagination. According to the literary accounts, Udayana, who lived about three centuries before Ashoka, was known for possessing a magical formula for controlling elephants, a great military advantage. This allowed Kaushambi to compete favorably with its neighboring states (*janapadas*) at a time when sixteen major states were vying for hegemony along the Ganges River system. King Pajjota of the neighboring state of Avanti decided to kidnap King Udayana in order to obtain this powerful formula. He had his carpenters craft a hollow wooden elephant, which was then beautifully painted. The elephant could be operated by ropes and levers from the inside, where sixty soldiers hid. A Vatsa hunter saw the beautiful creature near the boundary of the two states and quickly reported it to the king, who set out to capture it.

King Pajjota's plan worked perfectly, and his men captured King Udayana and locked him up in the royal palace of Avanti. The two kings worked out a deal whereby Udayana would receive his freedom in exchange for the magical formula. King Pajjota sent his daughter, Princess Vasula-datta, to learn the complex formula from the captive and memorize it, which would take several days. She remained hidden behind a drape, having been told that the captive was a dwarf. And King Udayana kept the drape in place, having in turn been told that his pupil would be a hunchback. Of course, the ruse failed, and the two fell in love. They plotted their escape carefully, using both wit and magic. Riding out of town on the back of an elephant that Udayana had been able to summon, they scattered gold coins from a purse to distract their pursuers. Miraculously, Udayana and Vasula-datta made it safely to Kaushambi, where she became his third and most loved wife.

This charming legend would have been extremely familiar in Kaushambi three centuries after the events it depicts. After all, it is still one of the best-known romantic tales in India. The legend represents just one chapter in the life of this king, who was not only a historic figure but served as a model for the Buddhist residents of Kaushambi. Like King Ashoka, who converted to Buddhism, Udayana underwent a transforming encounter with the teachings of Buddha and finally converted. During the rule of King Udayana, early Buddhist texts indicate, Buddha visited Kaushambi several times and delivered some of his more important sermons there. Under the great teacher's influence, King

Udayana initiated the process that would turn his city into one of the most important centers of Buddhism.

The Bird Altar

The third archeological find ranks as one of the most significant clues to the Hindu past of Kaushambi. Sharma (1960) reports that near the eastern gate of Kaushambi, just outside the fortification, the diggers found a sacrificial altar made of piled bricks. The altar had the shape of a flying bird, wings spread and tail stretched back, with its face turned to the side and pointing southeast. The construction was stunningly complex, far more elaborate than the rules of brick masonry would require. The bricks were piled in varying heights to achieve different surface levels for different parts of the bird. The bricks themselves varied in shape and size but were stacked up to an even surface through geometrical ingenuity. According to Sharma, the altar was very precisely designed, in terms of the numerical ratios of its different proportions, with the length (44 feet 8 inches) and width (33 feet 6 inches). Subsequent investigators (especially B. B. Lal) denied that the pile of bricks was an altar, but Sharma maintained his position.

The sacrificial altar at Kaushambi was of a type known as a *shyenaciti,* or hawk altar. According to Sharma, the altar is a recognizable example of a Vedic sacrificial space, carefully built to the specifications of texts that (as I have noted) mention Kaushambi, namely the Brahmanas (*Shatapatha, Taittiriya*, and others). In a sense, the *shyenachiti* is the very embodiment of these ancient texts, which were older than 800 BCE, and which detail and explain the even older ritual traditions of the Vedas.

The sacrificial rituals that formed the foundations of religious action at the beginning of Hindu religious history included sacrifices of such victims as animals, humans, and soma (an unidentified plant with profound mental and perhaps health effects). In the course of several centuries, the rituals became specialized and highly technical, and the Brahmana texts give detailed instructions for their construction, with names such as the Agnichayana (piling of bricks for the fire sacrifice), the Mahavrata (great year-long sacrifice), the Darshapurnamasa (new and full moon rituals), the Ashvamedha (horse sacrifice), and many more.

Indeed, the archeologists of Kaushambi uncovered, within the space of the large altar, the bones of humans, buffalo, horses, elephants, goats, and other sacrificial victims. With this discovery, a clear and unbroken line could be drawn between the religious practices of the third-century city and the primordial religion of the Vedas. And because a complex ritual such as the Vedic sacrifice, in its many forms, required numerous priests who sang hundreds of chants and hymns, the Hindu practitioners of Kaushambi clearly possessed wealth, institutional resources, and mastery over the texts and ideology of the Vedas. In other words, third-century Kaushambi Hindus knew and venerated their tradition of Vedic religion.

In summary, the three distinct archeological finds—the edict, the clay figurine, and the bird altar—help us situate Kaushambi in its own historic background—its perceived past. Viewed close up, each of these objects embodies time and tradition in a unique way. Together, they give nuance and texture to the glimpse of the religious life of Kaushambi that is available to us. They teach us, first and foremost, that the religious life at a given moment in India's history—the third century BCE—must be understood, among other things, in terms of the self-conscious preservation of venerable traditions. The earliest and most important tradition for Hindus was the tradition of the Vedas, the foundation of cultural existence for Kaushambi's Hindu residents. At the core of that Vedic tradition stood the sacrifice, with its complicated secrets.

4

King Janaka's Contest

A century and a half before the time of Buddha and the reign of Udayana, Kaushambi was not the best place to discuss the Agnicayana ritual. That distinction belonged to the state of Videha with its capital at Mithila, four days' journey east. That was the place whose king was willing to pay one thousand head of cattle and ten thousand pieces of gold just to find out who among the sacrificial experts within the Ganges River area was smartest at unlocking the hidden meaning of the sacrifice. Janaka was a king who could boast of remarkable generosity toward Brahmins along with the curiosity of a philosopher. In the course of his contests, where fortunes changed hands, esoteric ideas became public. One idea was so powerful, so manifestly persuasive, that modern thinkers still embrace it, three millennia later.

Videha, also known as Tirhut and Tirabhukti, was the easternmost region of Indo-Aryan settlement in the eighth century BCE. At that time it was not fully tamed by the fires of Agni, which was the Vedas' way of saying that the forests were not yet burned down for farmland. Instead, it was riddled with swamps and marshes, separated by broad swathes of jungle that was still thick with undergrowth. To the north, the Himalayan range walled in Videha, and it stretched south to the banks of the Ganges. The kingdom spread out, just east of the Gandaki River, to an area of about 25,000 square miles, about the size of West Virginia. Today the region is part of the Indian state of Bihar and extends to southern Nepal.

Although Videha was one of the best-known Ganges Valley states, its origins are entirely shrouded in myth. The most detailed account is told in the *Vishnu Purana*, a much later collection of myths, cosmologies, and pseudohistories. A son of Ikshvaku of the great Solar Dynasty (Manu was its founder), a man called Nimi, decided one day to perform a sacrifice. The greatest priest of the day, Vashishtha, turned him down because he was under commission to work for Indra, king of the Vedic gods. So Nimi turned to a second prominent priest, Gautama, who was Vashishtha's rival. When Vashishtha found out, he put a curse on Nimi so that he would lose his physical form, and Nimi reciprocated in kind. On the death of King Nimi, the *rishis* churned his discarded body and produced a boy, whom they called Mithi, the churned one. Mithi became king of the land that would eventually be called Mithila. He established a prolific dynasty of kings, all called Janaka (self-born), because the founder did not have a natural birth.

There is no archeological evidence for the actual founding of Mithila or for the events I will describe shortly having to do with the sacrificial contest. Despite its great renown, Mithila has not been excavated, and proper historical research in the area begins only with a much later dynasty, the Karnatas, who ruled between 1097 and 1325 CE. All of the information we possess about early Mithila comes from literary sources: the *Shatapatha Brahmana*, the *Brihadaranyaka Upanishad*, Panini's *Eight Chapters*, the *Ramayana*, the *Mahabharata*, Jain and Buddhist texts, especially the *Jatakas*, and the Puranas. As a cultural emblem, Mithila stands out as the native land of Sita, wife of the great epic hero Rama. According to the *Ramayana* (1.3), Rama and his brother Lakshmana took four days to reach Mithila from their own native Ayodhya. In Mithila, Rama won the hand of Sita in a *svayamvara*, a contest for winning the hand of a princess. Sita's father, King Janaka Siradhvaja, was the ninth Janaka in the dynasty, according to the Purana's list, and a forefather of the Janaka who was willing to spend a fortune on intellectual contests. Either in his court or somewhere in his state, the Brahminical school of the *White Yajurveda* produced its versions of the sacred Vedic texts: sacrificial manuals, commentaries, and speculations. The two most important works were the *Shatapatha Brahmana*, with its detailed explanation of the Agnicayana, and the *Brihadaranyaka Upanishad*—actually part of that Brahmana and one of the true masterpieces of world religious literature. I now turn to that Upanishad for the unfolding of this one specific contest.

The Contest

The *Brihadaranyaka Upanishad* tells us that King Janaka offered the competitors a prize of one thousand cows with ten pieces of gold hanging from the horns of each. It is difficult to say how many ritual experts attended. The truly distinguished competitors arrived from the state of Kuru-Panchala, the stronghold of Vedic learning, but they must have intimidated each other, because no one dared to claim the prize. The one who did would invite intense questioning by all the others, each drawing on questions from his or her area of expertise. According to a contemporary belief, failure to answer a question or asking more than one actually knew could result in the explosion of the pretender's head. Even short of such a catastrophe, the shame of exposing one's ignorance in the presence of eminent company was enough to inhibit the best thinkers of the region.

Surprisingly, the only man who was not deterred was local. Yajnavalkya, the text tells us, calmly instructed his young assistant to guide the cattle home. There is very little that we know about this man, outside of his performance at Janaka's contest. He was a Brahmin scholar and priest who lived outside of Mithila but was available to the king for consultations on religions matters. According to some of the contemporary textual sources, he was the author of the *Vajasaneyi Samhita* (known as the *White Yajurveda*) and his name was attached, centuries later, to an important school of jurisprudence. Yajnavalkya was married to two women, Maitreyi and Katyayani, but had no children. He lived a comfortable life, even before entering the contest, but would eventually renounce his possessions and family ties and retire to the forest to meditate. His wife Maitreyi, in one of the most personal Upanishadic narratives, would join him there.

Eight priests and scholars, some of them far more highly esteemed than Yajnavalkya himself, became outraged by his presumptuousness. They set on him with intellectual ferocity, probing to see how much he really knew. The first to attack, another local man, was a Hotri priest from the court of Janaka named Ashvala.

> "Yajnavalkya," he said, "tell me—when this whole world is caught in the grip of death, when it is overwhelmed by death, how can the patron of the sacrifice free himself completely from its grip?" Yajnavalkya replied: "by means of the Hotri priest—that is, by means of the fire, by means of speech. So this speech—it is this fire here; it is the Hotri priest; it is freedom; and it is complete freedom."
> (*Brihadaranyaka Upanishad* 3.1.3; Olivelle)

Ashvala knew what he was doing: the connection between his own role at the sacrifice, the fire he controlled, and speech was what he knew best. It had to be good to hear, especially with the king present, that complete freedom from death (for the sacrificer—the king!) would be gained through the Hotri's own ritual work. But there was still the matter of the cattle and Yajnavalkya's cockiness. So Ashvala continued with the questioning. Systematically and progressively, he grilled Yajnavalkya about the strength of the ritual and the role of all the other priests who officiated.

He also demanded to hear how were the days and nights, and the waxing and the waning of the moon—in short, time itself—overcome by means of the sacrifice? All of Yajnavalkya's answers resembled the first: the sacrificial priests were the answers, along with the psychological and cosmological objects they corresponded to. The Adhvaryu priest was sight and the sun; the Udgatri was breath and the wind; and the Brahmin priest was mind and the moon. All of these helped the sacrificer overcome time and attain heaven.

The questioning went on: How many verses, oblations, songs, and gods would be involved in the sacrifice later that evening? What were they and what did they mean? Yajnavalkya knew them all as though he could perform the ritual single-handedly. He answered without hesitation, economizing his words. The display was so authoritative that Ashvala, the king's priest, fell silent and sat down, defeated.

The next questioner, Jaratkarava Arthabhaga, was not as interested in the sacrifice as his predecessor had been. He began with a technical question about the ritual, but the terms he used were so ambiguous that Yajnavalkya could only interpret the questions psychologically: How many "graspers" and "over-graspers" were there and what were they? In the sacrifice, the grasper was a cup, and the overgrasper was an extra cupful. Both of these referred—experts said—to soma juice. But Yajnavalkya ignored this technical detail and explained the eight graspers and overgraspers as follows: Exhalation, speech, tongue, sight, hearing, mind, hands, and skin were the graspers. They were the sense organs with which we perceive ("grasp") the world around us. The objects they grasped were the overgraspers: inhalation, words, flavor, appearances, sound, desire, action, and touch.

The surprising conclusion, and the reason for the strange name "over-grasper," was that the object of the sense actually controlled the sense organ to the same extent that the sense organ produced the object. The relationship worked both ways. Your eyes allow you to see a tree, but the sight of the tree controls the eyes. To put this in modern terms, we do not just discover a world with our senses; we are constituted as subjects in that relationship. Yajna-valkya did not elaborate any, and the questioning moved to other topics, but this idea continued to resonate quietly until it resurfaced over a century later when Buddha discussed the psychology of suffering, and still later when Samkhya and Yoga philosophers developed it in much greater detail. Here

Yajnavalkya, almost casually, sowed the seed for an astounding idea, then moved on.

Arthabhaga was fascinated with the topic of death, and he led the conversation to these dangerous grounds:

> "Yajnavalkya," Arthabhaga said again, "tell me—when a man has died, and his speech disappears into fire, his breath into the wind, his sight into the sun, his mind into the moon, his hearing into the quarters, his physical body into the earth, his atman [self] into space, the hair of his body into plants, the hair of his head into trees, and his blood and semen into water—what then happens to that person?" Yajnavalkya replied: "My friend, we cannot talk about this in public. Take my hand, Arthabhaga; let's go and discuss this in private."
>
> So they left and talked about it. And what did they talk about?—they talked about noting but action [karma]. And what did they praise?—they praised nothing but action. Yajnavalkya told him: "A man turns into something good by good action and into something bad by bad action."(*Brihadaranyaka Upanishad* 3.2.13; Olivelle)

Perhaps more than other new ideas of great magnitude, the concept of karma had been a carefully kept secret. The Vedas had not yet discussed the metaphysics of moral retribution—"as you do, so shall you become." For centuries, the Indo-Aryans had linked their moral actions to consequences, but there was no specific and dedicated metaphysical mechanism for justice. If your sin angered a god—Varuna was usually described as the controller of the moral order—he could strike you with illness or misfortune: Varuna's fetters were the common Vedic idiom for moral retribution. The *Rig-Veda* pegged the destinies of those who died on the ethical quality of their life. It described journeys to worlds of fathers or of gods or to a hell governed by the god Yama, who weighed good and evil on his scale. But karma in the Vedas—literally "action," referred simply to ritual acts: sacrificing, following the rules. Suddenly, in a late Vedic text, Yajnavalkya alluded to a secret new doctrine about pure moral retribution: a mechanism that was built into action itself. This reference may have been the first mention of this quintessential Indian idea.

Possibly, when Yajnavalkya took Arthabhaga aside, he spoke to him in even greater detail about the physical process of dying, of assuming a new birth and relying on the moral quality of one's previous actions to achieve a good birth. Later, long after the contest was over, Yajnavalkya explained these matters to King Janaka (*Brihadaranyaka Upanishad* 4.4.3, 5, 6; Olivelle):

"It is like this. As a caterpillar, when it comes to the tip of a blade of grass, reaches out to a new foothold and draws itself onto it, so the atman, after it has knocked down this body and rendered it unconscious, reaches out to a new foothold and draws itself onto it." ...

What a man turns out to be depends on how he acts and on how he conducts himself. If his actions are good, he will turn into something good. If his actions are bad, he will turn into something bad.

On this point there is the following verse:

> A man who's attached goes with his action,
> to that very place to which
> his mind and character cling.
> Reaching the end of his action,
> Of whatever he has done in this world—
> From that world he returns
> back to this world,
> back to action.

In Buddhist philosophy and later Hindu thought, the concept of karma would attain great prominence. But no Indian thinker could improve on Yajnavalkya's early insight that desire was the driving force behind the psychology of karma, perpetuator of the cycle of birth and rebirth, death and redeath. It was Yajnavalkya, too, who first drew the conclusion that to banish desire was to overcome death and attain immortality, which was an archaic way of speaking about unity with Brahman. But more on that would be said in the contest.

Three more men addressed Yajnavalkya with difficult questions, and all were satisfied with his answers. Then it was Gargi Vachaknavi's turn. As far as Gargi was concerned, the exchange may have taken a turn for the overly abstract and was perhaps too detached from concrete reality. So she steered Yajnavalkya back to the world around us, keeping her questions sharp and concrete. "Tell me," she asked, "since this whole world is woven back and forth on water, on what then is water woven back and forth?" Gargi was referring, of course, to the familiar Vedic cosmological metaphor that expressed the unity of the world, its essential interconnectedness.

"On air, Gargi."
"On what, then, is air woven back and forth?"
"On the worlds of the intermediate regions, Gargi."
"On what, then, are the worlds of the intermediate regions woven back and forth?"

"On the worlds of the Gandharvas, Gargi." (*Brihadaranyaka Upanishad* 3.6; Olivelle)

This rapid exchange did not last long. After the worlds of the Gandharvas came the worlds of the sun, the moon, the stars, the gods, Indra, Prajapati, then Brahman. When Gargi finally asked on what were the worlds of Brahman woven back and forth, Yajnavalkya cautioned her to stop or her head would explode. And so Gargi fell silent, for the time being.

For anyone who might wish to find a capsule of late Vedic cosmology, here it is. The universe was ordered hierarchically from fundamental matter to cosmic matter, and from that to gods, and finally to Brahman, as the most basic entity in all of reality. The exact relation between each layer of reality—the ontology—is difficult to define with accuracy because weaving is a metaphor, not a philosophical concept. It is clear, however, that fabric is not truly woven on anything other than itself, with nothing but space between the threads. Thus, at this very early point in Indian philosophy, the question was What holds it all together? not What is the dialectical relation between substance and form? But for Yajnavalkya, a true genius, the search for the essence of reality would have to lead beyond metaphors to more explicit theories. The next questioner, a great Upanishadic figure himself, gave him that opportunity.

Uddalaka Aruni

Uddalaka Aruni may have been the foremost Brahmin scholar in North India during the time of the Brahmanas and early Upanishads. He came to the contest from his native Kuru-Panchala, where he was a renowned teacher. There is literary evidence that he had students from Kaushambi and from as far away as Taxila. Even Yajnavalkya was his student (*Brihadaranyaka Upanishad* 6.3.7), but Aruni's best-known lesson involved his own son, Shvetaketu. This lesson—recorded in the *Chandogya Upanishad*, a contemporary text connected with a different Vedic school (the Tandya school, which specialized in the Samaveda)—is worth recounting.

Uddalaka sent his son at the fairly late age of 12 to study the Vedas with a guru. Twelve years later, the young man came back with more arrogance than knowledge. He was particularly ignorant of the matter his father considered most important—the essential ground of all being. Uddlaka set out to teach Shvetaketu a concept he called "the rule of transformation." In the copper of a coin one sees all copper; in one lump of clay one sees all clay. The differences are merely a matter of convention—differences in shape or in the names given to all the objects made of copper or clay.

Shvetaketu showed interest and asked for more information. His father had been trying to communicate by means of concrete examples a more universal lesson: that all of reality is the transformed appearance of one thing only—an essence, or atman. His lesson became more explicit:

> "Now, take the bees, son. They prepare the honey by gathering nectar from a variety of trees and by reducing that nectar to a homogenous whole. In that state the nectar from each different tree is not able to differentiate: "I am the nectar of that tree," and "I am the nectar of this tree." In exactly the same way, son, when all these creatures merge into the existent, they are not aware that: "We are merging into the existent." No matter what they are in this world—whether it is a tiger, a lion, a wolf, a boar, a worm, a moth, a gnat, or a mosquito—they all merge into that.
>
> "The finest essence here—that constitutes the self of this whole world; that is the truth; that is the atman [self]. And that's how you are, Svetaketu." (*Chandogya Upanishad* 6.9; Olivelle)

In a series of brilliantly evocative mind experiments, Uddalaka demonstrated the relationship between the complex and diverse world we live in and the one true reality in its utter simplicity.

> "Bring a banyan fruit."
>> "Here it is, sir."
>> "Cut it up."
>> "I've cut it up, sir."
>> "What do you see there?"
>> "These quite tiny seeds, sir."
>> "Now, take one of them and cut it up."
>> "I've cut one up, sir."
>> "What do you see there?"
>> "Nothing, sir."
>
> Then he told him: "This finest essence here, son, that you can't even see—look how on account of that finest essence this huge banyan tree stands here.
>
> "Believe, my son: the finest essence here—that constitutes the self of this whole world; that is the truth; that is the atman. And that's how you are, Svetaketu." (*Chandogya Upanishad* 6.12; Olivelle)

All of these hands-on illustrations ended with the same didactic formula: that is the truth, the Self (atman)—and that is what you are, *tat tvam asi*. The expression "tat tvam asi" may be the signature phrase of the monistic

Upanishads—those that recognize one true reality—as an entire corpus. Whatever is essential beneath the multiplicity of names and forms is also essential to the individual person. It is the Self of the subject, the essence of who we are.

In the contest in Mithila, Uddalaka told Yajnavalkya about a woman who had become possessed by the spirit of a Gandharva—a celestial musician. The Gandharva asked two questions of everyone present: What is the string on which this world and the next, as well as all beings, are strung together; Who controls the worlds and all beings from within? Could Yajnavalkya answer these questions?

Yajnavalkya responded with his usual aplomb that he could: the string was the wind. On the string of the wind, this world and the next and all beings were strung together. Uddalka accepted this answer and repeated the second question about the inner controller.

Yajnavalkya's answer to this question was both remarkably short and long. The answer was atman, the Self. The atman, who is present within but is different from all things, is the inner controller. That was the short answer. Inexhaustibly thorough, however, Yajnavalkya ran off the full list of all the things which atman differs from yet controls: earth, waters, fire, the intermediate region, wind, sky, sun, the quarters (the directions), moon and stars, space, darkness, light, all beings, breath, speech, sight, hearing, mind, skin, perception, and semen. This repetitive and seemingly pedantic answer—no one would dream of interrupting its flow—concluded resoundingly with a stunning psychological insight:

> "He sees, but he can't be seen; he hears, but he can't be heard; he
> thinks, but he can't be thought of; he perceives, but he can't be
> perceived. Beside him, there is no one who sees, no one who hears,
> no one who thinks, and no one who perceives. It is this self of yours
> who is the inner controller, the immortal. All besides this is grief."
> (*Brihadaranyaka Upanishad* 3.7.23; Olivelle)

Uddalaka Aruni, who had taught atman to his son Shvetaketu, accepted this answer and fell silent.

After Uddalaka Aruni finished, Gargi Vachaknavi spoke up again (or perhaps the editors allowed another version of her previous question to remain on the record). The question, again, concerned that reality on which all things in the world ("the things above the sky, the things below the earth...") were woven back and forth. The new version of Yajnavalkya's answer—"the imperishable"—is worth quoting because it can help dispel any misconception that Brahman was a God-like entity:

He replied: "That, Gargi, is the imperishable, and Brahmins refer to
it like this—it is neither coarse nor fine; it is neither short nor long; it
has neither blood nor fat; it is without shadow or darkness; it is
without air or space; it is without contact; it has no taste or smell; it
is without sight or hearing; it is without speech or mind; it is without energy, breath, or mouth; it is beyond measure; it has nothing within it or outside of it; it does not eat anything; and no one eats
it." (*Brihadaranyaka Upanishad* 3.8.8.; Olivelle)

Yajnavalkya then added that even if a man performed every sacrifice and religious obligation, without knowledge of this imperishable, his religious life
would amount to nothing. Once again, he repeated that the imperishable sees
but is not seen, hears but cannot be heard. Aside from the imperishable, "there
is no one that sees, no one that hears, no one that thinks, and no one that
perceives" (*Brihadaranyaka Upanishad* 3.8.11; Olivelle).

Next spoke Vidagdha Shakalya. He may have calculated that he was the
last person standing between Yajnavalkya and a great wealth, for he took longer than the others and assumed a condescending tone. He asked how many
gods there were. Yajnavalkya, citing the ritual invocation, answered: "Three and
three hundred, and three and three thousand."

Shakalya was unable to restrain his sarcasm: "Yes, of course," he said, "but
really, Yajnavalkya, how many gods are there?'" Yajnavalkya said there were
thirty-three, and when the same question was repeated, he continued: six,
three, two, one and a half, and finally one.

Because there was only one, Shakalya demanded to know who those original three and three hundred and three and three thousand had been. Yajnavalkya explained that these were only the powers of the gods. But Shakalya kept
pressing, demanding an explanation for each of the numbers Yajnavalkya
had given, who those gods were, what they represented. Yajnavalkya explained
them all. Arriving at three, he explained that they represented the three worlds,
two were food and breath, one and a half was the wind, and one was breath.

This was hardly a theological discussion. Instead, the challenger demanded
to see what Yajnavalkya knew about the meaning of the liturgy. Soon, however,
the tone of the debate changed, and the topic became both deeper and more
dangerous. Every question Shakalya asked was turned back against him, and
the risk of failing to answer was immediate death.

"The person whose abode is the earth, whose world is fire, and whose
light is the mind—should someone know that person, the final goal of
every atman, he would be a man who truly knows, Yajnavalkya?"

"I know that person, the final goal of every self, of whom you
speak. He is none other than this bodily person. But tell me,
Sakalya—who is his god?"

"The immortal," Sakalya answered.

Then Shakalya asked again about passion and about visible appearances and
space and a whole world of external objects and psychological faculties. Yajnavalkya knew them all and turned each against Shakalya by asking who the
respective god of each was. The discussion then turned to the question of
foundations—what was the foundation of some major Vedic gods (Yama,
Varuna, the sun, the moon), what was the foundation of the senses, and the
action organs. Finally, Shakalya asked:

"On what are you and your atman founded?"

"On the out-breath."

"On what is the out-breath founded?"

"On the in-breath."

"On what is the in-breath founded?"

"On the inter-breath."

"On what is the inter-breath founded?"

"On the up-breath."

"On what is the up-breath founded?"

"On the link-breath. About this atman, one can only say "not——,
not ——." He is ungraspable, for he cannot be grasped. . . . I ask you
about [who is] that person providing the hidden connection [upani-
sad]—the one who carries off these other persons, brings them back,
and rises above them? If you will not tell me that, your head will
shatter apart." (Brihadaranyaka Upanishad 3.9.26; Olivelle)

Shakalya could not answer that question, and his head exploded. Yajnavalkya
then invited the other Brahmins to challenge him further, but they all remained
silent.

But Yajnavalkya did not elaborate on the question that killed Shakalya.
Instead, he quoted obscure verses that compared a man to a tree: his hairs were
the leaves, the skin his bark. Then Yajnavalkya asked (Brihadaranyaka Upanishad 3.9.28: Olivelle):

> A tree, when it's uprooted,
> Will not sprout out again;
> From what root does a mortal man grow,
> When he is cut down by death?

But once again, no answer was given, and the *Brihadaranyaka Upanishad* tells us nothing further.

Of course, a contest at Janaka's court or other places like it was not the only or even primary source of religious knowledge. While Yajnavalkya worked and taught near the court, in the countryside and forests were wandering teachers (*parivrajakas*), ascetics (*shramanas*), Buddhists, Jainas, and even Ajivakas, who taught a radical form of materialism. Nor was the *Brihadaranyaka Upanishad* the only text of its kind. Scholars today usually count 14 major Upanishads, along with numerous secondary texts, many of which date considerably later. Some of these texts, like the *Brihadaranyaka* itself, were attached to other scriptures within Vedic literature. The *Taittiriya Upanishad*, for example, belonged to the *Black Yajurveda* as an attachment to the *Taittiriya Aranyaka*, itself appended to the *Taittiriya Brahmana*. Other Upanishads, such as the *Mundaka Upanishad*, which greatly influenced Vedanta philosophers centuries later, stood on their own.

The Upanishadic age was also characterized by a pluralism of worldviews. While some Upanishads have been deemed "monistic," others, including the *Katha Upanishad*, are dualistic. Monism holds that reality is one—Brahman—and that all multiplicity (matter, individual souls) is ultimately reducible to that one reality. The *Katha Upanishad*, a relatively late text of the *Black Yajurveda*, is more complex. It teaches Brahman, like other Upanishads, but it also states that above the "unmanifest" (Brahman) stands Purusha, or "Person." This claim originated in Samkhya (analysis) philosophy, which split all of reality into two coeternal principles: spirit (*purusha*) and primordial matrix (*prakriti*).

Furthermore, while most Upanishads promoted an impersonal ultimate reality, some were highly theistic and devotional. The *Isha Upanishad* (of the *White Yajurveda*) begins:

> This whole world is to be dwelt in by the Lord,
> Whatever living being there is in the world.
> So you should eat what has been abandoned;
> And do not covet anyone's wealth. (*Isha Upanishad* 1; Olivelle)

It is thus virtually impossible to speak of a single Upanishadic philosophy. Still, as a body of literature, the Upanishads represent a transition from the implicit and ritually centered speculations of the Vedas to a more philosophical—even ethical—outlook on existence. The philosophical schools (*darshanas*) that emerged a few centuries later (see chapter 10) owed a great debt to these seminal speculations.

5

Vedic Science

The Grammar of Reality

The same individual, Alexander of Macedonia, who brought his troops
to Taxila, the military legend and hero of Romantic historiography,
met his Indian counterpart in Chandragupta Maurya. The story of
Alexander's apogee and decline in South Asia, mirrored in reverse
by the rise of the Mauryan empire, has fascinated historians of political and military economies. But to students of culture, this encounter is not a reverse Salamis (where the Greeks finally defeated the
Persians), the end of an empire. Instead, it marks one of the most
fascinating beginnings, at least for crosscultural historiography.
Alexander's military men, the admirals Nearchus and Onesicritus, as
well as the Greek-Seleucid ambassador to Chadragupta's court,
Megasthenes, became the West's earliest scholars of India, bringing
to the subcontinent all the curiosity and prejudice of Greek men,
and taking back invaluable knowledge about life in India in the fourth
and third centuries BCE.

These men wondered about things Indians took for granted and
therefore ignored in much of their writing. What did Indians look like
and what did they wear? Nearchus wrote: "The dress worn by the
Indians is made of cotton produced on trees. But this cotton is either of
a brighter white colour than any found anywhere else, or the darkness
of the Indian complexion makes their apparel look so much white"
(quoted in Arrian's *Indica* 16; McCrindle, p. 219). What kind of a man
might Chandragupta (whom these Greeks called Sadrocottos) have
been and how was his palace constructed? What were the size and

main features of his capital city—Pataliputra? Their accounts are not universally regarded as reliable, but the description of the city matches aspects of the archeological evidence:

> At the meeting of this river (the Ganges) with another is situated
> "Palibothra," a city eighty stadia (9.2 miles) in length and fifteen
> stadia (1.7 miles) in breadth. It is of the shape of a parallelogram and
> is girded with a wooden wall, pierced with loop-holes for the discharge of the arrows. It has a ditch in front for defence and for
> receiving the sewage of the city. (Strabo 15; McCrindle, 67)

The city wall was epic in dimensions, with 64 gates and 570 towers. It was surrounded by a moat 600 feet wide and 45 feet deep, with water channeled from the Son River. The use of wood throughout the city, apparently teak, was particularly striking, in view of the diminishing availability of raw material (Kaushambi was built of burnt brick) and the warning against using flammable material for defense by Kautilya's *Arthashastra*, which the guidebook for prudent kings. The royal palace was also built of wood, Megasthenes tells us, and archeological evidence seems to bear that out. An enormous 80-pillar hall was discovered at Kumrahar (part of the Pataliputra complex). It certainly dates to a post-Chandragupta period, perhaps Ashoka or later, but the use of wood at that time only strengthens the plausibility of Megasthenes' observations.

Modern students of India's history enjoy more concrete detail about the Mauryan court and about physical geography and economy, architecture and crafts, about life in general under Mauryan rule than is available for any other period of Indian history until centuries later. For instance, the Greek envoy to the court of the Mauryas was especially impressed by the paved road that ran from the northwest frontier to Pataliputra and from there to the Bay of Bengal—well over a thousand miles in all. One should bear in mind that in addition to Megasthenes and the other Greeks, Indian sources from that period were also descriptive. Texts such as Kautilya's *Arthashastra*, the Dharma Sutras, and the large literary epics— the *Mahabharata* and *Ramayana*—provide ample information that bears on life around the time of the Mauryan empire.

Agricultural practices along the rivers, to focus just on the obvious, were highly pragmatic and diverse. Rice, barley, wheat, and sugarcane farming dominated, but many farmers grew flax, millet, sesame, long pepper, grapes, fruit trees, medicinal plants, and herbs. Land use and irrigation were sophisticated enough to generate enormous surpluses and build concentrated wealth in regional centers. Farming sciences and techniques improved weights and measurement, transportation, cattle breeding, irrigation, tool making, and other activities. The urban economy was equally, if not more, diverse. Specialists constructed or made furniture, pottery, jewelry, toys, clothes; there were marble cutters and metalworkers, specialists in precise minting and stamping of coins, traders, recreation and beauty workers, hairdressers, physicians, scientists, architects. Each profession was dependent on several others and divided in turn into subsidiary specializations, and all of them depended on police work, administration, and, of course, taxation.

The fourth and third centuries BCE were particularly important in the history of Hinduism and merit a close study. Beyond the obvious political significance of a unified empire and the cultural consequences of the conversion to Buddhism of King Ashoka (Chandragupta's grandson), the age produced a profound religious synthesis: The ritual and institutional authority of the Vedas, enriched with the philosophical speculations of the Upanishads, were foundering in the face of strong challenges. The Buddhists and Jainas had rejected the Vedas altogether and were steadily gaining influence and power. Meanwhile, the energetic eastward and southward expansion of the Indo-Aryans continued; worlds and fortunes were torn down and rebuilt. Indian appetite for action widened the gap between this life and the ideology of Vedic religious goals. How could one reconcile a dynamic world, propelled by gregariousness and political ambition, with a salvific vision in which quiet introspection or ritual speculation prevailed? How could both Veda and Upanishad remain relevant? The answer—sciences and dharma—were the great achievements of the Mauryan centuries.

The Rise of the Mauryas

On the political front, the three or four centuries between Janaka's contest and the rule of Chandragupta Maurya brought about momentous changes. The newly emerging regional identities replaced old tribal societies. Local clans eventually disappeared into chiefdoms and then kingdoms or republics. Clan-based names gave way to geographical names for the new entities, like Magadha, Kashi, or Ujjain. These changes stirred up conflicts between the older system of kin relationships and the new system of emerging political organization around a king and his administration. This is how dharma (morality, law) took shape as the ideological lynchpin of social interaction. These broad changes found a very detailed expression in the two epics that dominated oral culture during these midmillennium centuries—the *Mahabharata* and *Ramayana*.

The longer of the two, the *Mahabharata*, was a monumental collection of stories, myths, legends, and didactic narratives assembled between 500 BCE and 400 CE. The encyclopedic work centered on a relatively simple plot. Two groups of cousins from a single line of succession within the royal lineage vied for the throne of Bharata in Hastinapura. The five Pandavas—sons of King Pandu (Yudhishthira, Bhima, Arjuna, Nakula, Sahadeva)—had the legitimate claim. The Kauravas, led by Duryodhana, were the one hundred sons of Pandu's older brother Dhritarashtra, whose right to the throne was undermined by his blindness.

When the Pandavas performed a coronation (*rajasuya*) sacrifice on behalf of Yudhishthira, the Kauravas decided to end the rivalry. They set up a game of dice in which Yudhishthira—an awful gambler—lost his kingdom, wealth, his brothers' and his own freedom, and finally the freedom of their shared wife, Draupadi. After a series of humiliations, and another game of dice, the Pandavas were finally compelled to go into exile for thirteen years, followed by a year of living in disguise. After returning, Yudhishthira was willing to settle for far less than the rightful throne, but the Kauravas remained adamant. A catastrophic eighteen-day war broke out on the field of Kurukshetra, which the Pandavas won.

The central narrative has the earmarks of ancient princely legends, but scholars have carefully discerned the highly symbolic and theological layers threaded into the work. On these levels of the narrative, the *Mahabharata* tells the ancient myth of the cosmic battle between gods and demons over the Earth. The Pandavas embody dharma—the *varnas*, the laws of the king—while the Kauravas represent disruptive and demonic values. Alf Hiltebeitel has even identified a ritual-sacrificial structure to the epic, with the war representing a ritual on a vast sacrificial plain (Kurukshetra). The religious level of analysis invariably takes into account the central role of Krishna, the incarnation of Vishnu, in this vast epic. The *Bhagavad Gita*, inserted into the sixth book of the *Mahabharata* just before the commencement of the battle, embodies this lofty cosmic task of Krishna in the battle between good and evil.

The *Ramayana* is a strikingly similar epic and just as cohesive in plot structure, though far smaller in scope. Rama was the heir apparent to the throne of Dasharatha in Ayodhya. However, his father had made a promise to the youngest among his three wives that her son, Rama's brother Bharata, would become king. Manipulated into a horrible dilemma, the king was forced to offer the throne to the younger man and to expel Rama. The loyal hero calmly agreed to leave the city for a fourteen-year exile in the forest, along with his wife Sita and a second brother, Lakshmana. During their stay in the forest, Sita was abducted by Ravana, the ten-headed demon king of Lanka. The grieving Rama managed to secure the help of a tribe of monkeys, led by Sugriva and the miraculously powerful Hanuman. With this formidable army, Rama destroyed

Ravana and his forces, and finally reunited with his wife. The two returned to Ayodhya, where Rama finally ascended the throne. However, Sita was first compelled to prove her purity—her faithfulness to her husband—by walking unscathed through flames.

Like the *Mahabharata*, which it probably predates, the *Ramayana* is a multilayered work, with an ancient bardic core of heroic folk narratives about a prince of the state of Kosala. The epic is attributed to the chief among the ancient poets (*adikavi*), Valmiki, and the central five books display a relative uniformity of style. But there are more recent layers—the first and last books of the epic, in which Valmiki himself is an actor and which the theology of the epic moves to the fore. Here Rama is no longer just a prince but an incarnation of Vishnu and, like Krishna in the *Mahabharata*, a warrior for dharma against evil in defense of the Earth.

Over the centuries, these two epics have figured prominently as central pillars of Hindu religion and culture. Many of the best-known myths and narratives about gods, demons, and holy men have found their way into these collections. The epics are still narrated in temples, performed on stage and in other ways, even filmed for television and cinema. But in some ways they are also snapshots of political, social, and religious moments at a given time in India's history. They address vital questions, including these: Who is a righteous king? What is the relation between power and authority? How important in political life is the family, the clan, or the tribe? How should the followers of dharma interact with indigenous populations? What is a good marriage?

In some sense, the two works foreshadow the ascendancy of a single great royal house, such as the Mauryas. However, at the heyday of the two epic capitals—Hastinapura and Ayodhya—the Magadhan Pataliputra was only a tiny village, unobtrusively tucked between the Ganges and the Son rivers. This is what the earliest Buddhist texts tell us. The little village was not even significant within its own kingdom of Magadha. The capital city of Magadha had been Rajgriha, until Ajatashatru's son Udayin moved it to Pataliputra, where his father had built a fort.

The kingdoms that dominated the central to eastern regions of the Ganges River in the century or so before Chandragupta were Kashi (Varanasi today), Kosala, and Magadha itself, along with the chiefdom of the Vrijjis. These political powers fought for supremacy and control of resources along the fertile river valley. The kingdom that would eventually prevail, and then become the seat of empire, was Magadha.

In 321 BCE the Mauryas, specifically Chandragupta, ascended the throne of Magadha, displacing the last ruler of the previous dynasty, the Nandas. Several

Hindu and Buddhist sources report the young Chandragupta's rise and consolidation of power. But while the Buddhists hailed this first great Indian ruler as a Kshatriya, descended from the Moriya clan, which was related to the Shakyas (to which Buddha, also a Kshatriya, belonged), the Hindu sources claimed that the Mauryas were, in fact, low-caste Shudras. History, always a value-saturated narrative, was especially contested in this case because Chandragupta's grandson, Ashoka, eventually converted to Buddhism and propagated the Dhamma (Pali for Dharma) of Buddha throughout his empire. Hindu writers found it more natural that a person of low caste would convert. For Buddhists, the Kshatriyas were true nobility. Many scholars agree that the young Chandragupta was aided by a cunning advisor, Kautilya (also known as Chanakya or Vishnugupta), whose name was connected with a text—the *Arthashastra*—that was fully redacted and edited only centuries later.

After overcoming the Nandas, who were Brahmins, and establishing dominion over the kingdoms that bordered Magadha, Chandragupta moved his army into the Indus River system, hundreds of miles to the northwest. He applied pressure to the Seleucid territories that had been vacated by the retreating Greeks and in 303 BCE achieved a pact with Seleucus that gave him control over the entire northwestern region of the subcontinent (including areas of present-day Afghanistan and Pakistan). The Mauryan empire covered both major centers of North Indian civilization—the Indus and Ganges river systems and the watershed in between.

While political and military events on a grand scale continued to unfold, everyday life proceeded as it had for centuries. Children came into the world and old people departed, men earned their livelihood and built things, women ran the household and raised the children. There is no reason to think that life in India differed markedly from life in Greece or Persia, or anywhere else. The exotica that Westerners have often looked for in all things Indian—beginning perhaps with Greek travelers' astounding exaggerations —played no role in the actual life of ordinary men and women.

Religion and Science

The centuries of the rise of empire in India increasingly blurred the sharp distinction between what sociologists like Max Weber call "rationality" (worldly action) and salvation. Religion was no longer just Vedic speculation, Upanishadic mysticism, or the magical cults of the *Atharvaveda* and the villagers in the countryside (see chapter 8). Action and metaphysical speculation were united, and the unifying force—at least that conceived and inspired by

Brahmins—was science. This was not a science of empirical investigation for its own sake or for the sake of formulating abstract principles about nature. Instead, it was a science that brought together a keen sense of the richness of raw empirical existence with a determination to order this reality according to meaningful principles, for the sake of both intellectual coherence and religious goals. Of course, the two (worldly action and ultimate salvation) did not blend seamlessly. Consequently, at the heart of the new scientific ideology was the consciousness of a gap, often conceived as "loss" or as forgetfulness.

For example, the science of statecraft (*niti*, political science), which Kautilya used to promote Chandragupta, portrayed itself in relationship to an Absolute. According to an important and familiar myth from the *Mahabharata* ("Shantiparvan," chap. 59), the world was created in the first of four yugas (eons), which the text called Krita Yuga (*krita* were the four (maximum) units of the successful gambler's die). Krita Yuga was a time of a perfect world wherein people followed the right path (dharma) naturally, despite the absence of a ruler or of punishment. In the course of the following eons, things deteriorated progressively, and humans became greedy, deluded, and sinful. The gods, concerned about the situation, asked the help of the creator, Brahmadeva. He responded by composing a monumental book of law, consisting of one hundred thousand chapters. Chief among the topics was *dandaniti*, the science of keeping law and order—in short, government.

Unfortunately, because with the passage of time humans not only became progressively more degenerate but also lost their health and longevity, the text had to be abridged. It was first reduced to ten thousand chapters, then cut in half. Brihaspati further reduced it to three thousand chapters, and finally the book was boiled down to a mere one thousand chapters.

According to experts on the *Arthashastra*, this account may hint at the existence of possible texts on government that predated the work associated with Kautilya. The *Barhaspatya Shastra*, for example, is such a text. But ideologically, the myth is equally important for linking the known science of government with a fundamental religious conception—divine authority. That does not mean that the recruitment of spies or the launching of military expeditions—typical *Arthashastra* topics—is religious in any substantive way. What the myth suggests, instead, is that the organization, the ordering, of government is a world-shaping enterprise. It requires classifying, numbering, ranking, dividing, and otherwise imposing order on a potentially chaotic domain—that is, scientific ruling. The science of government (rather than governing itself) was thus both descriptive and prescriptive. Again, this does not mean that either Kautilya or Chandragupta imagined himself doing the work of God, but that work and effort were not necessarily random. Nor were they subservient to the need to control mere natural drives and appetites. Dharma, the great achievement of the new scientific age, brought together both that which existed as a matter of fact and the structure of how things ought to have been. In that basic sense, it was the model of all sciences.

The Sciences of the Vedas

Like many other important cultural phenomena, science in India began with the Vedas. As the sacrificial ritual gained complexity and spread through ever-widening regions, the Brahmins who supervised the cult had to protect and preserve it. They needed to establish precise methods for calculating performance dates and times, guarantee uniform sacrificial altars and procedures, clarify and preserve the language of the ritual. Six ancillary sciences developed around the Vedic religion: metrics, performance and use of text (*kalpa*), astrology, etymology, phonetics, and grammar. These sciences were described as the feet, hands, eyes, ears, nose, and mouth of the Veda, respectively. In other words, the six sciences made a transcendent reality—the idea of Veda—concrete and knowable and thus ensured the preservation of the sacred cult.

According to tradition, grammar was the most important of the six Vedic sciences or Vedangas (limbs), and indeed, it was a grammarian, Panini (sixth or fifth century BCE), who towered as one of the greatest scientists of the ancient world, Asian or European. Though truly a science of linguistics, in a more general sense Vedic grammar was a tool for both decoding and encoding reality: deciphering the meaning and form of language (broadly conceived as symbolic communication) and setting down appropriate (precise and logical) rules for speech and ritual utterances. In a general sense, this scientific enterprise reflects the rise not only of the most sophisticated linguistics until modern times but also of advanced mathematics (including geometry), law (and ethics), and logic. The complexity of India's social arrangements—the caste system and the stages of life—in a word, dharma—cannot be fully understood without a look at these older sciences.

Geometry

Geometry emerged from the *kalpa* sciences. The geometrical texts (Shulbasutras) were parts of the larger Kalpa Sutras, composed by the same Brahminical clans (for instance, Baudhayana and Apastamba). Although the builders of the ancient Indus River cities (Harappa, Mohenjodaro) had undoubtedly mastered advanced engineering skills, the first mathematical texts emerged two millennia later and derived their name from the cord (*shulba*) that was used for measurement in the construction of the fire altars (*vedi* and *agni*). There were several types of altar: falcon, heron, carrion kite, chariot wheel and poles, a circular tub or vessel called *drona*, a tortoise, an altar shaped like the stretched hide of an animal.

All such altars had to consist of five layers of bricks in specified numbers—as discussed earlier. The total height of the altars was that of the knee of the sacrificer, who was an adult male. However, at special times the altar's number of layers and height were doubled or tripled. The shapes were difficult to achieve with square bricks: the circle of the chakra altar or the curved wings of bird altars resisted straight lines and cubic shapes. Millennia before the Renaissance builders struggled to round the square (by building domes over chapels) Vedic mathematicians succeeded—up to a point. But they had other agendas too: With changing environments, altars had to vary in size, while sacred ratios had to be kept constant. This required close familiarity with trigonometry, the mathematics of ratios, with fractions, squares and roots, and numerous practical algorithms. What the West has called the Pythagorean theorem was a familiar tool for manipulating altar sizes, though it was never proven for its own sake.

A distinct profession, inferior socially to the Brahmins, emerged to handle these operations. An example of the type of problem these professionals needed to solve, in this case where an altar is increased in size, can be seen in the *Apastamba Shulbasutra*. That text indicates that the corresponding sides and lines of similar figures were proportionate and give the following principle in connection with the bird altar with a curved wing: "The transverse side is 1/7 of the side of the wing and the lateral side is 1/4 of a purusa. Its frame should be expanded diagonal-wise. The planks should be inclined by 1/7 of the paksanamani—the slope or gradient of the wing" (*Apastamba Shulbasutra* 19.8; Amma). Sarasvati Amma explains this rule by means of a diagram (fig. 5.1), with comments:

> Here, what is meant by the paksanamani is the vertical height of the tip of the inclined wing from the horizontal. ABCD is half the wing, where CB lies along the vertical. If CB is produced to meet the horizontal through A in E, BE is the paksanamani. The bricks which have as their transverse side 1/7 of AB are to have the same inclination. To effect this the frame for making the bricks is to be given

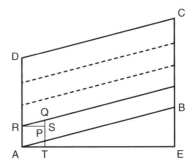

FIGURE 5.1. Altar Geometry. From *Geometry in Ancient and Medieval India*
by Dr. T.A. Sarasvati Amma copyright 1979. Reprinted by permission from Motilal
Banarsidass, Delhi, India.

a namani = 1/7 the paksanamani. I.e. if APQR is a brick and QP is
produced to meet the horizontal through A in T we get a triangle APT
similar to the triangle ABE.

$$PT/BE = AP/AB = 1/7$$
$$\text{Or } PT = 1/7.BE$$

Many of the problems were far more complex than this example. But in
every case, behind the math stood fundamental philosophical assumptions,
including:

1. Models (diagrams, altars) possess some of the key qualities of the
   reality they model, as long as the proportions are correct.
2. Numbers express both the practical manifestation of the craftsman's
   accuracy and the metaphysical guarantee that the correspondence
   in fact applies.
3. Geometry—the science of applying numbers to objects in space—
   provides a certain level of control over both empirical and metaphysical
   realities.

These were ancient principles, never worked out explicitly, but decisive in
shaping Vedic thought. The single most influential Vedic statement—the
Purusha Sukta (*Rig-Veda* 10.90; see chapte 6)—exhibits these principles in
mythical terms by insisting on precise numerical units for its cosmology. In
medieval India, no temple planner and builder could ignore these theoretical
principles, and the elaborate mathematical pyrotechnics that translated into
complex structures ultimately rested on just this simple idea: that the ratio
conceals a true relationship, that is, a correct ration between the building and
the world.

Grammar

Just as Vedic builders knew that objects came in all sizes and many shapes, the grammarians knew that languages come in countless forms. The *Rig-Veda* shows the influences of both time and geography, the contact with non-Indo-Aryans (Mundas, Dravidians) and with the speech of non-Brahmins. To some extent, that sacred text reflects the normal changes that languages, even elite sacred languages such as Greek and Latin became, undergo. But these trends were checked by the drive of the Brahmin grammarians to perfect their language by removing irregularities and establishing grammatical uniformity.

A deep religious motivation was at work; in fact, an entire ritual (an offering to the goddess Sarasvati) existed to expiate the linguistic errors priests might have committed in the major sacrifice. Early Indian grammar, contemporary with the early Vedic literature, thus seemed to reflect a creative tension between the natural evolution of a language and the top-down linguistic planning by an intellectual class with a strong ideal in mind. The scientific work took place in every aspect of grammar, but the domain of sound (phonetics) is instructive, particularly with reference to the priestly function of the language.

The Vedic expert was in a precarious position, because the precise performance of the chanting and recitation was vital to the effectiveness of the ritual, as were the actions themselves, and the proportions of the altar. Several techniques evolved to preserve the language of the ritual, guard the precise oral performance, and ensure that memorization of ritual formulas was accurate, while also clarifying obscure meanings.

Because Vedic literature was oral or *shruti* (heard), several mnemonic techniques emerged to protect accurate transmission from teacher to disciple. For instance, a given text could be committed to memory as a continuous phrase, without pauses between words; or it could be broken into word units, or pairs of words. More than eleven methods developed over the centuries, and students who memorized a Vedic text in several ways were then able to compare their versions in order to identify and eliminate inconsistencies.

However, many of the words, especially when they ran together or when they formed compounds, resulted in ambiguous meanings. Such ambiguities had to be cleared up if the ritual was to be performed correctly. For instance, the compound *sthula-prishatim* (big-spot-cow) could be a big cow with spots or a cow with big spots. Different types of compounds in Sanskrit grammar were indicated within the recitation by means of distinct accentuation and pitch. Only a trained grammarian could recognize all the differences, which explains the high esteem of the profession.

These and hundreds of other problems made grammar (*vyakaranam*) the most respected among the six Vedic sciences. According to Panini, the greatest of all Indian grammarians, only the expert who knew the procedures for deletion (*lopa*), addition, and sound modification was qualified to preserve the Vedic language. Panini himself, most scholars agree, probably lived around 500 BCE, though his place of origin is under some dispute. One tradition claims that he came from the Shalatura region in northwestern India (today in Pakistan). But he was intimately familiar with idiomatic expressions from a wide range of areas, from Kashmir to the Punjab and on to the eastern parts of the Ganges River system. He also appeared to know of at least ten grammarians who preceded him, though there were probably well over sixty.

Panini composed a work consisting of nearly four thousand sutras (aphoristic formulas), organized into eight chapters. Appropriately, the work was entitled *Ashtadhyayi* (Eight chapters). To help in memorization and transmission, the text was condensed and technical, virtually unreadable today without the aid of later commentators, primarily Patanjali and Katyayana. The *Ashtadhyayi* both described the Indo-Aryan language spoken at the time of Panini (late Vedic) and established normative rules and metarules for correct usage of this language, which was not yet called Sanskrit. The author listed the primary elements of language, including roots, phonemes, morphemes such as suffixes and infixes, word groups (compounds) of varying kinds, and others. He then described in great detail the procedures for applying the rules of grammar to these and other units of language. Panini's linguistics were both highly concrete and abstract: he recognized not just specific language behavior that he had observed (including his own) but also numerous classes of increasingly abstract principles that accounted for such behavior. He spoke of phonetic, syntactical, and grammatical units as categories ("empty boxes," as it were) to which additions, augments, doubling, affixations, and other operations could apply in a manner that could be described abstractly—almost like a computer algorithm. His grammar, in other words, looked a great deal like positional mathematics or algebra.

For example, two synonyms for the verb "to eat" have the verbal roots *khad* and *ad*. The first conjugates in the present third-person singular by requiring the addition of an *a* sound between the root and the appropriate conjugational suffix *ti*. This produces *khadati*. However, in the case of the second root (*ad*), no such sound is added, and the conjugated verb "he eats" is *atti*. But interestingly, because Panini's grammar recognizes place markings (where infixes might go) as a structural reality (a box or slot), one must not say that the second verb lacks the addition, but instead that it has added a "zero" (*lopa*) at the appropriate slot. This may seem like trivial hair-splitting, but it is not.

Just like modern structural linguistics, or algebra, Panini attributed significance to a location, even if it was empty. The importance of this detail can be demonstrated by means of decimal math. If you place a zero after a one, as a place marker, not as a quantity, you end up with a different number: o placed after 1 is 10. More important, not only is the number different, a whole new philosophy opens up with this radical idea, which may explain why decimal arithmetic took so long to arrive in the West and why the popes forbade the use of zero. Numbers are not only symbols that stand for quantity or size; they are also the surface manifestation of a deeper thought structure (the role of a position in a numbering system). This deeper thought may reflect yet more fundamental truths about the world, such as the notion that classification and computation are connected to hidden (and universal) truths. Zero, for example, could represent an awareness of the structure imposed on the world by mind or intentional thought, without any regard to the objects of consciousness. Both Advaita Vedanta and Buddhist Madhyamika philosophers would later explore the metaphysics of this idea, but positional classification (grammar, math) always retained its significant pragmatic and operational implications. Zero would not arrive in Indian mathematics for another millennium, but India was the place where it first appeared. The underlying thought—that "place" or structure is as important as what goes in it—was already ancient by then. The grammarians knew it, and it would prove decisive in the way Indian society was organized as well.

Political Science

Altar geometry, calendrical computations, and grammar do not have a great deal in common on the surface. But all are Vedic sciences, and all share a fundamental use of rationality: The universe is nonrandom, and a deep and abiding structure holds surface phenomena together. Grammarians did not describe that structure in numerical terms, but the specialized and coded metalanguage of linguistics was a functional equivalent of mathematics. A similar intellectual orientation prevailed in the *kalpa* sciences, which would eventually cover such diverse fields as political science, domestic rules, and dharma.

At the end of the fourth century BCE, Chandragupta obtained and consolidated his power with the aid of a Brahmin counselor who was as savvy as Machiavelli and as scientific as Panini. The lessons of Kautilya—who is not mentioned in Megasthenes description of Chandragupta's court—were probably just the core of the text that today goes by the name of *Kautilya Arthashastra*. But Kautilya's approach would likely have been just as systematic as the fully developed text that was augmented and edited centuries later. Kautilya may have taught his client, the emperor, virtually everything a king could ever imagine:

> This single (treatise on the) Science of Politics has been prepared mostly by bringing together (the teachings of) as many treatises on the Science of Politics as have been composed by ancient teachers for the acquisition and protection of the earth.
>
> Of that (treatise), this is an enumeration of Sections and Books:
>
> Enumeration of the Sciences, Association with Elders, Control over the Senses, Appointment of Ministers, Appointment of Councilors and Chaplain, Ascertainment of the Integrity or the absence of Integrity of Ministers by means of Secret Tests, Appointment of Persons in Secret Service, Rules for Secret Servants, Keeping a Watch over the Seducible and Non-seducible Parties in One's Own Territory, Winning over the Seducible and Non-seducible Parties in the Enemy Territory, The Topic of Counsel, Rules for the Envoy, Guarding against Princes, The Conduct of a Prince in Disfavour, Behaviour towards a Prince in Disfavour, Rules for the King, Regulations for the Royal Residence, Concerning the Protection of the King's Own Person,—these constitute the First Book "Concerning the Topic of Training." (*Arthashastra* 1.1.1–2; Kangle)

This quotation represented a fragment, perhaps one-tenth, of the full list of topics covered by Kautilya. The full enumeration was mesmerizingly thorough. And the topics included not only government matters but city planning, architecture, strategic military formations, and many other specialized areas of expertise. Knowledge of technical detail and application of power united in the administration of a kingdom—especially a vast empire such as the Mauryan. But political science was not just about the effective application of power. Like the other sciences, it reached for something more essential, an underlying truth that may have been explicit when *niti* (political science) had originally consisted of the full one hundred thousand chapters. In this sense, Kautilya's advice resembled sciences that have nothing to do with governing: it categorized, enumerated, added, divided, and even drew geometrical designs on the political map. Two examples may perhaps illustrate this approach: foreign policy, and the *raja-mandala* (royal circle).

Foreign policy was organized around an abstract principle called *shadgunya* (the six measures). It was explained in the seventh book of the *Arthashastra*:

> The circle of constituent elements is the basis of the six measures of foreign policy.

"Peace, war, staying quiet, marching, seeking shelter and dual policy constitute the six measures," say the teachers.

Among them, entering into a treaty is peace. Doing injury is war. Remaining indifferent is staying quiet. Augmentation of (powers) is marching. Submitting to another is seeking shelter. Resorting to peace (with one) and war (with another) is dual policy. (*Arthashastra* 7.1.1–2, 6–11; Kangle)

The six measures depended on the foreign political context in which the ruler happened to find himself in relation to his neighbors. The map was elaborately worked out in another section of the text, where the doctrine of the circle of twelve kings was worked out. The kings were listed as the potential conqueror (1), the enemy of 1 who borders on his kingdom (2), the friend of 1 who borders the rear of 2 (3), the ally of 2 who lies beyond 3 (4), the ally of 3 who lies behind 4 (5), and so forth to twelve. The principle was simple. Your contiguous neighbor was a threat—your enemy—and his enemy was your friend.

Some historians believe that this formula originated in the political realities of an ever-expanding Magadha. Modern European historians might be tempted to see a similar formula in the maneuvering that preceded World War I. Be this as it may, the *Arthashastra* did not pretend to describe the world exactly as it was. Instead, a strong normative streak ran through the mathematical precision with which political realities were catalogued. There was a resemblance here to a thorough grammar book that would always fail to describe how everyone in fact spoke. Grammar rules may have been perfect when a Brahmin composed a text; practice was another matter. What both sciences shared, at bottom, was a recognition that structure (location or norm) and context mattered as much as substance.

The Sciences of Society

If altar construction, calendars, language, and political action could be sorted out scientifically, why not human life? As a matter of fact, Vedic scholars classified virtually every aspect of life, including food, animals and plants, medicines, countries, and so forth. According to Brian K. Smith, this classification of the priests was totalistic—it covered everything, and was ultimately based on the poetic and ritual rationality exhibited by the hymns of the *Rig-Veda* and by the rules of the sacrifice.

And indeed, the sacrifice acted as an intellectual nexus around which to organize the known world. However, the taxonomic procedure varied widely from one cultural context to the next; no single system prevailed. Linguistic principles may have resembled mathematics, but the classification of language elements such as verbal roots was far removed from true number systems. Politics was different yet, and so were calendrical calculations. All of these, in turn, differed in notable ways from how Brahmins classified society by means of the *varna* and *ashrama* systems.

It should hardly surprise us that the life of ancient Hindus would also be sorted out by means of ritual principles. Beginning immediately after conception and continuing well beyond death, existence was marked with ritual landmarks that separated one stage from the next. All led to gradual perfection (*samskara*), or the successful progress of the soul in its ongoing journey. These rituals were described in great detail in the texts called Grihya Sutras, which formed parts of the Kalpa Sutras that had emerged from different Vedic schools. For instance, the *Apastamba Grihya Sutra* was connected with the *Apastambiya Kalpa Sutra,* which came from the Taittiriya school of the *Black Yajurveda.* This school coexisted alongside the *White Yajurveda,* whose elaborate fire altar instructions I described earlier. The *Apastamba Grihya Sutra* was probably the oldest, and remains the best preserved, among the manuals that regulated the lives of high-caste Hindus during the years around 500 BCE.

Two levels of reality provided what we might call the raw material on which the many prescriptions of the *Apastamba Grihya Sutra* were meant to operate. The first was biological: conception, pregnancy, birth, nurturing of the child, and on to death. The text did not presume to control (speed up, improve) the substance of all such natural processes, only to mark their significance; every aspect of life was regarded as meaningful in a formal way. Furthermore, because life was complex and even risky, the texts reflected and expanded on magical rituals designed to improve fertility and health and prolong life. As the second level of the text's concern, the authors looked at what villagers and city dwellers were practicing in the way of folk traditions and fashioned a science of prescribed rituals, the *samskaras* (rituals of perfection) that covered virtually every aspect of life:

For example, on the fourth month of a married woman's first pregnancy, an elaborate ritual called the parting of the hair took place. After a series of ritual actions involving the domestic fire, the text prescribed:

> He makes her sit down to the west of the fire, facing the east, and puts her hair upwards (i.e. beginning from the front) with a porcupine quill that has three white spots, with three Darbha blades [of grass], and with a bunch of unripe Udumbara fruits, with the

Vyahritis or with the two next verses. (*Apastamba Grihya Sutra* 6.14.3; Oldenberg)

The ritual did not end there, of course; it was very elaborate. Other Grihya Sutras varied slightly, and probably applied to different regions of India. None of the texts provided explicit explanations for such odd details as quills, spots, the number three, and the direction of the hair; a careful study of these rituals by modern anthropologists could yield rich symbolic results.

Still, the overall principle of the text's discussion of the stages of life is clear: de facto existence, even when fortified by magic, is not sufficient. It must be sacramentalized, conceived as leading to religious perfection through obedience to concrete rules and hidden principles—a science of growth, so to speak. The psychological rationale, vis-à-vis karma, was sophisticated. As one matures and progresses from stage to stage in life, one must accumulate the fruit that accompanies the actions of that stage, though the final stage will require the shedding of all fruits of actions! Why the paradox? Why accumulate so many prescribed acts if the ultimate goal (liberation) is free of karma? It seems that the one fruit that most concerned the authors of the *ashrama* (stages of life) system was the regret bred by a life that had not been fully lived.

Varna Dharma

Overlapping with this ritual system, which regulated every phase of life, was a broader organization aimed specifically at males of the three upper social groups. This second system consisted of only three categories: the Vedic student (*brahmacharin*), the householder (*grihyastha*), and the renouncer (*samnyasin*). According to Patrick Olivelle, these three *ashramas* represented life choices rather than sequential steps in the life of a single individual. As such, they differed markedly from the system of *samskaras*. The *samskaras* described a totality: one literally grew through all of the sacramental steps in sequential order, for the sake of a successful and sanctified life. In contrast, the older model of the *ashramas* was optional or exclusive. A man could choose to be either a householder or a renouncer. In time, Olivelle argues, the graduated approach of *samskaras* influenced the *ashrama* system, a fourth was added (forest dweller, *vanaprastha*, which comes before the stage of the renouncer), and they became conceived as stages of life.

By describing the *ashramas*, the writers of the Dharma Sutra texts developed a system of abstraction that moved from ritual perfection or purity to a loftier idea, dharma. Here, rules of conduct, duties, moral order, law, and the definition of human nature combined to prescribe a normative life for male members of the upper castes (the "twice born," those who had undergone initiation), each according to his stage in life. Religion and ethics thus wove the fabric of a man's existence into the patterns of society as a whole, because the rules of the *ashramas* (*ashrama-dharma*) connected to one's caste obligations (*varna-dharma*). A few centuries after the Dharma Sutras were composed, entire libraries of law books (Dharma Shastras) and commentaries emerged to elaborate the relationship between the two domains.

Contemporary with the Grihya Sutras and originating in the same Brahminical ritual schools were Dharma Sutra texts, with names such as Apastamba and Gautama. These expanded the scope of *kalpa* sciences to a wide range of topics bearing on social and legal matters. A few centuries later, probably after the fall of the Maurya empire, more elaborate and systematic texts, called Smritis, further developed the science of dharma. These works, also called Dharma Shastras, and written in *shloka* metrical style instead of the aphoristic style of the sutras, became the repositories of comprehensive Brahminical social principles.

The most prestigious among these texts was *Manu Smriti*, or *Manava Dharma Shastra*. Named after the mythical progenitor of humankind, it represents a work of collection and editing by numerous authors over several centuries, probably between 200 BCE and 200 CE. *Manu*, as the text is often called, was a large text of 12 chapters, ranging in topic from cosmogony and cosmology to theories of the afterlife and virtually every aspect of life in between. The authors touched on the rites of the Grihya Sutras (*samskaras*, domestic rituals), of course, as well as stages of life, but also discussed criminal law and procedure, the conduct of the king, sins and expiations, and general prescriptions for conducting both domestic and public rituals. The authors recognized two types of social category—*varna* (caste) and *jati* (birth group or subcaste). While the broad conception consisted of the four primary *varnas* (Brahmin, Kshatriya, Vaishya, Shudra), the text identified a far larger and more complex social reality. The subsidiary castes, *Manu* theorized, were produced by the intermixing of the primary ones according to a number of principles.

Rigidly demarcated rules of conduct kept the four *varnas* separate and carefully ranked. The four categories were separated by professional, dietary, and social boundaries that were fortified by the king's laws and favored the higher over the lower. In some cases, for instance, criminal laws, the rules that described legal privileges, were virtually mathematical in their precision (table 5.1).

Although such formulas are impressively precise, scholars such as J. D. M. Derrett or P. V. Kane have questioned whether the laws of Manu reflected true

TABLE 5.1. Justice Grid in the *Manu Smriti* (Number of *Panas* to Be Administered as Punishment for Verbal Abuse)

	Victim			
Perpetrator	Brahmin	Kshatriya	Vaishya	Shudra
Brahmin	12	50	25	12
Kshatriya	100	12	50	25
Vaishya	150–200	75–100	12	38–50
Shudra	150–200	75–100	38–50	12
	+ corporeal	+ corporeal	+ corporeal	

legal practice among historic Indian kings. After all, the four *varnas* represented a social ideal—not the actual state of affairs. Other scholars—anthropologists, sociologists and theologians—have speculated about the foundations of such a unique social arrangement as the caste system. Was it guided by a religious ideology, such as concern for ritual purity, or did it merely reflect the economic dominance of higher-status social groups? The topic of caste has been controversial, of course, and a painful one for many modern Hindus. But the authors of *Manu Smriti* were resoundingly clear and confident about the nature of society—about *varna-dharma*. It is hard to fathom the precise foundations of their *varna*-based sociology. It may be that just as Panini developed a science that bridged actual linguistic practice with ideal language, the authors of Manu tried to reach for a similar goal: linking or mediating between a cosmic ideal (recall the Purusha Sukta, Rig-Veda 10.90) and the true social reality around them. Thus, dharma texts would come to represent the flowering of a trend that began in the age of the Vedas, namely organizing a complex and observable reality on the basis of rational (Veda-based) principles. At the core of this scientific rationality was a recognition that the ideal and the real were conceptually distinct but could be mediated through science, ritual, and law.

6

Kanishka and Krishna

Roughly halfway between New Delhi and Agra, on the main tourist route of northern India and under the capital area's smog umbrella, is the ancient city of Mathura. To millions of religious tourists, it is known as the birthplace of Krishna and center of Krishna devotion, along with Vrindavan nearby. Archeological excavations began relatively early here, a full half a century before Mortimer Wheeler transformed archeology from trophy collection into science.

Nine miles north of Mathura, at the village of Mat, in 1911–12 archeologists uncovered a large religious building, which may have been a shrine. Led by Rai Bahadur Pandit Radha Krishna, the diggers uncovered numerous objects, particularly large statues, which were carted off to museums. The diggers were so thorough in their excavations of the place that later, after the emergence of scientific archeology, it was virtually impossible to date the origin, development, and cultural context of the shrine.

Fortunately, a number of inscriptions on the objects removed from the dig have helped researchers with the dating. It is now clear that the shrine served the kings who ruled in Mathura at roughly the first and second centuries CE, probably the Kushanas. Among the statues removed from the site (just outside the shrine itself), the most impressive was a headless figure, over 6 feet tall, identified by an inscription as the most distinguished among those Kushana kings, namely Kanishka.

Kanishka was certainly one of the more remarkable political figures in India's history, a king who ruled over vast tracts of land in northern India. His coins and inscriptions were found as far east as Kaushambi, but his capital was Purushapura (near Peshawar in Pakistan today). He was no Indo-Aryan and certainly no follower of the Brahmins' Vedic religion, but he ruled at the very heart of Indian civilization in Mathura, the most powerful and important king between the Maurya and Gupta dynasties.

Like the architectural features of the Mat shrine, the headless Kanishka betrays what we might call a sensibility "foreign" to India. Despite its height, the sculpture appears squat in its proportions and two-dimensional. The long coat looks Central Asian (Scythian) in style, as are the quilted boots. The figure stands with feet spread apart, holding a sword in his left hand (rather awkwardly) and the sheath in his right. The sculpture bespeaks power and confidence. But implicitly, it also displays the obverse aspects of power—it is headless; the head was probably removed by succeeding kings who wished to forget Kanishka, and it was never recovered.

The reign of Kanishka is one of the most thoroughly studied periods of early Indian history, and the wealth of material the Kushanas left in Mathura, has been a fertile source of information. But to scholars today, the sculpture of Kanishka and the Kushana government in general raise puzzling questions: How does a "foreign" king come to rule in the heartland of Hinduism without annihilating its traditions? How did diverse religious and political cultures coexist in a place like Mathura and what was the role of the king within such a pluralistic society? Indeed, the centuries between the Maurya and Gupta dynasties saw an unprecedented level of political and cultural upheaval, including the coming and going of several non-Indo-Aryan powers. No city represented this dynamic mix more thoroughly than Mathura. But this was also the same Mathura where the first great devotional cult emerged in India—dedicated to Krishna Vasudeva.

In this chapter I will show that the two trends, devotional theism and cultural diversity, were tightly interwoven. If diversity and royal (foreign) power raise the questions of authority and legitimacy (*raja-dharma*), devotion to a personal god (bhakti) emerged as one of the most decisive solutions. Kanishka and Krishna are thus related as question and answer.

Mathura and History

The last of the Mauryas came to a violent end, assassinated by his Brahmin advisors. The Shungas, the dynasty that arose in Magadha following the

Mauryas, was Brahminical, but it was short-lived, and its territories shrank just as quickly. In Mathura, attention shifted from the now irrelevant Magadha in the eastern Ganges and toward the northwest regions of India. Situated at the upper Yamuna on the so-called Delhi-Aravalli Axis, Mathura was a prime trading location, enjoying cultural and artistic exchanges with the energetic cultures in Gandhara, Bactria, and beyond. For over three hundred years, Mathura had acted as a fulcrum for intense political and economic jockeying as different powers came and left, with no single hegemony lasting for long. After the Shungas departed, there were the Kanvas, then various Indo-Greek powers (called Yavanas), Parthians and Kshatrapas, the Shakas and Kushanas. Most of these groups were foreign, in the sense that they did not originate in the many states into which the Indo-Aryans had divided. But the political challenge to stability in Mathura came from local forces as well, such as Kalinga in Orissa (eastern India), the tribals of Rajasthan to the west, as well as the Malava republic and the Satavahanas from the Deccan in the south.

Because it was the political leader who provided the wealth to sponsor great architectural projects and fill them with art works, to mint coins and write inscriptions, the archeology of Mathura gives evidence of the diversity of succeeding political organizations. At the same time, the clients of such material investments were often religious, so the same archeological remains, along with texts, indicate that Mathura was host to a dazzling wealth of religions and cultures. Jain, Buddhist, Zoroastrian, and Brahmin institutions, including monasteries, temples, and charity halls, were sponsored. The non-Indo-Aryan rulers and traders brought ideas and religious objects, along with artistic styles, from Gandhara and the Hellenistic West Asian lands.

New Hindu theistic cults—primarily cults of Krishna-Vasudeva, Balarama, Vishnu, and Shiva—also began to replace the older Vedic gods and sacrificial religion. Indigenous or tribal religions, with their numerous deities, spirits, and nature-based mythologies, also prospered in the nearby countryside. Most of the rulers who originated in the northwest showed a marked preference for Buddhism; chief among them was Menander (Milinda), who figured in one of the most important early Buddhist texts, the *Milinda Panha* (*Questions of Milinda*). Nonetheless, many of these rulers were generous with other religions, including Jainism and the Brahmins' Vedic religion. This was certainly true for Kanishka.

Scholars place his ascent to his throne at about 78 CE, but it may have been 70 years later. He was probably the son of a chief of the Kushanas, a subgroup of the Yuch-Chi, a Central Asian tribe that had been pushed west and then south by a wave of migrations and conquests by other Asian tribes from further east. Shortly before Kanishka's rise to prominence, the Kushana subgroup, one of five into which the Yuch-Chi had split, had unified all five under its domination. From Bactria, Kanishka expanded the Kushanas' political influence eastward past the Indus River region to Mathura and beyond. In Mathura itself, Kanishka consolidated power in a central but unstable region, establishing a rule there that lasted for well over a century.

Kanishka was a renowned patron of Buddhism who, like Ashoka three hundred years earlier, converted to that peaceful religion after a violent military life. He also established a reputation as a lavish sponsor of all the religions and cultures in his state. His immediate successor, Huvishka, built a *punyashala* (hall of merit) large enough to feed over a hundred Brahmins in one sitting, as well as making expensive donations to Hindu guilds and temples.

Despite the tolerance of Mathura's rulers in theological matters, and their fiscal generosity toward Brahmins, the Hindu (Brahmin) establishment felt threatened on at least two fronts: first, the sanctity of Vedic public rituals (*shrauta*), and second, the sanctified social order—the *varna-dharma*. Mathura under the Kushanas was a city of wealth, professional skill, and economic status. Those who could amass money gained status: a low-caste Shudra could become a landlord, while a high-caste Brahmin or Kshatriya could—through a lack of initiative, bad luck, or ideological aversion to money—be reduced to servanthood.

The primary fissure was not between foreign ruler and Indo-Aryan subject but between Vedic dharma and a multiplicity of competing worldviews. The politics of identity were not nation-centered at that point in India's history. In fact, the Indo-Aryan Mauryas from Magadha to the east had been remembered by Brahmins as impure and despicable. The *Mahabharata*, for instance, regarded these eastern rulers as virtual non-Aryans, because they were inhospitable to Brahmins (8.30.73). The Guptas, who would follow the Kushanas as the new northern power (based again in Magadha) would have to deal with the same Brahminical litmus test for purity—the founder of the dynasty, some scholars believe, actually performed a famous Ashvamedha (horse sacrifice) to attract a Brahminical stamp of approval. But after the fall of the Shunga dynasty and the arrival of northwestern powers, for three hundred years in the heartland of Aryan Brahminism, the Vedic worldview coexisted in a precarious balance with competing religions. Those who championed dharma had three major options: reject all other worldviews; ignore them; or integrate them somehow into a comprehensive synthesis. All three options came into play, but in pursuit of the third, which is most interesting to scholars of Hinduism, the Brahmins had to tackle the following issues:

- Who is the good king?
- Can the Veda be salvaged in a changing world?

- How is dharma to be protected in the face of wealth, violence, and monastic forms of escapism?

Over the centuries, several answers emerged. The law book of *Manu* (*Manu Smriti*), for instance, produced a magisterial synthesis of numerous trends and ideas leading to a comprehensive dharma philosophy. At its core, *Manu's* dharma had to overcome the perceived gap between the immutable perfection of Veda and the contingent multiplicity of the historic world. *Smriti*, "recollection," is one such bridge. The books designated by this name, law books for instance, organize human conduct along the lines of an ostensible Vedic norm.

However, the most satisfying solution was not law (dharma) but bhakti, the tradition of devotional practice that championed a particular god, and in Mathura this god was primarily Krishna Vasudeva, an incarnation of Vishnu. The rise of Krishna bhakti was, among other things, the Brahmins' theological response to non-Brahminical rule, to militarism, to Buddhism, and to the loss of Vedic influence. Of course, ultimately the Krishna bhakti cults and dharma (the law books) were two interrelated aspects of a monumental creativity that carried India from Vedic religion to classical "Hinduism."

Ancient Sources of Devotion

As already shown, Vedic poets were great connoisseurs of complexity. With loving attention to detail they sang the praise of the sensory world and the equally rich worlds of the imagination. Everything was vast, intense, conflicted. But the *rishis* were not just poets—they were thinkers as well. Innovative systems of classification sustained intellectual coherence and supported the philosophical insight that the cosmos rested on deeper and more solid principles. These could be revealed (to the qualified) through such intellectual tools as numbers, similarities, analogies, or distinctions such as purity versus pollution and center versus periphery. Two types of late Vedic conceptions were particularly interesting from the perspective of those defenders of dharma who had to cope with the challenges of the Kushana period. The first was a separation of reality into three worlds, and the second was the permanent conflict between the *devas* (gods) and *asuras* (demons) over the three worlds. The way these two interlocking issues had been articulated and resolved in the Vedas and Brahmanas would bear directly on the Kushana period. And, as it turns out, it was Vishnu who had mediated between the two powerful ideas and thereby provided early models for coping with cultural differences.

Vishnu had been the Vedic god who established the three worlds with his strides, but his strides had been a response to the overwhelming power of the *asuras* over the *devas*. This is how the *Rig-Veda* (1.154) presented Vishnu's accomplishment:

> Let me now sing the heroic deeds of Vishnu, who has measured apart the realms of earth, who propped up the upper dwelling-place, striding far as he stepped forth three times.
>
> They praise for his heroic deeds Vishnu who lurks in the mountains, wandering like a ferocious wild beast, in whose three wide strides all creatures dwell.
>
> Let this song of inspiration go forth to Vishnu, the wide-striding bull who lives in the mountains, who alone with but three steps measured apart this long, far-reaching dwelling-place. (*Rig-Veda* 1.154.1–3; Doniger)

The early theology of Vishnu, articulated poetically in this ancient hymn, set in motion a nonaggressive ideology of reconciliation between competing forces and worlds. Vishnu both establishes the three worlds with his strides and mediates or spans them. He both confronts the demons as the hero (ferocious wild beast) of the gods, but he deceives them by assuming other, ostensibly powerless, forms. His incarnation as the finger-sized dwarf who stretched out to cover the three worlds is the perfect example of subtlety.

By the time Vishnu's paradoxical theology developed, the Vedic poets had already adopted a number of strategies for coping with what contemporary cultural studies calls "difference"— the kinds of conflict that arise in a situation of competing cultures, ideas, and forces. The most fundamental was confrontational: Indra had killed the demon snake Vritra with his *vajra* (weapon), just like a warrior-king. Indeed, Vishnu, too, in later mythology would take over the identity and role of Indra as king of the gods; he famously goes by such names as Madhusudana, "Slayer of the Demon Madhu"; Vanquisher of Enemies; and other names connected with royalty and militarism. But there were intellectually more creative options for bridging differences. Extending or pervading space (the three strides) in a subtle manner (in disguise) is an interesting alternative to force. Divine intervention in human affairs may have been the idea behind such a mythology. There was also mediation, as when Vishnu is described as the cosmic pillar or axis that reaches from the lowest world to the highest, or when he is identified (in the Brahmanas) with the sacrificial post, which was also the ritual equivalent of the world's central axis.

When the sacrificer, according to the Brahmanas, gained unity with Vishnu, he also obtained, through the mediation of that god, an identity with the universe as a whole.

For those who wished to use the Vedas as a guide for coping with impinging non-Aryan cultures, there had been ideas about confrontation, encompassment ("Our ideas include yours"), pervading ("Your ideas are only a surface form of ours"), and mediation ("There is a single way of representing both your and my ideas"). But theologically speaking, this was just the start. A deeper and more abstract synthesis emerged during the age of the Upanishads, particularly the *Shvetashvatara Upanishad* (c. 500 BCE). God, in this case Shiva, would act as a synthesizing force in a world that was no longer portrayed simply in mythical terms.

The *Shvetashvatara Upanishad*

One of the great protophilosophical texts from the late Vedic period was the Upanishad with the strange title *Shvetashvatara* (Man with a white mule). This text, originating in the *Black Yajurveda* school, was a stunningly ambitious early monotheistic work that sought to answer the many great questions of the day by means of one theological answer: Rudra (Shiva).

Shiva (or Rudra in his earlier name) was a relatively modest figure in the Vedic corpus, at least in terms of the number of appearances he had made. Some scholars have traced Shiva to the pre-Indo-Aryan figure found in Harappa: the so-called Lord of Beasts on the ancient Indus Valley seal. But in the *Shvetashvatara Upanishad*, Rudra was now the supreme and only Lord, the author and foundation of all existence, the philosopher's final shelter. In promoting Shiva, the author showed a mastery of all the synthesizing techniques one could bring to the task of harmonizing his unitary view with a plurality of known (and competing) contemporary doctrines. The text began with the great questions:

> What is the cause of brahman? Why were we born? By what do we live? On what are we established? Governed by whom, O you who know brahman, do we live in pleasure and in pain, each in our respective situation? (*Shvetashvatara Upanishad* 1.1; Olivelle)

The author would not abide an eclectic or pluralistic approach to these most basic questions. He knew what the Vedic priests would say, or the followers of Yajnavalkya, or any other thinker of the Vedic age, but he remained uncompromising:

> Those who follow the discipline of meditation have seen God, the
> self, and the power, all hidden by their own qualities. One alone is he
> who governs all those causes, from "time" to "self." (*Shvetashvatara
> Upanishad* 1.3; Olivelle)

There was only one answer that subsumed—or did it negate?—all other theories. But in order to promote this answer, the author had to cover all his bases, that is, address the schools of thought and doctrines that represented alternative approaches to his questions. There was the monistic approach of Yajnavalkya and Uddalaka Aruni from the early Upanishads: atman and Brahman. There were the prominent Vedic gods from the *Rig-Veda* and the Brahmanas: Agni, Savitar, Prajapati, Vishvakarman, Hiranyagarbha, and Purusha and the various ritual ideas that accompanied them. The author was also familiar with the emerging philosophical schools of Samkhya and Yoga, which had promoted dualistic (*purusha-prakriti*, spirit-matter) metaphysics and elaborate psychology.

In other words, the full range of Indian religious thought lay before the *Shvetashvatara*'s author, and he was not content with any of it. He wished to promote a new idea, a theology of one God—Shiva—and none of these intellectual precedents could express what he sought to achieve. What were the logical options for a theologian who wished to argue that all of reality was only one God? "There is only one Rudra; he has not tolerated a second who would reign over those worlds by his sovereign powers" (*Shvetashvatara Upanishad* 3.2; Olivelle). How could one reconcile this near-Hebraic monotheism with the dualism of Samkhya, with the mythical Rigvedic Purusha, who has a thousand heads, and with all the rest? A Near Eastern theologian might have declared war on the others, at least intellectually. Not so the author of this text. Instead, he quoted the others extensively, reinterpreted them, encompassed or identified with them, or when necessary ignored the differences. If the task was enormous, the author's solution requires some expertise to decode. For example, about the Samkhya and Yoga schools, which would not have their own texts for another half millennium, the author said:

> We study it—
>   As a wheel that is one-rimmed and threefold, with sixteen tips,
> fifty spokes, twenty counter-spokes, and six sets of eight, whose single
> rope is of many forms; that divides itself into three different paths;
> and whose delusion regarding the one springs from two causes.
> (*Shvetashvatara Upanishad* 1.4; Olivelle)

> Compressing his breaths in there and curbing his movements, a man
> should exhale through one nostril when his breath is exhausted. A
> wise man should keep his mind vigilantly under control, just as he
> would that wagon, yoked to unruly horses. (*Shvetashvatara Upanishad*
> 2.9; Olivelle)

The first passage, with its elaborate enumeration and oblique homologies, alludes to Samkhya psychology, which explains the multiplicity of experienced reality as a kind of evolution of carefully numbered elements (*tattvas*) that emerge in a complex process from *prakriti,* the fundamental ground of all matter. Over and against this primordial materiality stands *purusha*, absolute spirit. It rests perfectly, unperturbed by the activity of matter. *Prakriti* and *purusha* are two coeternal and coexistent realities. Where does the one Shiva fit in? Clearly, the promoter of Shiva's supremacy found a way here to integrate Samkhya psychology into his own theory by reducing the difference to our failure to understand the One (Shiva). The fact that Samkhya recognized two principles (*purusha* and *prakriti*) at the ground of all existence did not represent a major obstacle. The author is happy to integrate Yoga ideas where they suit his purposes. Even worshipers of Shiva must learn to meditate, to curb their senses and yoke their wandering minds. The second verse demonstrates this: the practice of Yoga (cognate with "yoke") is a physical means for training the mind, or disciplining the senses, to enable one to perceive truth.

The author of the *Shvetashvatara Upanishad* quotes the Vedas extensively; his most remarkable quotation refers to Purusha, whom we have seen at the center of late Rigvedic mythology:

> The Person [Purusha] had a thousand heads, a thousand eyes, and
> a thousand feet. Having encompassed the earth on all sides, he ex-
> tended ten fingers' breadth beyond it. (*Shvetashvatara Upanishad* 3.14;
> Olivelle)

This passage, known as the Purusha Sukta (*Rig-Veda* 10.90) was probably one of the most prestigious and familiar texts of the Vedic corpus. By the third century BCE, it was the moral and intellectual foundation of social morality (*varna-dharma*) and a rationale for metaphysical, especially monistic, specula-tion. The author of the *Shvetashvatara Upanishad* quoted it for an obvious reason—its assertion: "The Person [Purusha], clearly, is the immense Lord" (3.12; Olivelle).

If one had wished to persuade one's audience that one's theistic ideas were compelling and orthodox, there would have been no better way than to identify

God with familiar and prestigious Vedic concepts such as *purusha*. In fact, one of the most compelling philosophical mysteries in the *Rig-Veda* found its answer here in the person Rudra. "There was neither non-existence nor existence then," sang the author of Rig-Veda 10.129, before asking: "Who really knows? Who will proclaim it here?" This was the great agnostic hymn of the *Rig-Veda*, but its mystery was bound to end at some point. The *Shvetashvatara Upanishad* gave the answer: "When there was darkness, then there was neither day nor night, neither the existent nor the non-existent—the Benign One alone was there" (*Shvetashvatara Upanishad* 4.18; Olivelle).

But there was more. The author's God, Rudra, could also be identified with Vishnu, at least implicitly, by subsuming that god's most distinct qualities: "It is he who protects the world at the right time, the lord of the universe hidden in all beings" (*Shvetashvatara Upanishad* 4.15; Olivelle). Vishnu was the defender of dharma who pervaded the world and incarnated in a variety of beings that did not look like God. Here he became immersed within the identity of the Upanishad's other God—Shiva!

Of course the author of the text did much more, and was far more sophisticated than a brief overview can indicate. However, his results were not seamless: scholars can certainly identify the many quotations, allusions, identifications, and analogies in his work. Still, the overall message came out clearly: Shiva was the God who encompassed everything valuable that earlier Hindu philosophers had discovered and written about atman and Brahman, about *purusha* and *prakriti*, about the sacrifice and the Vedic gods. Shiva was the one Truth that united diverse manifestations, the simple and true answer to all the questions that had been addressed in so many ancient ways. The author did not reject other ideas; he reinterpreted and subsumed them within his own theology of Shiva.

But the Upanishad's author was no mere archivist: he was a religious revolutionary as well. He mastered the disciplines and philosophies of ancient India and demonstrated his superior theology. However, only through the grace of God—a bold new concept—has he been able, he says, to obtain the final religious goal. Here, at the very end of the Upanishad, was where the emerging tradition of bhakti was leading. Salvation, the author concluded, was not just a matter of erudition, insight, or discipline. The essential new ingredient was bhakti:

> Only in a man who has the deepest love for God, and who shows the same love towards his teacher as towards God, do these points declared by the Noble One [*mahatma*] shine forth. (*Shvetashvatara Upanishad* 6.23; Olivelle)

The *Bhagavad Gita*

Three and a half centuries before Kanishka ruled in northern India, Ashoka had renounced his bloody approach to empire-building and converted to Buddhism. He then consolidated his rule under the banner of the Buddhist Dhamma (Dharma), spreading a vision of peace and compassion throughout the Mauryan empire. The *Bhagavad Gita* (Song of God), India's most highly revered scripture, could easily have been a Hindu response to Ashoka's double transformation. The *Gita* was, at one level, a brilliant argument on behalf of the Hindu king, who wished to remain engaged politically while grounding his ethos in ultimate religious values. But it was also, and remains today, the most coherent Hindu guide for resolving the conflict between the pursuit of social action and that of individual salvation.

The *Bhagavad Gita* is situated as a clearly distinct work within the sixth book of the vast *Mahabharata* epic, at the point in the narrative when the Pandavas have returned from their exile and demanded their kingdom, as the Kauravas had agreed. But now Duryodhana refused to abide by the old agreement. Yudhishthira, the eldest among the Pandavas and the rightful heir to the throne, backed down and reduced his terms to a mere five villages. But even that was more than Duryodhana was willing to concede. The Pandavas were then simply forced to declare war in order to reclaim what was rightfully theirs.

The *Gita* opens with the two vast armies confronting each other in Kurukshetra. The long list of names that dominates the first chapter includes numerous relatives, elders, and teachers; the conflict was tearing apart relationships, much as the Civil War did in the United States. The leading warrior among the Pandavas—it was inconceivable that they could win without him—was Arjuna. This great archer responded to the challenge by commanding his charioteer to drive between the two armies, where, surveying his elders and relatives on both sides, he announced that he would not fight: "It were healthier for me if the Dhartarashtras [sons of Dhritarashtra, the Kauravas], weapons in hand, were to kill me unarmed and defenceless, on the battlefield" (1.46; Van Buitenen).

The text thus began with a sharp moral dilemma, as though the author were placing the dharma of *Manu Smriti* itself on trial for ethical inconsistency. *Manu*'s laws *had* covered every aspect of life: a ruler was not only justified in fighting enemies of the state (or of dharma) but was obligated do so. Such enemies included those who violated treatises; stole land; violated the rights of the weak and the honor of women. The Kauravas had done all of this. And yet the same *Manu* also declared that one had to respect one's elders and never, under any circumstances, kill a guru (teacher). The internal contradictions of the moral life, of dharma, now exposed, could only drive a warrior to seek the life of a renouncer (2.5; Van Buitenen):

> It was better that without slaying my gurus
> I went begging instead for alms in this land
> Than that I by slaying my covetous gurus
> Indulge in the joys that are dipped in their blood.

Arjuna's charioteer (*suta*; also means "narrator")—a merely respectable military position—was no ordinary soldier. It was Krishna, who plays a rich and complex role in the entire epic. Krishna was the son of Vasudeva and head of a neighboring North Indian clan not far from Hastinapura—the Vrishnis. On the epic's narrative level, Krishna was a Kshatriya prince. But in some sections of the work, he is also an incarnation (*avatara*) of Vishnu, hence God himself. Human actors in the epic recognized this fact, but it played a relatively minor role in the unfolding of events: the villains simply ignored Krishna's identity as *avatara* when he acted as go-between, seeking from the Kauravas a compromise on behalf of the Pandavas. In fact, in no place did Krishna behave as a "God" who could impose external solutions on human conflicts. Instead, he acted as friend and mentor, and in the *Bhagavad Gita,* he sought to persuade to action the one warrior who could make a decisive difference in the outcome of the battle. The text is presented as a detailed transcript of God imparting his teaching to a skeptic in order to change history through human agency. In order to achieve this effect, the *Gita* as a whole had to resolve the moral dilemma at the core of religious life: as noted, the conflict between the pursuit of social action and that of individual salvation.

The second chapter of the *Gita* tells of Krishna's rather cursory efforts to address the literal problem at hand: should a warrior fight? Of course he should, if he is a true man! Arjuna's caste duty as a Kshatriya warrior bound him to fight. *Varna-dharma* (caste rules) trumped *kula-dharma* (family rules), including even the apparently universal rule (*sadharana-dharma*) against killing a guru. In fighting, Krishna argued, a warrior could do no wrong; heaven was guaranteed. But Krishna quickly moved to a deeper argument, beyond warriors and wars.

"Dharma" not only referred to the concept of duty—what a person ought to do or avoid doing; it also described the nature of that person, the nature of reality as a whole. A man's dharma is not only what he should do but who he is; the two things were interconnected. In fact, according to dharma, all of reality is a kind of grid in which all things are linked. On that level—of how reality is in fact (ontology) rather than how actors ought to act (ethics)—those who kill do not really kill, and those who are killed do not really die! Beyond the frightening

appearance of death and carnage, the soul continues on—serene and unperturbed (2.20; Van Buitenen):

> It is never born nor does it die
> Nor once that it is will it ever not be;
> Unborn, unending, eternal and ancient
> It is not killed when the body is killed.

There was no point, then, Krishna declared, in Arjuna mourning those he will
slay in battle, because the aspect of their being that is essential to them—
certainly not the body—will continue to exist. As if discarding old clothes, the
soul will give up the body for a new one in the new life it takes. That was the law
of transmigration, ancient and revered as the early Upanishads.

By now Krishna has led Arjuna to reflect about psychological and philosophical ideas. Krishna was past justifying the killing now, having argued that
the true reality of the soul can only be perceived by those who acquire a special
kind of discipline. Discipline meant Yoga: It required a subtle equanimity in
relation to sensory experience, a special detachment from the senses. This
mental state of balance was unusually difficult to achieve in the face of a sensory
reality dominated by pleasure and pain. But the reward was immense: "The
wise man whom they [sensations] do not trouble, for whom happiness and
unhappiness are the same, is fit for immortality" (2.15; Van Buitenen).

The truly balanced mind produces a unique type of existential knowing
that changes the knower forever. The very self of the knowing agent disappears
in the object of knowledge. Knowledge and Being dissolve into each other, or
into a single field. But Arjuna, now deeply engaged in Krishna's teaching,
remained skeptical. If the goal of the religious life was a meditative dispassion,
why was Krishna pushing him to act on the battlefield? Would it not follow that
he should retire into Yoga, like the sages of the Upanishads or the Buddhist
monks? Starting with the third chapter, the new dilemma of the *Gita* was no
longer ethical. The question instead was this: How does one pursue *moksha* or
nirvana—the goals of contemplative discipline—while remaining engaged in
worldly action?

It remains one of the defining questions in all of religious literature. In
answering it, the *Gita* had to integrate many of the leading intellectual traditions of the day: Vedic theories of action, Upanishadic philosophical speculation, Buddhist and Jain monasticism, Samkhya psychological metaphysics, and
Yoga practice. Like the *Shvetashvatara Upanishad* a century or two earlier, the
Gita did not produce a seamless doctrine out of all these: there were too many
layers of thought, and the redactors showed an admirable reluctance to throw
away or cover up the work of those who had gone before them. As a result, no

simple summary could ever do justice to the ambitious synthesis of the *Bhagavad Gita* or the complexity of its exposition.

Krishna's answer to Arjuna's poignant question is, in a nutshell, "we don't really have a choice in the matter; action takes place all around us." This answer comes straight out of Samkhya philosophy. Primordial materiality, *prakriti*, the underlying matrix of everything that exists, is intrinsically dynamic, by virtue of its constitutive elements, the three strands (*gunas*). This does not mean that action must bind us through karma by the fetters of its consequences. We are, ultimately, free. This was, in fact, the *Gita's* great innovation: it asserts that we are not complete slaves to action or to its consequences. Krishna's teaching described the threefold discipline, Yoga, that allows us to combine action with freedom. These were the discipline of action (*karma-yoga*), the discipline of insight (*jnana-yoga*), and the discipline of devotion (*bhakti-yoga*). *Karma-yoga* showed Arjuna how to act without regard for the fruit of action. By renouncing such considerations as rewards or benefit, the actor avoids the binding trap of karma. But this difficult skill depends on the second discipline, the more basic one of insight, which allows the realization that the world of the senses—the phenomenal world—is distinct from the truly real. In the Upanishads, such an insight would have marked the distinction between the embodied soul (*jivan*) and the essential Self (atman). Only atman is ultimately identical with the true essence of reality, with Brahman. Combined, *karma-yoga* and *jnana-yoga* produce a dispassionate wisdom that allows the individual to disengage from those aspects of reality that bind him or her to false ideas and to perpetual rebirth.

The third discipline, *bhakti-yoga,* moves the *Gita* beyond the integration of Upanishadic and early Buddhist philosophy to a new realm. *Bhakti-yoga* places the first two disciplines in a theistic context. Disciplined action is not merely free from the thought of its rewards; it is turned into a positive offering: "Whatever you do, or eat, or offer, or give, or mortify, Kaunteya [son of Kunti, Arjuna], make it an offering to me, and I shall undo the bonds of karman, the good and evil fruits. He whose spirit is yoked to the yoga of renunciation shall come to me" (9.27-8; Van Buitenen).

It seems, then, that the teachings of Krishna in the *Gita* expanded Vedic ideas of action and Upanishadic theories of knowledge. In the mouth of Krishna, the *Bhagavad Gita* developed a sophisticated monotheism that embraced the other sources and deepened their potential implications. Krishna—God—was the answer to Arjuna's dilemma. Krishna theology, to put it in more abstract terms, acted as the ideology that could accommodate philosophical pluralism under one umbrella: "Even they who in good faith devote themselves to other deities really offer up their sacrifices to me alone, Kaunteya, be it without proper rite" (9.23; Van Buitenen). Even the most elevated religious practitioner, the Upanishadic sage who pursues *moksha*, is in fact immersed in Krishna: "Having become *brahman*, serene in spirit, he does not grieve, he does not crave, equable to all creatures, he achieves ultimate *bhakti* of me" (18.54; Van Buitenen).

Krishna, the supreme God of the *Bhagavad Gita*, encompasses all things in the universe: objects, living beings, gods, even doctrines. He is the pervader and integrator of the substance and structure of all there is. Chapter 11 of the *Gita*, in which Krishna reveals himself to Arjuna as the supreme God, makes this vividly and even frighteningly clear (11.23; Van Buitenen):

> At the sight of your mass with its eyes and mouths,
> Multitudinous arms, thighs, bellies and feet,
> Strong-armed One, and maws that are spiky with tusks
> the worlds are in panic and so am I!

But even as the *Gita* formulated its grand theology, the older material, out of which Krishna was fashioned, in a sense, continued to show. Among the text's many links to older traditions is the mention of Purusha, that Rigvedic Person (*Rig-Veda* 10.90) who also embodied all of creation. Krishna as *purusha*, or for that matter as Ishvara or Agni, was thus both a respectful tip of the hat to Vedic culture (*Bhagavad Gita* 11.3; 11.18) and a glimpse at the layered history of third-century theology. Still, Krishna was not just *purusha*, he was the "highest *purusha*": This was the text's way of informing its audience that Krishna was superior to both the transient and the intransient, to both the Vedic and the Upanishadic traditions (15.18)

The number of integrative techniques in the *Bhagavad Gita* is impressive. The pluralistic maze of North Indian cultures and religions provided rich fodder for Krishna theology and for bhakti. The text quoted older traditions, interpreted them, identified God with ancient gods and ideas, encompassed contested doctrines—in the epiphany of chapter 11, many were literally swallowed—compared, superseded, replaced, underpinned, or simply identified. The text's approaches were ontological (comparing realities), epistemological (contrasting ways of knowing), mythological, political, and psychological. The result was a complexity and polyvocality that could only be compared to a Bach six-part invention or 50 simultaneous chess games.

Krishna in Mathura

The huge *Mahabharata*, with its ascendant gods who replaced the Vedic pantheon, and the *Bhagavad Gita*, with its new devotion to Krishna, reflect the transitional period between the Maurya and Gupta empires. Both texts give evidence of the emergence of a new normative tradition for an age that had seen the prominence of heterodoxies (Buddhism and Jainism) along with the coming and going of political powers. The *Bhagavad Gita* thus defined the ideal king—in the figure of Arjuna—as the man who combined devotion to God with vigorous political and even military engagement. Krishna in the *Gita*, and the *Mahabharata* in general, represented the divine embodiment—the *avatara*—of the fight waged by a transcendent God, namely Vishnu, for righteousness (dharma).

Toward the end of this chaotic but formative period, during the Kushana rule, the political and religious ideology of the *avatara* assumed a more concrete and local face in Mathura. It was there that the *Harivamsha* (Genealogy of Hari, or Krishna), a formidable devotional text, began its history—remaining oral for a long time. The *Harivamsha* describes the life of young Krishna, who as an adult figured so heavily in the story of the *Mahabharata*. In a sense, the *Harivamsha* was what we might call a prequel to the *Mahabharata*. The *Harivamsha* collected numerous narratives (legends, myths, folktales, histories) and integrated them into one of India's most familiar and best-loved traditions: the story of the boy Krishna growing up among the cow herders and villagers. In religious iconography, Krishna has usually been depicted with these episodes in mind—playing a flute or crawling as a child to steal some butter. Far more rare is the heady representation of Krishna as Arjuna's charioteer and mentor.

Krishna was born to Vasudeva and Devaki, but his uncle Kamsa—the usurping ruler of Mathura—vowed to kill him. The infant was smuggled out and raised by the villagers Yashoda and Nanda. The stories of Krishna's youth in the village across the Yamuna continued to develop for centuries, especially in the Puranas, chief among which was the *Bhagavata Purana* (the tenth book). While still an infant, Krishna killed a treacherous wet nurse, uprooted two trees, and overturned a cart. Later, he overcame the serpent Kaliya, who had poisoned the water of the Yamuna River, where the shepherds brought their animals to drink. Krishna finally killed Kamsa, who had blighted the entire region with his evil rule. However, at no point did the young Krishna represent an overwhelming and inevitable divine power. Upending *adharma* (evil) through the incarnation of God always required equally matched forces, where the outcome was both tenuous and a shade short of inevitable. The point of the *avatara* theology was precisely to downplay the power of God in favor of a more subtle process. After all, the demons are still all around us. Just as Vishnu had to deceive the *asuras* as a dwarf in the Vedas, now it was as the boy Krishna.

Scholars do not agree whether several historical traditions converged to create the religious figure of Krishna. Were there several Krishnas (the Vrinshi prince, the cow herdsman from Vrindavan, the incarnation of Vishnu) or was the cowherd identity merely a disguise for the one and only Krishna (the Kshatriya incarnation of Vishnu)? Were the stories of the young Krishna folkloristic (local and independent of the great texts) or were they symbolic narratives about a subtle and paradoxical God?

Whichever of these two alternatives one adopts, it is clear that the *Harivamsha*, like the *Bhagavad Gita*, was profoundly concerned with questions of legitimacy and dharma: What are the characteristics of the righteous king and how does religion figure in legitimizing kingship?

When the young Krishna, in one of the best-known episodes, challenged Indra, the Vedic god of royalty and the storm, a new political ethos tested itself against the old. Indra had represented power and the benefits that attend the service of power (through Vedic rituals). Krishna showed the villagers that Govardhana Hill, near the village, was as worthy of worship as Indra himself, and then, when the angry god attacked with a violent storm, the young Krishna blithely held up the huge hill with one hand, protecting the villagers from the storm. The episode, often represented in art, was every bit as political as it was religious—if one adheres to what is, in fact, a Western distinction.

The political implications of the *Harivamsha* and *Mahabharata* are far more explicit in the notorious episode of Jarasandha, which is recounted in both. Jarasandha was the powerful and evil king of Magadha—historically, the place in the east where the Mauryas had ruled. He forced Krishna to escape Mathura and journey west to Dvaraka. Only much later did Jarasandha meet his end at the hands of Yudhisthira's powerful brother Bhima. But the implications of Krishna's exile from Mathura were politically and historically telling, as *Mahabharata* scholar Alf Hiltebeitel points out. The Kushana period in Mathura saw a Buddhist and Jain dominance, which Kanishka made political by converting to Buddhism. A period of diminished Hindu influence was a symbolic exiling of Krishna, the autochthonous God of Mathura. The new political arrangement also trivialized the concept of righteous kingship, as embodied in the doctrine of Vishnu's incarnation. Hindu scholars and thinkers did not declare war on Kanishka or the heterodoxies he promoted—he was rather generous with Brahmins as well. Instead, Brahmin theologians showed a remarkable ability to acknowledge religious and political pluralism while integrating many perspectives into a unified worldview.

7

Performing Arts
and Sacred Models

Around the year 350 CE, almost six hundred years after King Ashoka's
pillar was erected in Kaushambi, it was still standing. The Magadhi
language inscription, chiseled in Brahmi script, was accessible to virtually no one, and its message—unity in the Buddhist monastic
community—was quaintly out of date. But it was still a prestigious,
perhaps hallowed monument when an official named Harishena
from Magadha composed a longer inscription in Sanskrit and had it
cut into the same stone. Harishena was working for the current king in
Magadha, Samudragupta, who was, self-consciously perhaps, the
perfect Hindu counterweight to the Maurya who had converted to
Buddhism. Samudragupta, in print so to speak, told the world he was
the perfect Hindu king.

Son of Chandragupta I, who had taken over the regional kingdom
of Magadha when it was a mere shadow of its former greatness,
Samudragupta began to expand it by means of military and political
maneuverings, including a felicitous marriage. The period of the
Guptas, traced to the starting year 320, is attested through coins, inscriptions, and rich archeological remains that document the greatest
political and cultural era of Hindu polity. The pillar in Kaushambi
(now in Allahabad) was a resounding glorification of Samudragupta
not just as a king but as a Hindu king. First, of course, is the litany
of military successes, which were impressive even by the standards
of the Mauryas. Samudragupta accelerated his father's initial efforts
and subdued the Naga rulers of Mathura and Pawaya as well as the

Vakataka kings in the south. He vanquished border kingdoms, including Nepal in the Himalayan range, and overran numerous tribes, even the fierce Malavas in what is now Rajasthan. Surpassing all other northern kings, he extended his reach as far south as Sri Lanka. Still, most of the kingdoms and states listed on the pillar were not defeated in a military campaign but either agreed to pay tribute or reached some other political arrangement with the ascendant power.

Following this extended curriculum vitae of military accomplishment, the inscription speaks of loftier themes. Samudragupta is compared to the four *lokapalas*, the Vedic gods who guard the main directions of the world: Kubera, Varuna, Indra, and Yama (four others guarded the intermediate directions). According to the dharma texts of that age, primarily *Manu Smriti*, the good king was the virtual embodiment of these divinities—especially in his capacity as upholder of dharma (law). The righteous king guarded and protected the weak against the "laws of the fish" (*matsyanyaya*), whereby the larger devour the small. He supported the poor and helpless subjects of his domain. In short, the *dharmaraja* (righteous king) was the perfect ruler, who had once been embodied in the person of Yudhishthira in the *Mahabharata* and in the life and work of Rama in the *Ramayana*. As far as the citizens of the new empire were to be concerned, that was how Samudragupta was to be regarded. The pillar made this clear. The king was even Purusha, that Rigvedic Person who was the foundation of all existence. By this time, Purusha had become merged into the identity of Vishnu, the model for the perfect king. Samudragupta was Vishnu incarnate, the guardian of dharma. His royal seal, logically, portrayed Garuda, the bird that served as Vishnu's vehicle.

Samudragupta's 20-year reign (until 375 CE) represented the early period of the Gupta dynasty, which lasted until the early decades of the sixth century—faltering toward the end under the constant pressure of Hunas (the Huns, the same peoples who sacked Rome). The heady early decades have left archeologists with relatively modest remains; the great architectural and artistic treasures associated with the Guptas date to the later years. However, two types of discovery from Samudragupta's time, or very shortly after, are unusually illuminating. The first is a monumental stone sculpture of a horse, found in Khairigarh on the northern border of Magadha with Nepal. Blocky and crudely carved, the horse lacks the graceful flow of earlier Gandhara or later Gupta stonework. The sections of the horse's anatomy are schematically differentiated, and the entire sculptural composition projects a static and heavy feel. An inscription on the base traces the horse to Samudragupta, which makes it particularly interesting to contrast with the horse on the famous Ashvamedha coins of the same king.

These coins, found throughout the region, show a surprisingly similar horse, though far more graceful in artistic execution. The horse stands facing a sacrificial post, above which an inscription reads: "The king of kings who has performed the Vajimedha sacrifice wins heaven after protecting the earth." On the flip side of the coin, the crowned queen stands on a circular mat holding a fan and a towel in her hands. The inscription on this side declares: "Powerful enough to perform the Ashvamedha sacrifice."

The king minted other coins. Following the Roman standard and Kushana precedent, the coins consisted of 121 grains of gold—an expensive standard that would decline in later years, for a variety of economic reasons. The coins depicted different themes, including Purusha surrounded by a *chakra* (solar disc) in the manner of Vishnu, as well as coins depicting Garuda. Nonetheless, to solidify his stature as the paradigmatic king, the very embodiment of Vishnu, Samudragupta minted the Ashvamedha coins and may have performed the ancient Vedic rite itself. And as everyone knew, the man who was able to perform that most prestigious, daring, and controversial of all Vedic rituals— the horse sacrifice—was indeed a great Hindu king.

The Horse Sacrifice

From the earliest days of Indian chieftainship and kingship, the horse sacrifice served as the primary symbol, alongside the rite of inauguration (*rajasuya*), of royal dominion and legitimacy. Unlike most other rituals, the horse sacrifice required both Brahminical knowledge and Kshatriya brawn. All the old Vedic schools prescribed this ritual, an indication of wide-ranging influence. Detailed accounts can be found in two major Shrauta Sutras (Katyayana and Apastamba, named after the Braminical families who composed them, as noted in chapter 2), as well as the *Vajasaneyi Samhita* and the *Shatapatha Brahmana* and *Aitareya Brahmana*. The ritual is eulogized in two famous Rigvedic hymns (1.162, 163). The *Brihadaranyaka Upanishad* opens with the sacrificial horse as a vital metaphor. And the *Mahabharata* contains an entire book dedicated to the Ashvamedha.

At over one year long, the ritual itself could be enormously complex and expensive, and therefore rare. It consisted of numerous subsidiary rites, preparations and purifications, transitional rites, and penances—most of which had to be performed unerringly. Reduced to its most basic components, the Ashvamedha has two parts, the first preparatory, the second culminating (conducted a year apart).

All four major types of priests (*Adhvaryu*, *Hotri*, *Udgatri*, and *Brahman*), along with numerous helpers offered their services to the king for this ritual. In the preparatory rites, the ritual experts chose a young white stallion with black spots—a valuable animal said to be worth one thousand cows. A special sacrificial structure was built along an east-west orientation. To the east of this structure, expert builders constructed a fire altar, according to the specifications of the appropriate geometrical text (Shulbasutra). At a point in time that was precisely indicated by astrologers—also able mathematicians—the king and his wives entered the sacrificial house in an elaborately staged manner, from the proper direction and in the correct sequence, in order to attend a minor sacrifice. That night the king, following precise instructions, slept in the embrace of his favorite wife, but had to avoid sexual activity.

On the next day, a series of carefully scripted rituals consecrated the horse. It was tethered with a special rope to a post and addressed as a god (Prajapati or Purusha): "You are the one who includes all. You are the world" (and so on). Officials then sprinkled the horse with water. A black dog killed, passed under the legs of the horse, and dragged to the river from which the water had come for the sprinkling. After a number of additional actions, including whispering mantras into the horse's ear, the animal was released. The king and his priests drove off the horse in a northeasterly direction.

Surrounded by a herd of one hundred geldings and protected by four groups of one hundred Kshatriyas who were related to the royal court, the horse ranged freely for a full year. If it felt like galloping, it did, and when it wished to graze lazily, it did so as well. The movements of the animal, free as the spirit of the king himself, could under no circumstances be curtailed. The warriors ensured this freedom. If the animal wandered into a neighboring state, it was still vital to continue the ritual, even when defending the horse meant war.

After a full solar year and following the return of the horse, the second and more elaborate portion of the Ashvamedha ritual would take place. This would begin with several preparatory rites that lasted a whole month. They included the initiation of the king to the state of ritual purity, the consecration of numerous lesser animals, and their sacrifice. In some texts the number of such sacrifices reaches as high as 609 animals. The central sacrifice began with the anointing of the horse with clarified butter. Three of the king's wives did this, and the horse was also decorated with 101 pearls, while the priests chanted a basic mantra: "Bhuh, bhuvah, svah." The priests then began a prescripted contest of riddles. The horse was sprinkled with water, then suffocated ("pacified") to death. Its corpse was positioned on the ground with its legs pointing to the north, while the body stretched from east to west.

As other animals were sacrificed, the king's wives encircled the horse nine times, addressing it as "mother" and fanning it with fans (*chouri*) like the one depicted on Samudragupta's coin. The "nine gates" or openings of the horse's body, through which its life had departed, were cleansed. The chief queen then ceremonially lay down next to the horse in a position that mimicked copulation; the two were covered with a single blanket. The other women and the priests then exchanged lewd verses from a carefully scripted text, as follows.

> "Hey, maiden, hey, maiden, the little female bird . . ." and she insults him back: "Hey, officient, hey, officient, that little bird . . ."
>
> And then the overseer . . . insults the chief queen: "Hey, chief queen, hey, chief queen, your mother and father climb to the top of a tree . . ." She has as her attendants a hundred daughters of kings; they insult the overseer in return: "Hey, overseer, hey, overseer, your mother and father play in the top of a tree" [and so on]. (*Shatapatha Brahmana* 13.5.2.1–2; Doniger)

The horse was sectioned along the lines indicated by the king's wives with golden needles. It was vitally important for the priests to avoid breaking a single bone; the horse, after all was a sacred object and symbol. Following a series of additional performances, the priests returned to their own memorized script and exchanged a series of philosophical questions and answers.

Later into that evening, the entire arena was still buzzing with ritual activity, chanting, and singing, until the blood of the horse was poured in offering into the sacrificial fire from its hoof. The meat of the horse was roasted in the fire and eaten as the events of the day came to an end. For 12 days after the conclusion of the central ritual, additional ceremonies took place; many of them (called *prayashchitta*) served as expiations for any mistakes that might have slipped by the priests during the central ritual.

Predictably, perhaps, the ancient Indian texts provide their own theories for the horse sacrifice. The *Taittiriya Brahmana* says that the horse and its sacrificer were in fact one being and that the horse, in essence, was the god Prajapati. Through the ritual, then, the sacrificer became God. The *Shatapatha Brahmana* says, in contrast, that the horse was dear to Prajapati because it was the most precious (and martial) of animals. In fact, the horse had been created out of Prajapati's own left eye, when the eye swelled and fell out (*ashvayat*; the horse was *ashva*). Of course, the ancient texts were renowned for fanciful etymologies and puns that served the purpose of explanation.

No theory of magic, scapegoating, or symbolism can ever account for what takes place at any ritual unless the theorists can be present to talk to the participants. The actual performance is always richer than the script, and the actors have surprising thoughts about the entire affair. What would an anthropologist from another planet say after reading a description of a Broadway play, a baseball game, or a high mass? Could the alien tell how literally we take these performances, or exactly what various items mean to us? What would the anthropologist make of the color schemes on baseball uniforms? In fact, in 350 CE or so, when Samudragupta's Ashvamedha may have taken place, it was an extremely old ritual, perhaps 1,500 years. It is virtually impossible to fathom what the participants make of the objects and actions in the vast and esoteric ceremony. At a minimum, the following can perhaps be conceded:

- The ritual was not precisely the "thing itself" (dominion, God, prosperity, the three worlds), but it was somehow connected with these.
- The ritual was astoundingly detailed, and only the priests, as a group, knew everything. The other actors had to be directed.
- Precision and attention to detail, including the inexplicable (directions, numbers, material used, timing, vocal intonation, rhythm), were paramount. A mistake could incur the wrath of the director (Brahmin priest).
- The entire event was consciously theatrical. A stage was built, and people behaved as they would never behave offstage (the exchange between wives and priests is the most notorious example). The musical (instrumental and vocal) accompaniment to the ritual reinforced this impression of theatrical production.

Because the Ashvamedha combined drama, mystery, and pomp, it could be co-opted in a variety of manners—just as a medieval Christian passion play could evolve into a Bach oratorio. The meaning of the ritual was above all what the performers wished it to be. For Samudragupta, it was a twofold declaration of great magnitude: I am the strongest and wealthiest king in India, and I am the *dharmaraja*—the royal embodiment of law!

Gupta Theater

On the same pillar in Kaushambi, Samudragupta also boasted of his great artistic exploits. The inscription praises his singing abilities and his virtuosity on the lyre. He is called King of Poets and described as a great patron of the arts. This was a precedent-setting boast for a conquering emperor: support and promotion of the arts. Indeed, under Samudragupta and his successors, the arts—literary, dramatic, musical, and plastic—did flourish. The Gupta years have often been called the golden age of Indian cultural history, and it would not be an exaggeration to say that the achievements of that age were unprecedented. Two of India's most important theoretical thinkers worked during that period—the Buddhist philosopher Vasubandhu the elder, and the art theorist Bharatamuni (a century or two later). The most renowned figure associated with the Gupta rulers themselves was the dramatist Kalidasa, who composed his six works during the late years of Samudragupta and the early years of his son Chandragupta II (375–415 CE). Scholars believe that Kalidasa modeled the heroes and events of at least two of his *kavya* works (*Raghuvamsa*, The Lineage of Raghu, and *Meghadhuta*, The Cloud Messenger) on the achievements of Samudragupta. For instance, the description in *Raghuvamsa* of the king's conquest of the world matches the list of Samudragupta's campaigns on the Kaushambi pillar.

But Kalidasa's dramatic art (*natya*) was hardly a simple eulogy of this or that king. The king in Hindu political life embodied highly prized values that were not always easy to reconcile. How could he combine violence (military or judicial) with virtue, and how might political action in general (*niti*) conform with transcendent religious values? As others had before him, Kalidasa defined the perfect king and the perfect public life. But he was a creator who worked through relatively new artistic media—drama (*natya*) and poetry (*kavya*)—which gave him both freedom and precision, and explains the power of his work even today.

Kalidasa was a devotee of Shiva at a time when the kings he served were Vaishnavas (devotees of Vishnu) who regarded themselves as the very embodiment of Vishnu. However, the two theologies often overlapped, or could be made to do the same metaphysical work. For example, Kalidasa sang the praise of Shiva's eight manifest forms (*ashtamurti*), which included the four elements, the sun, the moon, and others. This doctrine embraced the symbolic split between two cosmic halves—Shiva's feminine side, equated with nature (*prakriti*) and his masculine side, which roughly corresponded with *purusha*. The same dualistic principle figured in the metaphysics of Vishnu. In both Shaiva and Vaishnava theology, the unity of two cosmological principles represented a mystery, reconciled only as paradox. For Kalidasa, the king stood at this metaphysical boundary line. The ideal king, in other words, had to resolve the contradictions that inhere in reality: soul and nature; morality and love; action and ultimate felicity.

The best known among Kalidasa's works, *Abhijnanashakuntala* (Shakuntala and the Ring of Recollection), is a beautiful and moving staging of these ideas in action. The story of the play was an ancient one, reworked dramatically by the fifth-century dramatist: King Dushyanta, ruler of Hastinapura, was on a hunting expedition in a lush forest, near the hermitage of the sage Kanva. In pursuit of a deer, the king caught a glimpse of the beautiful Shakuntala, who was the daughter of the sage Vishvamitra and the celestial nymph Menaka but lived as the adopted daughter of Kanva. After a period of unfulfilled mutual longing, the two finally consummated their love sexually, which rendered them husband and wife, according to the Gandharva standard. Dushyanta gave a ring to his beloved, sealing their relationship. Some time later, Shakuntala, in great excitement, failed to honor an ascetic named Durvasas. The notoriously temperamental holy man cursed her with being forgotten by the king, who had already left the hermitage.

Time passed, and Shakuntala's pregnancy advanced, but no word came from her husband at the palace, as he had promised. Finally, accompanied by members of the hermitage, she traveled to the court in order to join her husband, but Dushyanta did not remember her identity. He disavowed the pregnant woman. At this time, Shakuntala was mortified to discover that the ring had been lost during the journey. There was no way to make the king remember her. At that worst of moments, her friends abandoned her, while the king, out of mere duty, agreed to let her wait out the pregnancy at the palace. But Shakuntala suddenly vanished, snatched by a celestial nymph on a ray of light. Some time later, a fisherman discovered the ring lodged in the stomach of a fish, and Dushyanta remembered his beloved.

Years of pain and regret went by for the love-struck king, until one day he set out in pursuit of hostile demons. The chase took him to the heavenly hermitage of Marica, where he met a mischievous boy—his own mirror image. Then he saw the boy's mother, Shakuntala, pale and emaciated from sorrow, but undeniably his beloved.

To understand the power this play had over contemporary audiences, one must forget Shakespeare. There are no conflicts here among individuals, no betrayals. Nor is there pride, jealously, or greed. Dushyanta is neither Lear nor Othello. The drama, after all, was generated by an innocent oversight, followed by the curse of an ascetic, so seemingly peripheral that it is voiced by a character who never even makes it onto the stage! The movers in the drama, to a large extent, are ideas: dharma, fate, love, memory, karma. Even the vivid descriptions of the heroes read more like symbolic representations than the features of a unique individual (act 1, verses 17, 18; Miller):

> A tangle of duckweed adorns a lotus
> A dark spot heightens the moon's glow,
> The bark dress increases her charm
> Beauty finds its ornaments anywhere.
>
> Her lips are fresh red buds,
> Her arms are tendrils,
> Impatient youth is poised
> To blossom in her limbs.

These images may read like clichés, but can the modern reader explain precisely why? What is the "obvious" reference of moon, buds, blossom? For the audiences of the Gupta theaters it was nature, *prakriti*. Shakuntala stood for the matrix of reality in the familiar cosmic dualism of *prakriti* and *purusha*. What, then, did the king represent? His charioteer told the audience early in the play, during the hunt (act 1, verse 6; Miller):

> I see this black buck move
> As you draw your bow
> And I see the wild bowman Shiva,
> Hunting the dark antelope.

An audience of connoisseurs could not fail to see the point, much like the central allusions of an elaborate sacrifice. It was God himself. However, both types of performance were multilayered. The king who hunted and the beloved who blended into the lush vegetation of the forest—the reference in those tropes was Prithu and Prithivi: the primordial king (manifestation of God) who mastered the Earth in a mythical chase (she changed shapes to elude him of course). Again, behind the characters and the action stood familiar philosophical ideas: spirit and nature, *purusha* and *prakriti*, the king, Earth, dharma and karma—the consequences of every single act.

In the hands of the Gupta dramatist, these ancient themes received a new twist. Kalidasa wrote about love-in-separation—that seems clear—but more important than distance was forgetfulness: the lover who forgets his beloved (act 5, verse 31; Miller):

> I cannot remember marrying
> The sage's daughter,
> But the pain my heart feels
> Makes me suspect that I did.

What does it mean, on a philosophical level, that the soul forgets matter? The metaphysical idea of epistemological failure, central to Yoga and Samkhya philosophies, suddenly is existentially realized here. Forgetfulness in the drama acts as the symbol of a longing toward something vaguely felt, an inkling of an essential union now lost. Abstract concepts are anchored in artistic experience, however rarefied. And so when the lovers' reunion takes place, it is not simply a happy ending but the skillful evocation of those mythical meanings anchored to memory (act 7, verse 22; Miller):

> Memory chanced to break my dark delusion
> And you stand before me in beauty,

Like the moon's wife Rohini
As she rejoins her lord after an eclipse.

Drama Theory

The kings of the royal Gupta line were indisputably generous sponsors of religious and political pomp, as well as the arts. In fact, the distinction between religion, politics, and art have been overstated in the West's understanding of classical India; the staged dramas of Kalidasa were as fundamentally religious as the horse sacrifice. This is not only because of the more or less obvious mythical and metaphysical themes expressed in his dramatic art, *natya*. The identity ran at a deeper level, where all human activity was conceived as structured ("woven warp and woof," in the words of the old Upanishad) along the lines of a religious design.

An influential contemporary work of art theory—Bharatamuni's *Natyashastra*—clarified the relationship between art and religion in a number of ways. Bharatamuni opened his enormous work with the familiar assertion that his subject matter, *natya* (drama), was sacred in owing its origin to God the creator himself, Brahma. Responding to the request of the agitated gods, Brahma created *natya* through the power of his mind, as a fifth Veda:

> I shall make a fifth Veda on the Natya with the Semi-historical Tales
> (*itihasa*), which will conduce to duty (*dharma*), wealth (*artha*), as well
> as fame, will contain good counsel and collection [of traditional
> maxims], will give guidance to people of the future as well, in all their
> actions, will be enriched by the teaching of all authoritative works
> (*sastra*) and will give a review of all arts and crafts. (*Natyashastra* 1.7;
> Ghosh)

In other words, the dramatic sciences (*natyaveda*) would equal the Vedic science, including even the sacrifice (*yajna*), as a source of religious norms and insight. The place of performance would become a sacrificial ground, surrounded by gods, while the play would be conducted with authoritative precision. The staging of *Shakuntala* or any other play, dance, or musical performance would thus become a religious event. Even today, a proper concert begins with the invocation to the god Ganesha or the performer's guru, a minor consecration of the stage as an altar and of the performer as religious devotee. But this is still the surface of the matter. On this level, even criminal trials in ancient India could be regarded as a sacrifice. The paradigm was ubiquitous.

In contrast, the true sacrifice—the Vedic *yajna*—aimed at transcendental goals, and the careful staging of the performance was no mere pomp; it was a calculated instrument for achieving invisible ends by uncertain means (*adrishta-artha*). The sacrifice was conceived, as I will show in chapter 10, as a majestic mystery. What could the transcendental (esoteric) goals of *natya* be?

Bharatamuni, about whom we know virtually nothing, probably composed his vast work during the later Gupta years. By the standards of Indian art theory and poetics, this was still early; he was clearly a trailblazer. At the heart of his analysis was a deep metaphysical and psychological insight about aesthetic experience, as follows. Art contained and aimed at something essential on the psychological level. That goal emerged as the product of the play's complexity. Bharata claimed that the performance consisted of at least four distinct agendas:

- Meaningful bodily gestures
- Emotions and sentiments
- The use of sound and language
- Staging (costume, makeup, lighting, stage design)

The successful play was a difficult coordination of all such elements. The unity toward which the play aspired he called *rasa*. The ancient word had meant *juice*, the juice of plants, their sap, and therefore their essence. Multiplicity merged into an essential unity. Later theorists, especially the Kashmiri philosopher Abhinavagupta, would develop *rasa* into a far more sophisticated and even mystical concept. In the sixth century, it was still the unity at which artistic performance aimed. This may seem dry, even dull, to modern readers, but in fact, nothing could be further from the truth.

Categorizing what he called sentiments (also termed *rasa*, but slightly different in meaning), Bharatamuni classified at least eight major types: romantic, comic, pathetic, violent, heroic, terrifying, disgusting, and wondrous. He explained that each emotion has specific causes, effects, and ontological qualities. In fact, each emotion could be either natural or ideal. The natural fear of encountering a tiger in the woods had virtually nothing in common with the ideal fear depicted in a play. The play might have utilized a group of gestures to evoke the sense of fear, but it does not try to imitate the natural emotion or its psychological displays. Instead, theater distills natural emotion, through conventional gesture and highly specialized technique, to produce aesthetic fear. Bharatamuni initiated a science of idealized emotions that related to natural emotions—in similar ways, perhaps, to the ways Panini's grammar related to the actual spoken languages of his time.

The sentiments and the ways he says they are depicted on stage are not obviously evocative. A modern Western audience would have no way to tell what emotion the actors were performing, because conventional and stylized gestures and speech were used to produce something essential, almost transcendent—not to *imitate* a living situation. Many of these gestures eventually made their way into the iconography of sculptures and temple reliefs, which represented religious ideas through conventional postures (fig. 7.1).

The motivation for suppressing individual spontaneity in stage gestures in favor of rigid convention was the assumption that the audience's aesthetic appreciation of the drama—the goal of performance—was a deep state, not simple enjoyment. Dramatic arts mirrored social philosophy: The dharma-based society was not a joining of intentional and rational individuals. It was not the liberal society of England or France. Instead, its basic unit of reality was the *varna*, or the social type. The structure of society, the pattern of relationships, was more valuable, perhaps more "sacred," than the "substance," namely individuals. Caste came before looks, wealth, or even gender as a marker of identity. In drama too, as in dharma, the category preceded its content, though philosophers were always at liberty to argue that the two were continuous.

The Temple as Trope

Regardless of the rare grand spectacle like the Ashvamedha, Gupta-era rituals shifted away from Vedic ceremonies to temple-based worship (*puja*), which usually focused on one or two gods. Among the oldest temples funded by the Guptas was one located far from Pataliputra in what is today the village of Nachna, about 100 miles southwest of Kaushambi. Although the temple was dedicated to Shiva, it is known as the Nachna Parvati Temple.

The temple consisted of a square inner structure, surrounded by a walled-in courtyard designed for circumambulating the central shrine—a common plan and practice in Hindu temples to this day. The temple was modestly sized, with the external dimensions of the entire complex measuring 10 meters by 10 meters. The entrance at the front of the temple was from the west, according to an archaic floor plan; later temples had the entrance at the east. The shrine probably housed a lingam—an iconic representation of Shiva—but stands empty today. Still, images carved onto the stone walls, the windows, and the door frame are consistent with the worship of Shiva.

Shiva and Parvati (his consort), along with worshipers, are depicted in relief on the lintel of the doorway facing the arriving visitor. The door guardians and the river goddesses (Ganga and Yamuna) flanking the doors marked the religion of Shiva worship, as did the *ganas* (Shiva's army) on the side wall, and the Yakshas—who had displaced the rivers from their customary flanking

FIGURE 7.1. Drama (Dance) Gestures. Dancing Siva. Early 8th c. Location: Temple of Kailasanatha, Kanchipuram, Tamil Nadu, India. Photo Credit: Vanni / Art Resource, NY

position to the top of the door jambs. The Yakshas were probably vestiges of the ancient veneration of the forest and water spirits that inhabited the wood with which ancient worship places had been constructed.

Shiva was, of course, lord of Mt. Kailasa, and Parvati was daughter of the mountain. The mountain stood at the center of the cosmos, bridging the three worlds—a theme that resurfaced again and again. The temple in Nachna represents these theological ideas in vertical space. Archeologists believe that the temple once displayed a superstructure atop the central shrine, though it must have collapsed and the stones been plundered. A plinth (base) surrounded the temple, grading into the wall of the lower temple story to create the visual impression of a natural slope. The structure itself evoked the texture of a mountain: The moldings and dentils were shaped and rounded like a rocky hill, with boulder-like carved walls. The thinking that went into this plan was explicit, as visitors can see from an inscription on another contemporary temple: "A temple which, having broad and lofty spires, and resembling a mountain, and white as the mass of the rays of the risen moon shines, charming to the eye, having the similarity of being the lovely crest-jewel, fixed in its proper place" (Mandasor shrine inscription; Fleet 1970, p. 128).

A more sophisticated and better preserved, though only slightly newer, temple from the late Gupta years stood in Deogarh, about 100 miles west of Nachna. The highly refined wall reliefs depicted familiar themes and mythical episodes linked to the theology of Vishnu. Visitors can still see Vishnu reclining on the serpent Ananta, while his personified weapons battle the demons (Madhu and Kaitabha) who had stolen the Vedas during his sleep. Nearby are Nara and Narayana, as well as Vishnu flying on the back of Garuda to defend Gajendramoksha—the elephant king. Positioned along the wall in the clockwise direction of the worshiper's circumambulation of the shrine, the relief figures create a narrative about the beginning, middle, and end of a spiritual journey, leading ultimately to *moksha* (spiritual liberation). This iconic theology had been developing for a number of centuries after the Vedic age, and finally gained a foothold in the temples of India in the form of art and ritual.

But the Deogarh temple was both more and less than a theology in stone. Like the older one, it faced west, but here the mountain-shaped tower survived the centuries, if somewhat damaged. Clearly, the mountain motif went beyond Shiva and Parvati, extending to the architectural philosophy of many temples, regardless of the residing deity. The floor plan provided a good indication of this universal philosophy. Unlike the simple square of the Nachna Parvati Temple, here the design, called *pancyatana*, attained greater complexity. At the center still stood the small shrine (in later temple architecture called the *garbha-griha*, womb house). Surrounded by a walled courtyard, it measured about 16 meters by 16 meters, with four small shrines at the corners. The whole structure rested on a plinth and was accessible from all four directions. The basic geometry of the floor plan, not the mythological art on the walls, contained the more powerful idea.

Temple geometry reached back directly to ancient Vedic altar geometry and to the Shulbasutra texts. During the early Gupta years, that geometry was still rudimentary—a square and a circle. Subsequent centuries saw the explosion of both design forms and theoretical explanations within specialized texts such as the *Mayamata, Shukranitisara,* and *Vishnudharmottara*. The altar form itself had been dominated by the center-point. From the center, the altar stretched out to form the most basic shape, the square. But variations on the square soon developed, with creative use of angles and curves. The builders even developed algorithms for drawing a circle on the area of the square by using a rope and following ingenious calculations.

That early circle plan had been related to the wheel-shaped altar (*cakra*), and the wheel lent itself easily to the symbolism of time or to the marking of astrological constellations (*nakshatras,* mansions), through which the sun passed on its journey. With the circle acting as time, or as the canopy of the heavens in which the sun passes, the square became the earth, the foundation. Together, according to the imaginative work of the art historian Stella Kramrisch, they formed a cosmological totality—the circle in the square. Early temple architects could not design a circular tower; their *shikaras* (central towers) were four-sided constructions. But the idea of the circle, resting on top of the building's foundational square, remained implicit in the design if not the actual execution.

During the Gupta era, these aesthetic and cosmological ideas developed into an explicit science of design. The contemporary founder of that science, one of India's most erudite encyclopedists and a great admirer of Kalidasa, was Varahamihira, who was born in 505 CE in a village outside of Ujjain—one of the most prosperous North Indian states. Scholars dispute who ruled during the productive years of his life, when he wrote his encyclopedia, the *Brihat Samhita* ("Great Collection"). It may have been Harsha Vikramaditya. According to traditional sources, Varahamihira died in 587. He was a devoted worshiper of the sun god, known as Aditya, and valued both astronomy and astrology as mathematically oriented devotional sciences. He wrote the *Brihat Samhita* after completing two vast works on astrology/astronomy and attaining great fame.

The *Brihat Samhita* was a monumental collection of knowledge that covered virtually all of the sciences of the day, ranging from astronomy to

geography, calendrical calculations, meteorology, flora, agriculture and economics, politics, physiognomy, engineering, and botany and reaching even
such prosaic topics as dental hygiene and maintaining clean toothbrushes.
Any modern reader who wishes to get an intimate sense of how sixth-century
Indians lived their lives—from their loftiest thoughts to the most mundane
details—can leaf through the hundreds of pages that make up this vast work.
There are descriptions of architectural designs, sculpture making and iconography, metallurgy, painting, perfumes, cosmetics, medical remedies, umbrel-
las, personal ornaments, patterns of bird migrations, forests, and deforesta-
tion, as well as endless lists of the animals that still roamed the forests of
northern India. The *Brihat Samhita* combined lists with sensory descriptions,
adding calculations and theories as it painted a detailed picture of India in
Gupta times.

The author was a collector and cataloger, not a creative scientist (except in
astronomy and astrology). As the name of the work itself (*samhita* means
"collection") indicates, its data came from numerous sources, some of them
probably quite old. This undoubtedly applied to Varahamihira's description of
temple planning and construction; much of this material could be found in
other contemporary and even older sources such as the *Agni Purana*. But the
prestige and systematic nature of the *Brihat Samhita* gave its material the
authority of prescriptions. Its detailed instructions became the cornerstone of
a new tradition called *vastu shastra*—the science of building.

Varahamihira insisted that the square of the house, or of the central
structure in the temple—the *garbha-griha*—had to measure in units that could
divide precisely into 81 equal squares.

> In order to divide the ground-plan of a house into 81 squares draw ten
> lines from east to west and ten others from north to south. Inside the
> diagram, thirteen deities are situated, and thirty-two in the outer
> compartments. Thus, there are 45 deities in this figure. (*Brihat
> Samhita* 53.42; Bhat)

The squares are then grouped in zones dedicated to different gods. Brahma—
the creator—occupies the central nine squares, more than any other. To his
immediate east (in three squares) is Aryaman; to the south of Brahma is
Vivashvan; to the west Mitra; to the north Prithivi-dhara. These gods, and all
the rest (see fig. 7.2), saturate the entire space of the building with sacred value,
lending each section its unique qualities and marking the eight directions
with specific theological meanings. The floor map is thus more than a builder's
blueprint; it is a cosmological map. But this is still just a theoretical map.
The real territory, the power grafted onto the map and the essence of the

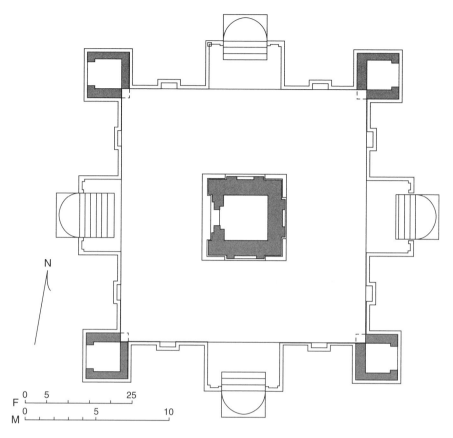

FIGURE 7.2. Temple Floor Plan. From *The Art of Ancient India* by Susan Huntington copyright 1985. Reprinted by arrangement with Shambala Publications Inc., Boston, MA www. Shambala.com.

building (house or temple), is the *vastu purusha*—the Person of the house, or God.

This is the same Purusha who figured in the *Rig-Veda*, the Upanishads, the *Bhagavad Gita*, and elsewhere. Here is his resting place: He lies across the map on the floor, with his head at the northeast corner, in the following manner.

> Fire (Agni) is situated on his head; Water (Apah), on the face;
> Aryaman, on the breast; Apavatsa, on the chest; Prajanya, on the
> eye; Jayanta, on the ear; Indra, on the chest (neck?); and the Sun,
> on the shoulder [and so on]. (*Brihat Samhita* 53.51-54; Bhat)

The text continued in great detail, and the finished design looks like the Vedic Purusha stretched across the floor plan, (as shown in fig. 7.3):

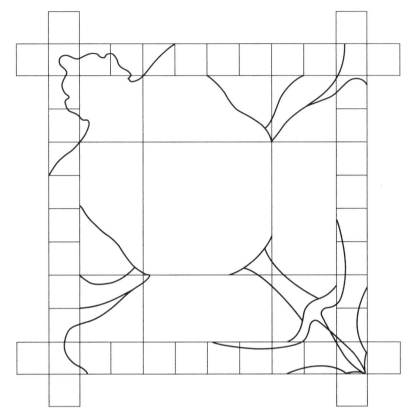

FIGURE 7.3. Purusha Figure on Floor Plan. From *The Hindu Temple* by Stella Kramrisch copyright 1976. Printed by permission from Motilal Banarsidass, Delhi, India.

The symbolic temple plan extended beyond two-dimensional space. Temple measurements in vertical space were just as important as the floor plan:

> The height of a temple should be double its width, and the height of the foundation above the ground consisting of steps (over which the edifice is built) equal to a third of this height. The Sanctum Sanctorum should be half the width of the temple. (*Brihat Samhita* 56.11–12; Bhat)

Builders could find in Varahamihira's encyclopedia instructions for measuring the door, for placing the two door guardians (Nandin and Danda), for carving decorations with various forest motifs (trees, foliage, creepers), and many other topics. But most basic of all, the temple had to evoke a sacred mountain.

In fact, Varahamihira explicitly identified the temple with mountains in the names he gave the first three types of temple within his classification: Meru, Mandara, and Kailasa. These were mythological mountains familiar to every Indian of the sixth century and central to numerous Purana episodes. The instructions for building Meru, for example, specified a six-sided structure with 12 stories and internal windows. Its four doors faced the cardinal directions, and its height was double the length of the side. Mt. Meru had been depicted in the Puranas as a vast golden mountain at the very center of the cosmos. It was, in a mythical sense, the axis of the world—a joining point between the heavenly and earthly planes.

Virahamihira knew that Mt. Meru was mythical, and he knew that his own temple plans were representations. He thought of temple planning as a way of mapping the sacred, but like a good mapmaker, he remained aware of the difference between the symbol and what it symbolized.

Kalidasa and Bharatamuni would never have claimed that the dramatic displays of emotions on stage were natural feelings. As aesthetic distillations, they were evocative representations. The priests and officials in the vast and detailed Ashvamedha also knew the difference between ritual action, mantra, and symbols and whatever transcendent reality lay somewhere beyond. The philosophy of ritual action (Mimamsa), which I have not yet discussed in this book, was already a full millennium old, and it, too, had clarified the distinction between ritual action and spiritual reality.

When the sciences of iconography—the artistic representation of gods and goddesses in temple and artistic contexts—reached its first bloom during the Gupta years, the same distinction between the sign and the signified prevailed. Theologians and artists, keenly conscious of the precise proportions that went into a proper icon (*murti*), knew that the object was the work of man. It was not secular, of course, but its power came from evocation—a subtle artistic and ritual process.

Still, it is important to bear in mind that at this time when symbolic thinking dominated high religious culture, there were probably more Indians who believed that the object of veneration was intrinsically powerful, indeed divine. This is the subject of the next chapter.

8

The Second Rationality

Hinduism was never a single doctrinal highway running through a wilderness of heterodoxies. Too much in India was taking place simultaneously, and no center held it all together. While kings built temples, cities, and empires, and while Brahmins were bridging this world with other, more perfect ones through sacred sciences, other people were equally busy. Doctors, artisans, and craftsworkers, members of the low castes and remote tribes, villagers, and women everywhere created worldviews no less compelling than the few that came to dominate the scriptures. These many groups—only some qualifying for what sociological jargon calls "marginalized"—did not actually occupy a separate universe. Of course, in the absence of a literary tradition, there is little we can know about the philosophy of a remote tribe or a fifth-century housewife. Still, in subtle and indirect ways, their productivity did, in fact, make it into the pages of sutras and *shastras*, where one can find its traces if one knows where to look.

From the first appearance of Vedic literature and all the way to the popular temple pamphlets sold in India today, the ideas and actions of these groups played counterpoint to Brahminical ideologies. A mere sampling of the most prominent examples from the Vedic to the Gupta periods, which this chapter will undertake, is impressive. It includes eclectic speculations in the "Fourth Veda," the *Atharvaveda*, along with its associated ritual text the *Kaushika Sutra*. Nearly as important as these two was the *Rig Vidhana*, the early medical text*Charaka Samhita*, and more broadly, early Tantric ideas that were scattered in a variety of sources. Extratextual evidence for the non-Brahminical worldviews can also be found in art works, architecture, iconography, and other physical remains.

But what exactly is the difference? What are we comparing when we juxtapose the thought of, say, a Brahmin grammarian with the diagnosis of a physician or the ritual conduct of a woman who worships a local village goddess? Since Robert Redfield's distinction between "great" and "little" tradition emerged in the 1950s, scholars have contrasted cities and literate elites with peripheral and folk cultures. This analytical distinction has influenced a whole generation of India scholars since Milton Singer and M. N. Srinivas conducted their studies fifty years ago. Today, researchers prefer more nuanced analyses of culture, rejecting inviolable theoretical boundaries. That new skepticism applies well to the material at hand. The Vedic mathematician who plans the altar and the grammarian who invents linguistic categories do not necessarily stand over and against the villager who chants for rain in the same way that reason opposes superstition. Science, magic, and religion, as Stanley Tambiah has shown, can all be encompassed in a broader way of talking about symbolic rationalities and worldviews. And besides, the elite's counterparts were often right there, working with them: the brick maker and the altar planner, the physician and the alchemist.

To oversimplify a complicated picture, then, one may say that two distinct types of rationality run through the historical-religious record. The first, more prestigious one (*vaidika,* great), could be termed analogical rationality, and the second (*laukika,* little) participatory rationality. Consider once again Vishnu's three steps across the three worlds: earth, atmosphere, and sky. The Greek equivalents, often invoked even in Indian studies, are microcosm, mesocosm, and macrocosm. Brahmin scientists and thinkers often thought of their intellectual tools (numbers, words, dramatic gestures, rules of dharma) as ways of mediating or bridging the objects of the world with a more fundamental reality (such as Veda or Brahman). Theirs was a powerful and sacred semiotics: the sign standing in between the signifier and signified.

Others understood the matter differently, and theirs was the second rationality of this chapter's title. When the object does not signify or represent another reality, it can do something else: contain or participate in it. The space where "micro" and "macro" come together can be the intrinsically powerful sensory world around us. For the villager—according to some scholars—this may just be magic or witchcraft, but for the Tantric and medical theorist, there is indeed some essence in the world that can be scientifically known and put to good use for the sake of fertility, health, or long life. To such "second rationality" thinkers, the world does not represent a mere shadow of truer and transcendent realities, acting as their symbol; instead, it holds them as the fruit holds its juice.

The two rationalities coexisted in the works of Brahmins, and probably even in the actions of villagers. As Laurie L. Patton has recently shown, the rationality of the Vedas is far more "magical" and that of magic far more "rational" than most Indologists have acknowledged. But this chapter, to put it bluntly, tells the story of just the second rationality—participation.

The Fourth Veda

Two or three centuries after the *Rig-Veda*, but before the other Vedic texts *Yajur* and *Saman*, a fourth Veda took shape. Like the others, it came down to us in a number of versions and apparently originated from four families or schools (*shakhas*) of priests. Though lacking the greater prestige of the others, the *Atharvaveda* testifies to the intellectual and religious ambiguities coursing through literate Hindu cultures a century or two before the rise of Buddhism. Just as the prestige of the Vedic cult and its scriptures owed its impetus to the wealth of chiefs and kings, the last Veda, with its magic, sorcery, and medicine, also depended on royal patronage. Along with the priests who could perform the sacrifices, kings required other specialists with different skills, men like the court physician or the standby sorcerer. Even the king's main priest, the *purohita*, tended to be an Atharvan priest, a specialist in *abhichara* (magic or witchcraft), as an important law text (*Yajnavalkya Smriti*) informs us. Another law book, *Manu Smriti* (11.33), recommends that the king use magic as a stealth weapon during war, and the *Kautilya Arthashastra* actually reveals some of the sorcery methods these specialists used on behalf of the king.

For instance, in order to obtain the highly desirable capacity to see at night, one could carry out the following prescription:

> Taking the right and the left eyes of one, two or more of the following, the cat, the camel, the wolf, the boar, the porcupine, the flying fox, the *naptr* [nocturnal bird], the crow, the owl or other creatures roaming at night, one should prepare two separate powders. Then anointing the right eye with (the powder of) the left (eye) and the left with (that of) the right, one is able to see at night and in darkness. (*Kautilya Arthashastra* 14.3.1–2; Kangle)

But servicing such pragmatic needs did not come without a measure of revulsion and a deep intellectual ambivalence, which persisted for centuries. For instance, *Manu Smriti* regarded the physician as an impure person and excluded him from the rituals of virtuous and pure people. Still, despite the conflicted attitude toward magicians and doctors, and despite the loaded reputation of the Atharvan priest, the *Atharvaveda* ignored any clear distinction between high and low cultures. Instead, the text's authors produced an eclectic collection (*samhita*) of enormous scope that reflected the beliefs and practices of diverse populations and encompassed every sphere of life. Some of the *Atharvaveda*'s ideas overlap with ideas in the other Vedas, in Brahmanas and Upanishads; many of these ideas pertain to the speculative first rationality and need not concern us here. The authors' widely cast net, however, pulled up unique practices that were not clearly discussed elsewhere and that starkly illustrate the pragmatic and conceptual features of the second rationality.

The authors of the *Atharvaveda* were interested in everything except the Vedic sacrifice. The range of their topics was staggering. Health concerns included fever, jaundice, dropsy, diarrhea, constipation, rheumatism, colic, pulmonary diseases, paralysis, skin diseases, internal diseases, leprosy, wounds, fractures, bleeding, snake bites, poisoning, worms, hair growth and loss, sexual dysfunction, mental illness, and many more. But the authors covered every other private and public topic imaginable, including amulets, grooming, longevity, dietary styles, coiffeur, sorcery and counter-sorcery, warfare, demons, numerous "women's procedures" (*strikarmani*), love, romantic rivalry, conception and reproduction, family matters such as keeping domestic harmony and prosperity, teacher-pupil relations, royalty (including consecration), the role of the *purohita* priest, charity, Brahmins, gaining esteem and wisdom, house construction, avoiding disasters, public works, agriculture, rain, cattle, trade, winning at dice games—to name a mere fraction. It is hard to imagine an area in life, however trivial, that did not concern the authors of this enormous collection in their desire to serve their clients or to provide the necessary formulas for those who wished to improve their lives without the help of specialists. It seems, however, that the single most important topic, framing all the rest, was expiation: uttering the words that would relieve the users of the text from the consequences of an error in the performance of the primary ritual.

But the chanting of an Atharvana mantra was only half the ritual. Precise action had to accompany the words, however powerful these may have been. The four schools (*shakhas*) that authored the *Atharvaveda* also produced a manual of practice called *Kaushika Sutra*. According to an important ancient commentator on the *Atharvaveda*, Sayana, the *Kaushika Sutra* emerged as a *samhita vidhi*, a guidebook of practical instructions for the *Samhita*'s verbal material. Indeed, the *Kaushika Sutra* consisted of 14 chapters that covered many of the same topics. In brief and exceedingly obscure aphorisms (sutras), it provided instructions for the ritual use of Atharvan mantras. Combined, the verbal formula and the choreographed action give the appearance of mutually reinforcing magical arts.

Headaches, Enemies, Worms

Virtually any topic can be used to illustrate the close fit between the two manuals. The *Kaushika Sutra*, in fact, quotes specific *Atharvaveda* formulas. Some scholars have suggested that the rituals were actually grafted onto the verbal script of the *Atharvaveda samhita*, after the fact. The following examples illuminate the possibilities. Against headaches:

> The healer gives to his patient a liquid made of honey, fat, clarified
> butter, and sesame oil to drink. The patient, wearing a hat made
> of woven *munja* grass, carries a sieve containing empty kernels of
> barley, which he spreads using his right hand. After spreading the
> barley, he puts the hat on the sieve and holds on to a bowstring and
> axe, still with his right hand. He passes before the healer, who is
> guiding him. Then the patient places the sieve and the hat along with
> the bowstring on his head, where he feels the pain. When the pro-
> cedure is complete, he returns home, where he pushes a small
> amount of clarified butter up into his own nostrils. Finally, he sup-
> ports his forehead with a staff of bamboo that has five knots.
> (*Kaushika Sutra* 26.1–9; my translation)

During the performance of this procedure; several *Athravaveda* mantras must be chanted, including the following two:

> Free him from headache and also from cough, (produced by light-
> ning) that has entered his every joint! May the flashing (lightning),
> that is born of the cloud, and born of the wind, strike the trees and
> the mountains!
>   Comfort be to my upper limb, comfort be to my nether; comfort
> be to my four members, comfort to my entire body! (*Athravaveda* 1.12;
> Bloomfield)

What does the ritual mean? Can a modern reader even begin to capture the sense of these strange actions as the performers did? A sieve with barely kernels and a hat on top of a hurting head—this is precisely the kind of exotica the Victorian-era scholar James Frazer collected over a century ago for his huge compendium of magic: *The Golden Bough*. Few scholars today think, as Frazer did, that the ritual represents bad scientific thinking. Stanley Tambiah regards the actions as symbolic expressions of a complicated analogy. I have explained magical rituals in a previous book (*The End of Magic*) as techniques for changing states of consciousness. Ancient Brahmins also knew what a symbol does, but we may never know what the patient and the healer (who were not Brahmin scholars) thought.

The belief in ghosts and invisible spirits (*bhuta-preta*) still remains one of the most pervasive features of folk medicine in India, though the rituals have lost much of the early investment in detail. The following case illustrates this domain of magic. Against demonic enemies (*Pishachas* and *Rakshashas*): "The patient digs a trench around a fire and walks around it three times while offering oblations of rice into the flames" (*Kaushika Sutra* 31.3; my translation). As he does this he recites the following verse, among others: "Do you well offer within the fire this oblation with ghee, that destroys the spook! Do you, O Agni, burn from afar against the Rakshasa, (but) our houses thou shall not consume!" (*Athravaveda* 6.32.1; Bloomfield).
Against worms in a child:

> The healer winds a young worm around a bamboo stalk [Karira], then mashes this part of the stalk, roasting it with the worm. Then he places both in the fire. At the same time, he throws some dust over the child. The dust is then gathered and removed from the village. The healer places the child in the lap of his mother on the west side of the fire. He warms the palate of the child by means of clarified butter that has been smeared onto the bottom of a club. Then he taps the child three times. (*Kaushika Sutra* 29.20–22; my translation)

I have shortened here the description of a very long healing procedure; the deeply symbolic ritual is accompanied by the following mantras.

> I have called upon heaven and earth, I have called up the goddess Sarasvati, I have called upon Indra and Agni: "they shall crush the worm," (I said).
>
> Slay the worms in this boy, O Indra, lord of treasures! Slain are all the evil powers by my fierce imprecation! (*Athravaveda* 5.23.1–2; Bloomfield)

Veda for the Masses

While the traditions of the *Atharvaveda* probably incorporated numerous indigenous, South Indian, and folk practices, the flow of ideas moved in both
directions. Schools of Brahmins, particularly Shaunaka's and Katyayana's, took
it upon themselves to situate the hymns of the scriptures, even the sacred *Rig-
Veda*, in common ritual contexts. They channeled *shruti* (revelation) into con-
cise manuals for pragmatic ends: improving health, making money, fighting
demons and enemies, and winning lovers. The work of turning the scriptures
into more practical recipes would eventually play a key role in creating post-
classical or Puranic Hinduism and enriching the Tantric traditions. The *Rig
Vidhana* ranks as one of the best examples of this trajectory in the synthesis
between Veda and popular cultures. That text is literally a manual of Vedic
hymns for everyday use. For example: "One should worship the rising sun [with
the verse] beginning with Ud u [*Rig-Veda* 1.50] daily. Verily this [hymn] is
destructive of the heart disease and conducive to excellent health" (*Rig Vidhana*
1.99; Bhat). The *Rig-Veda* hymn ("Ud u") to which this magical/medical
prescription refers is addressed to Surya, the sun. It includes the following
verse.

> As you rise today, O sun, you who are honored as a friend, climbing
> to the highest sky, make me free of heartache and yellow pallor
> [jaundice]. (*Rig-Veda* 1.50.11; O'Flaherty)

The *Rig Vidhana* spell then continues and turns darker:

> Having muttered the half-verse beginning with Dvisantham [*Rig-
> Veda* 1.50.13cd] one should think of him whom one hates; [then] the
> evil-doer obtains enmity within a week. (*Rig Vidhana* 1.100; M. S. Bhat)

This passage refers to the final part of the *Rig-Veda* hymn:

> This Aditya [the sun] has risen with all his dominating force, hurling
> my hateful enemy down into my hands. Let me not fall into my
> enemy's hands! (1.50.13; O'Flaherty)

A single example out of a rich text only hints at how the scripture might be put
to practical use. The *Rig Vidhana* does not provide explicit and detailed ritual
formulas, like the *Kaushika Sutra*, so one is left without a recipe for magical
actions. Nonetheless, because the power of Rigvedic mantras exceeds those of
the *Atharvaveda*, it is conceivable that no action is required—the words themselves will do the job. Either way, the text clearly illustrates the argument that

the difference between "religion" and "magic" blurs in practice—as does the distinction between elite and folk cultures.

Yakshas and Goddesses

Among its many guiding themes, the *Atharvaveda* promoted several that would later influence Ayurvedic medicine. The medicinal use of water and plants ranked foremost among these. Water, which possessed the healing and generative powers of nectar, or essential liquid, was the very best medicine: "The waters chase away disease, the waters cure all (disease): May they prepare a remedy for thee" (*Athravaveda* 6.91.3; Bloomfield). Closely allied with water were the plants, whose sap was the coursing water of the earth. These, too, acted as cure for every illness: "The plants, whose womb is the *avaka* (*blyxa octandra*), whose essence are the waters, shall with their sharp horns thrust aside evil" (*Athravaveda* 8.7.9; Bloomfield).

These were not isolated statements on behalf of water, sap, and liquid medicine. In fact, Vedic cosmology and cosmogony elevated water to a supreme role, and as the sacrifice became increasingly influential in later Vedic religions, water (and fire) gained correspondingly important intellectual value. Or to be more precise, a whole range of liquids figured in these religions, from soma as the best down to snake poison at the bottom. Popular ideas about nature and farming intersected with Brahminical theories around the subject of water, and the mythical figures of the Yakshas embodied this synthesis.

The Yakshas and Yakshinis were demigods, ambiguously associated with water, vegetation, and fertility, but also meat-eating—perhaps as autochthonous forces. Early Indian (Hindu, Buddhist, and Jain) sculptors often depicted them iconographically as peripheral figures surrounding the main gods, or as space fillers who embodied vegetative decorative motifs. But in time the Yakshas evolved into more complex divinities. Already in the *Atharvaveda* they were more than just fertility icons: "The Great Yaksa, steeped in concentration on the surface of the water in the middle of the world, on him the various gods are fixed like branches around the trunk of a tree." (*Athravaveda* 10.7.38; Sutherland). This was a deeply metaphysical idea, an abstraction far removed from simple nature and vegetative essence. *Yaksha* thus represented a fascinating development: a natural symbol that was co-opted by metaphysics. According to A. Coomaraswamy, this denaturing of the symbol would continue, and *yaksha* would eventually become conflated with the supreme concepts of Brahman, atman, *purusha*, and other metaphysical principles that defined essential being.

But the Yakshas' rise to prominence at the center of Hindu cosmology was an exception to the rule. Evidence for cults that prospered on the margins of Brahminical consciousness tends to be nonlinguistic. Some of the earliest figurines linked to an Indian goddess cult are from Zhob and Kulli in Baluchistan, at the northwestern edge of the South Asian cultural sphere. One figure, apparently a mother goddess, shows a female with elaborate hairstyle, naked breasts, and hands placed on her hips. The eyes are small stones attached to the face. More famous are the figurines from the Indus Valley cities (Mohenjodaro and Harappa), with their rich ornamentation—neck collars, chains, bangles, and anklets. No evidence remains of the ritual and doctrinal aspects of the cults, or the precise economic conditions that supported these goddess religions. The Baluchistan goddesses were probably associated with newly prosperous village agriculture, while the Indus River economy centered around powerful urban centers.

The figurines themselves remain ambiguous—were they objects of veneration or magical tools? Still, their broad distribution throughout the subcontinent attests to the prevalence of female-centered religious activities. Diggers in Kaushambi have unearthed female terra-cotta figurines, and the Patna Museum (where Pataliputra once stood) owns pre-Mauryan mother goddess statues that have been dug up in Buxar of the Sahabad district nearby. The Buxar one has a round face with punched earlobes and prominent breasts, and may have served a local fertility cult. Near Pune, in Maharashtra, an ancient nude female figure accompanied by a bull—another symbol of fertility—was uncovered.

Despite the lack of direct textual evidence, such archeological objects support the contention of some scholars that mother goddess religions were directly implicated with fertility or fecundity. Some of these religions predate the *Rig-Veda*; others prospered beyond the boundary of Brahminical religious hegemony. But as goddesses became incorporated into the mythical and devotional literatures of Hinduism, their association with rivers, vegetation, cattle, and sexuality did not diminish. Clearly, "fertility" is too narrow a term to describe the range of values these goddess embodied and would eventually encompass in popular Hinduism.

Nonetheless, the rise of the goddesses was slow. In the *Rig-Veda*, few goddesses, with the possible exception of Ushas (Dawn), enjoyed the same prestige as males. Although Aditi is described as the mother of the gods, a supporter of creatures, and a housewife (*Rig-Veda* 1.166), not a single hymn is dedicated specifically to her. Similarly, Vach (speech) did receive a small number of late hymns but assumed the character of a rather impersonal principle (10.71; 10.125) Only Ushas (Dawn) inspired enough devotion to receive 20 exclusive hymns: "Let me obtain great riches of glory and heroic men, Dawn, riches that begin with slaves and culminate in heroes. Fortunate in your beauty, incited by the victory prize, you shine forth with the fame of great achievements" (1.92.8; O'Flaherty).

With the rise of the late Vedic sacrificial cult Prajapati, Soma and Agni superseded the more naturalistic gods, and female-centered Vedic ideas and practices were edged out even further. Not until centuries later did goddesses finally emerge in the epic literature (*Mahabharata, Ramayana*) and the early Puranas—especially as the consorts of the new gods of Hinduism (Brahma, Vishnu, Shiva, Rama, etc.). But goddess cults had never actually disappeared, and the religious practices of women never fully retreated from the pages of the scriptures.

The Goddess finally emerged in her own theological text in an extraordinary Gupta-era work, *Devi Mahatmya*, which can be found embedded today within the *Markandeya Purana*, a much larger (and later) collection. The *Devi Mahatmya* was unusual for a number of reasons. It was the first exclusive exaltation of the Goddess, ranking her above the most prestigious and widely worshiped male gods—Shiva and Vishnu. The text itself is both a fairly cohesive work, which was unusual, and a synthesis of many existing older ideas. In that sense, it resembles the *Shvetashvatara Upanishad* and the *Bhagavad Gita*. Another way of putting the matter is that the Goddess, Durga, like Krishna before her, was both a discrete and a synthetic figure.

The text collected and retold three versions of the old myth about the war between the *devas* and *asuras*, immediately after creation by Prajapati. Given their inability to vanquish the demons, the gods in this version created a divine female entity of overwhelming power:

> And from the bodies of the other gods, Indra and the others, came forth a great fiery splendor, and it became unified in one place.

> An exceedingly fiery mass like a flaming mountain did the gods see there, filling the firmament with flames. (*Devi Mahatmya* 2.10–11; Coburn)

In vivid detail, and with literary power to move generations of Devi worshipers, the author swept up every known theological principle into the figure of the Goddess, who would shortly take on the demons and annihilate them. The author's agenda of subsuming revered religious ideas under one feminine principle was primarily verbal in this text. Whatever the Goddess was named, that was what she represented. But to add more authority yet, the names were voiced in the mouths of the other gods:

"Hail to the Goddess, hail eternally to the auspicious great Goddess! Hail to *Prakrti*, the auspicious! We who are restrained bow down to her. . . .

"The Goddess who is known as the *maya* of Visnu in all creatures, Hail to her, hail to her, hail to her: hail, hail!

"The Goddess who is designated 'consciousness' in all creatures, Hail to her, hail to her, hail to her: hail, hail." (*Devi Mahatmya* 5.7, 12–13; Coburn)

Researchers do not fully know what the author or authors of this text were trying to accomplish within the immediate political and social context of the *Devi Mahatmya*. From a religious point of view, the text reflects the elevation, in certain circles (perhaps Tantric), of the Goddess to the center of philosophical and devotional thought. This development raises profound questions about divinity in India and in general, and the role of gender in conceiving ultimate reality. Like the Purana in which the text is embedded, the *Devi Mahatmya* broaches the serious methodological question of what tools we may bring to the way we understand Hindu gods. Can we use psychoanalysis? Are the myths of Durga strictly political? I will address these questions in the next chapter.

While Durga worship was never restricted to women, most of the practices that dominated the religions of women during the Gupta period probably still persist in many regions in India. Among the most significant, especially as an alternative to the male-dominated Vedic cult of the sacrifice, was the *vrata*. Textual specialists know the term primarily from its use in the Dharma texts (*Manu*), where it is a ritual of penance that erases the effects of sins. However, *vratas* were extremely pervasive in ancient India both in and out of Dharma text traditions. The great Dharmashastra scholar P. V. Kane claimed that there were nearly 25,000 Puranic verses on the subject, and he himself collected numerous examples out of the two thousand or more *vratas* known to exist.

The *vrata* was a vow that involved voluntary ritual undertakings, often including fasting, pilgrimages, prolonged chanting, or other inconvenient or even painful actions toward a desired goal. Though hardly restricted to women, *vratas* tended to be more popular among women, who enjoyed a more limited access to Vedic rituals. In fact, at the heart of the *vrata* was a subtle calculation of exchange that resembled the sacrifice. But unlike the high solemn rituals, most *vratas*, despite their dazzling diversity, focused on worldly matters: health, fertility, happiness, auspiciousness. The wife fasted for the health or longevity of her husband or the sister for that of her father and brothers.

FIGURE 8.1. Kolam Patterns.

Despite the fact that women's *vratas* usually involved the quid pro quo of deprivation and desired benefits, rituals took no fixed form: they ranged from the construction of miniaturized models of the world (the village, a forest, a mountain) to the design of highly abstract geometrical diagrams known generally as *vrata mandalas*. Some of these diagrams, known today throughout India by a variety of names (*kolam, rangoli, mehndi*) were drawn on the threshold of the house for protection, or on the walls or in the courtyard. Pupul Jayakar has traced these forms both to the *Atharvaveda* (and *Kaushika Sutra*) and to early Tantric practices. Either way, the drawings, often strikingly elaborate and beautiful, act as an expression of the belief in the power of controlled technique, along with self-sacrifice, over matters that dominate in people's lives in this world (see fig. 8.1).

Ayurveda

Like the village priest of later times and like women, physicians always had to cope with the specific needs of daily life. The king, reluctantly perhaps, kept a physician on hand, but away from the court and the capital, doctors worked everywhere, and their work was usually judged with both eyes wide open: "Failure (in medicine) is the result of improper administration" (*Charaka Samhita*, sutra 15.4; Sharma and Dash). Among the practical sciences and crafts that proliferated in India between the time of the Vedas and the Gupta dynasty, medicine (Ayurveda) may have best exemplified the complicated overlap between metaphysical and empirical worldviews. Doctors had to treat physical ailments, of course, but medical theory went beyond the body in its physical context to speculate on the basic nature of reality.

The oldest collection of Ayurvedic knowledge was gathered by a certain Dridhabala during the Gupta period. This large work, called *Charaka Samhita*, consisted mostly of pre-Gupta material going back about seven centuries. The *Charaka Samhita* included eight books entitled "Sutra," "Nidana," "Vimana," "Sharira," "Indriya," "Cikshita," "Kalpa," and "Siddhi." These added up to 120 chapters, covering numerous specific diseases, diets and foods, pharmacology, physicians, anatomy and embryology, diagnosis, prognosis, medical philosophy, and more.

Like many other contemporary texts, the *Charaka Samhita* claimed divine origin. The introductory narrative describes an ancient sage, Bharadvaja, who went to Indra on behalf of his numerous colleagues. He explained that bad health was disrupting their ability to pursue spiritual goals and was shortening their life. The text then declares: "(Indra expounded) the immortal and sacred (science of life) consisting of three principles viz. etiology, symptomology and the knowledge of therapeutics as a means to well-being" (*Charaka Samhita*, sutra 1.24; Sharma and Dash). Thus begins the *Charaka Samhita*, emphasizing that Ayurveda is beneficial both for spiritual goals and for sound health.

But the nod to Indra's prestige is more than just formality. The Ayurveda assumes, as a basic principle, that a fundamental correspondence prevails between humanity and the cosmos. More concretely, a person is a replica, a microcosm, of the universe. Both consist of the same six elements: earth, water, fire, air, ether, and Brahman. The substances and processes that dominate within human bodies replicate, even instantiate, cosmic process. Ayurvedic theories emphasize three such fundamental types of substance within the human organism. These are the three humors (*dosha*: wind, choler, phlegm); bodily tissue (*dhatu*); and waste (*mala*).

To greatly simplify a complex science, Ayurveda claims that the most fundamental corporal process is digestion. Like cooking, digestion is ultimately a way of transforming matter from one state into another, within the fire of the stomach (*jatharagni*). Body tissue, muscle, blood, and bone represent various permutations of substance as it undergoes change in the furnace of digestion. When the process works smoothly, a kind of essential energy (*ojas*) circulates throughout the body. Illness can be conceived as a blockage that causes disruption of this material flow, slowing down the transformation of substance or its distribution in the body. Healing then is a reopening of channels and restoration of the body's ability to circulate matter. The *Charaka Samhita* recognizes numerous other types of ailments and medical metaphors, from injuries to invasive diseases. But Ayurveda was most innovative in the way it combined Brahminical homological theory with rich and pragmatic forms of empiricism in which liquids and essences course through the body. Both of these pillars of practical and theoretical science deeply influenced the development of Tantric religions.

To repeat and illustrate this important point: The *Charaka Samhita* brought to bear metaphysical (even mythical) as well as material thinking in its analysis and treatment of numerous medical conditions. The complex of conditions called *jvara* illustrates this synthesis with clarity. *Jvara* was regarded as the first and most important of all diseases and a cause, oddly enough, of both death and birth. Its appearance was associated with both physical and mental factors:

> Factors which are responsible for the manifestation of *javara*, in brief, are the three *dosas*, namely *vayu*, *pitta* and *kapha* and two *dosas* of the mind namely *rajas* and *tamas*. Living beings do not get afflicted with *jvara* without the involvement of these *dosas*. (*Charaka Samhita*, 3.12; Sharma and Dash)

The condition becomes manifest in the form of high temperature, lack of appetite, inordinate thirst, achiness, chest pain, and other symptoms. It often leads to a "descent into darkness" (*tamas*) and sometimes death (3.16; Sharma and Dash). The text thoroughly notes that *jvara* might also lead to listlessness, yawning, heaviness, mental fatigue, indigestion, and many other symptoms. Within the *Charaka Samhita*, the term *jvara* covered a wide range of ailments—the name was usually accompanied by a descriptive predicate—and different causes required corresponding treatments. But regardless of which specific fever was diagnosed, the general principles that characterized humoral medical philosophy (*dosha*) and the hydraulic-alchemical physiology applied across the board.

> Three aggravated *dosas*, viz. *vayu*, *pitta* and *kapha*—either individually or jointly in the combinations of two (*samrsta*) or three (*samnipata*) spread through the *rasa dhatu* and dislodge the *jatharagni* (digestive fire) from its own place. Being supplemented with their own heat and the heat of the *jatharagni*, the heat of the body gets accentuated. These channels of circulation get obstructed by them, and they being further aggravated pervade the entire body to produce excessive heat. Therefore the person's temperature increases all over the body and this condition is called *jvara*. (3.129–32; Sharma and Dash)

In order to alleviate this condition, the *doshas* have to be restored to balance, the digestive fire reinvigorated, and the channels of circulation unblocked. Depending on the type of fever (and humoral imbalance), the patient must drink different mixtures, along with having emetics, massages, and stronger medications. For instance, a fever dominated by *kapha* imbalance in the stomach and small intestine required emetics. For other types of fever, the patient might receive gruels and bitter herbs boiled in water after the emetic therapy. In sum, in virtually every case of fever, the operative assumption is that the body, particularly the digestive organs, needs to be restored to balance and to its efficient capacity for channeling substances or turning these into energy.

Tantra

Alongside the prestigious philosophies and sciences of the Brahmins, numerous cultural trends provided a fertile ground for the emergence of Tantric cults. The quasi-liquid physiology of Ayurveda, Atharvanic ritual techniques, the chemistry and craftsmanship of metallurgical, jewelry, and numismatic crafts—all situated within a theological context that recognized a divine feminine, or a gendered cosmic dualism—provided the intellectual matrix for a decisively different religious orientation. To be more precise, Tantra did not emerge as a distinct and organized tradition, and it did not even emerge in any textual form until post-Gupta years. The earliest physical evidence we have of a "Tantric" religious belief is the reference to the "Divine Mothers" in a famous inscription, the Gangdhar stone inscription of Vishvavarman, dated to the early Gupta years (423–24 CE).

Scholars generally define Tantrism as the use of specialized ritual techniques to achieve both spiritual liberation (*jivanmukti*) and worldly perfection (*siddhi*) without renouncing the world or denying its value. The origins of this religious outlook are shrouded in mystery, but it clearly owed more to the second rationality of the *Atharvaveda* and Ayurveda than to the Veda and Upanishads. The early Tantric emphasis on the body as a perfectible vehicle for the attainment of supernatural powers reflected the influence of the medical texts on the authors of Tantra, who may have been autochthonous magicians or Brahmin intellectuals who wished to explore another approach to religion.

The earliest extant texts those Tantric thinkers produced can be classified as early medieval. Among the more important early works were *Kubjikatantra* and the *Rasaratnakara* of Nagarjuna, who also wrote the *Kakshaputatantra* and *Arogyamanjari*. This ninth-century writer was not the great Madhyamika Buddhist philosopher. He is renowned, however, as the author of the extremely sophisticated medical text *Sushruta Samhita*. These early Tantric works already reflected long-standing traditions with well-developed ideas and practices. The references to alchemy (*rasayana*) provide an example of how the earliest Ayurveda technique—such as the use of mercury for healing and rejuvenation—became integrated into Tantrism. The *Rasaratnkara*, for example, focused on the purification of minerals by extracting their essence, along with a variety of other chemical procedures, including fixating (solidifying) mercury in order to obtain the elixir of immortality.

The literary flowering of Tantrism lasted from the seventh to the fourteenth centuries, but Tantra's overall influence on Vedic/Puranic Hinduism has always remained broad. Tantra was divided into sects based on the worship of Vishnu, Shiva, the Goddess, the sun, and Ganesha. The main Vishnu groups were the Pancharatra and the Bengali Vaishnava Sahajiyas. The best-known Shiva groups were the Kapalikas and Kalamukhas, while Goddess groups were usually called Shaktas. All of these groups further subdivided, particularly along regional lines.

But the emphasis of Tantra was always on the individual practitioner, and the very secretive relations between the Tantric student and the guru. This relationship begins with the all-important initiation (*diksha*) and the student's reception of a unique mantra. It was in Tantra Hinduism that mantras became so pervasive as a spiritual tool, for instance as a central feature of meditation, along with their accompanying diagrams (*yantras*, mandalas, and *chakras*).

Over the centuries, Tantric sects developed highly specialized doctrines and practices. But Tantra has also pervaded what Western scholars have considered normative (Vedic, Puranic, or dharma) Hinduism in so many ways that it has become virtually impossible to isolate. For instance, contemporary Hindu worship (*puja*) has evolved far beyond Vedic formalism into a ritualized emotional encounter—even identification with—the divine that owes its intensity to Tantra. Numerous pilgrimage centers have derived their sanctity and their power from the body of the Goddess (Sati), which literally fell to the earth in one of the best-known Tantric myths. The central place in medieval and modern Hinduism of beloved gurus, the architecture and rituals of temples, the power of mantras—all of these have been largely shaped by Tantric ideas and practices.

At the heart of these notions, to summarize, is the recognition that the world is intrinsically sacred. The world not only corresponds to the divine as symbol, it enfolds the divine, for the world was emitted from the same primordial matrix and needs only to be purified or refined to reattain salvation.

9

Maps and Myths in
the *Matsya Purana*

Unlike the ancient Mauryas, the Guptas gave substantial autonomy to regional administrators. Provinces, districts, even villages were essentially governed locally in this vast northern Indian empire. The end of the Guptas only accelerated this rise of regional governments with local cultural flavors. Four kingdoms made up the empire's territory until 606 CE, which was the beginning of the rule of Harsha, India's first king of whom we have a biography (Bana's *Harsha Charita*). During Harsha's 41-year reign—his capital city was Kanauj in the western Ganges region—an extraordinary pilgrim arrived in India.

Two Pilgrimage Centers

Hsuan Tsang was a Mandarin Chinese monk who had converted from Confucianism to Buddhism and undertook an Odyssean pilgrimage to the land of Buddha. Like his fifth-century predecessor, Fa-Hsien, Hsuan Tsang was an indefatigable traveler and a methodical chronicler with an eye for detail. He spent a great deal of time in the countryside along the Ganges where Buddha had wandered and taught. This pilgrimage finally took him to the district where the Ganges and the Yamuna rivers meet. The capital there was Prayaga, a sacred city whose name reflected its history as an ancient place of sacrifice.

The *sangam* (river confluence) was a holy bathing place in the seventh century, as it is today. But instead of listening to the bathers,

the Buddhist visitor chose to focus, somewhat derisively, on the broad reputation of the rivers at Prayaga. Perhaps he looked to amuse his Buddhist audience back in China. Two local features captured his attention above others.
The popular Hindu belief that death at Prayaga leads to salvation inspired an
unusual number of devotional suicides; and the supposed efficacy of austerities
at this sacred place produced unusual behaviors, like clinging to poles in the
middle of the river.

Hsuan Tsang described a city with hundreds of "*deva* temples" and only
two Buddhist institutions. In front of one temple stood a large banyan tree from
which devotees would jump to their death. Bodies, then bones, littered the
ground beneath the tree. The Buddhist tourist reported an old story about
a Brahmin who once decided to put an end to the popular superstition by
climbing the tree himself and jumping off in front of a crowd. The man's
friends had placed piles of clothing under the tree, so he survived the fall. This
allowed him to announce to the gathered crowd that the call to jump was only a
siren song: "What is seen as the *devas* in the air summoning one is the leading
of evil spirits, not the acquisition of heavenly joy" (Watters 1904, 1:362).

It seems, then, that one of the earliest dateable observations we possess on
Prayaga is a lightly sardonic exercise in comparative religion, as it were, by a
Buddhist rationalist who rejected both the concept of an eternal soul and the
superstitions such a belief might have inspired among Hindus. The temple and
tree are no longer there; toward the end of the sixteenth century, the Mughal
emperor Akbar built a fort on that site, causing the practice to move to the actual confluence. Still, Hsuan Tsang's records from Prayaga—of the names of
temples, bathing pools, and wells and of the economic urban scene—are all
valuable for historians and resonate with Hindu sources whose authors are
both nameless and undated.

The most explicit and evocative contemporary source of information on
that sacred place was the *Prayaga Mahatmya*. If Prayaga in the sixth and seventh
centuries resembled the place today, it bustled with pilgrims, priests, vendors,
beggars, guides, and thousands of local individuals just milling around along
the river. The priests and the guides had a mutual stake in promoting a robust
level of activity, and probably cooperated on the guidebooks, which they published to describe the virtues of the holy *sangam*. The earliest promotional
works aimed at tourists from that era were called *mahatmyas*; the *Prayaga
Mahatmya*—there were probably many others—has survived. It was put together, possibly from an oral recitation, by the editors of a very large later
text, the *Matsya Purana*. The *Prayaga Mahatmya* now (as it has been edited
and published in modern times) consists of chapters 103–112 of the larger
book.

Although the *Prayaga Mahatmya* is a relatively pragmatic document, a sort of brochure for religious tourism, its authors adopted a classical literary style. The work begins with a frame that places the narrative in a revered ancient context any Hindu could recognize: After the devastating *Mahabharata* war, the text begins, Yudhishthira was racked with guilt for having killed good men and numerous relatives: Bhishma, Drona, Karna, King Duryodhana, and many others. The great sage Markandeya was just then visiting Kashi (Varanasi), from which Yudhishthira ruled the entire world. To console the grieving king and offer him a way of removing the taint of his guilt, Markandeya told him about Prayaga. The sage's words on this subject make up the body of the *mahatmya*.

The text is remarkably straightforward. At its core it simply says: Bathe in Prayaga and your every sin will wash off. After death, you will attain either heaven or final liberation. The reason Prayaga is so powerful, the text explains, is twofold. Both the rivers meeting there—the Ganges and the Yamuna—are auspicious goddesses. Moreover, the place as a whole is the residence of the three main gods of contemporary Hinduism: Brahma, Vishnu and Shiva. As soon as Markandeya finishes the consoling narration, Yudhishthira and the other Pandavas make the short trip (80 miles) to Prayaga, where Krishna joins them. They bathe, give alms to the Brahmins, and then return home, having attained peace of mind.

The anonymous writer who put those words into the mouth of Markandeya was an excellent pitchman for Prayaga. Some of his praise for the pilgrimage center deserves to be quoted:

> Having bathed there they go to heaven, dying there they do not return to existence. Those who live there are protected by Brahma and the other gods.

> A man becomes liberated from his sins by the mere sight of that *tirtha* (pilgrimage center), remembering its name or rubbing its clay on his body.

> A man who remembers the Ganges from 1,000 yojanas [8,000 miles] obtains highest felicity, even though he has committed evil. (*Matsya Purana* 46.5, 10, 13; Sarma ed., my translation)

> On the eastern bank of the Ganges, there is a well, by the name of Samudra-Kupa, and the place Pratisthana (modern Jhusi) which is renowned in the three worlds. If one resides there for three nights, observing sexual purity and keeping himself dispassionate, he is

freed from all his sins and gets the merit of the performance of the
Asvamedha sacrifice.

Markandeya said—King! You should bear in mind what has just been
told you about Prayaga, for Brahma, Visnu and Siva, the Lord of
Devas are eternal. Brahma creates the universe, Visnu fosters it and
at the end of the kalpa, Siva destroys it. At the time of the destruction
of the universe, Prayaga is saved. One who looks upon the sacred
Prayaga as the Lord of all creatures, becomes omniscient and blessed.
(*Matsya Purana* 106. 30–31; 111.2–3; Taluqdar of Oudh)

The "division of labor" between the three major gods—Brahma, Vishnu,
Shiva—had by now become a standard theological formula, a religious cliché.
In fact, Vishnu and Shiva were worshiped widely, while Brahma was reduced to
an ancient mythical figure—the "creator." The author mentions the three, the
trimurti, as a standard way of extolling the virtue of Prayaga, and not much
more. At the same time, it is virtually impossible to ignore the slap here against
Kashi (Varanasi)—India's best-known sacred city and pilgrimage center. To
purify his sins, Yudhishthira left the holy city and dipped at Prayaga instead.
Such are the boasts, anyway, of local advertisers. Still, the *Matsya Purana* was
large and inclusive enough to accommodate a *mahatmya* for Kashi (in addition
to others), and the boosters for Kashi made similar claims on behalf of their
own *tirtha*: "*Moksha* can be obtained in Prayaga, or here, by taking shelter in
me. Although Prayaga is best of *tirthas*, this place is considered supreme"
(*Matsya Purana* 73.56–7; Sarma ed., my translation).
    Like Prayaga, Kashi makes austerities (*tapas*) redundant. To illustrate this,
the authors of the *Kashi Mahatmya* tell the story of a *yaksha* (sprite) named
Harikesha, who was expelled by his father from his home due to his virtuous
nature. Seeking to win Shiva's protection, he came to Kashi, where the god was
known to reside, and undertook severe austerities. He stood motionless, ram-
rod straight, for one thousand divine years until ants devoured his flesh, leaving
nothing but white bones, still standing erect. Parvati, who was Shiva's consort,
reminded the Supreme Lord (Maheshvara) that it was not fit that one should
have to practice such extreme austerities in a place like Kashi. Shiva listened
sympathetically and granted Harikesha divine vision—the ability to perceive
the three worlds. He also gave the *yaksha* the lofty position of lord of the celestial
attendants (Ganapati). In short, the story concludes, "The sacred Kasi is the
fulfiller of cherished desires. It is free from diseases and the place of asceticism
and yoga. Lord Siva, enshrined there is shining in His full glory" (*Matsya
Purana* 185.51; Taluqdar of Oudh). Already in the early eighth century, the

authors of the *Kashi Mahatmya* made extravagant spiritual claims on behalf of the bathing steps (*ghatas*) and ponds along the river's bank in Varanasi: Dashashvamedha, Lolarka, Keshava, Vindumadhava, and Manikarnika. Today there are many more, but little has changed inside the water. Hundreds of bathers arrive half an hour before sunrise, ritually prepare a space in the water for themselves, and enter. In the water, they mumble mantras about the rising sun and about Hiranyagarbha, the Golden Germ, which brought about, and now mimics, creation.

> Golden of color, pure, purifying,
> In which Kashyapa was born, in which Indra
> They have conceived Agni as a germ, of varied forms;
> May these waters be gentle and kindly to us. (*Taittiriya Samhita*
> 5.6.1.1–2; Sastri ed., my translation)

The merit these bathers acquire in Varanasi at dawn equals that of the greatest austerities painfully practiced elsewhere, or the most exacting obedience to dharma, or the most passionate devotions to God.

Although Kashi and Prayaga openly competed for religious supremacy, both shared the same bravado: The great paths to realization—the same three promoted by the venerable *Bhagavad Gita*—all would materialize merely by visiting the *tirthas* and by performing ablutions with a resolute mind. Such claims were not novel; they were the very stuff of the religious syntheses that so characterized the subcontinent for centuries. Traditions joined and formed new ones by acknowledging others, by claiming to encompass their merit, or by adopting their names and powers, as Devi did gloriously in her own *mahatmya*. But the *Matsya Purana* added one more twist to these unifying techniques: "One who reads this Mahatmya in the morning, and remembers the Prayaga every day, attains bliss and goes to the world of Siva, after being free from his sins" (*Matsya Purana* 112.6; Taluqdar of Oudh).

After *tapas*, dharma, and bhakti have been encompassed by *tirtha-yatra*, the pilgrimage to Prayaga has now been encompassed in turn by the reading of the priests' brochure. Literature, both written and oral, can finally boast the same powers it attributes within its own pages to a holy place and custom. The author, or more precisely, the narrator (*suta*), has become the conveyor of salvation, and his book—the Purana along with its *mahatmyas*—has become an efficacious scripture. In this way, medieval Hindu religious literature has tapped into the aura of Vedic oral sanctity. At the same time, it transported the reader (devotee no doubt) from a real place to the imaginary geography of the entire universe. The map became as important as the territory! This was not unique to the *Matsya Purana* with its pilgrims' *mahatmyas*. All the major Puranas did this.

According to modern scholars, the Puranas claim to possess five topics (called *pancha lakshana*): primary creation, secondary creation (after a destruction), genealogies (gods, ancestors), the ages of Manu, and aspects of history, including lunar and solar dynasties. In fact, as Velcheru Narayan Rao has argued, each Purana is dominated by additional, often richer material that is merely framed by these five topics. For the Brahmins who collected diverse narratives and odd bits of information, the primary frame, the *pancha lankshana*, was a way of legitimizing—Brahminizing—their collections.

Geography and History

The two pilgrimage centers teach us an extremely useful lesson about myths in medieval India. Both Prayaga and Kashi are real places, but both are saturated with myth. The geographical place was enriched, not contradicted, by the mythical way visitors regarded both places. Even pilgrims probably knew that physical reality and myth were neither entirely different nor completely identical—that the Yamuna was both just a river and more than a river. But this is no easy feat of mind. The intellectual act that posits a paradoxical relationship between geography and myth combines two dominant forms of rationality: representation and participation. An object or place can represent some other reality—the place where a god lives, where a hero died, or where a part of a goddess fell to the earth in some ancient time. Varanasi is such a place, and so, in their ways, are Jerusalem and Mecca. Still, the physical location must also be intrinsically powerful in some way; it may sit on top of a mountain, may face sunrise across a vast river, or may be the seat of some extraordinary object. Among people who think in terms of both symbolism and participation, myth should not be sought only in the leap of the imagination to transcendent times and places. It is, rather, continuous with experience.

Like other Puranas, the *Matsya Purana* lists the sacred places that pilgrims visit to feel the presence of the goddess. In the ancient myth (*Mahabharata* 12.282–3), Daksha performed a sacrifice to which he failed to invite both his own daughter (Sati) and her husband, Shiva. When Sati arrived unannounced, she was insulted by her father, which drove her to commit suicide. In grief and rage, Shiva destroyed Daksha's sacrifice, and then danced madly with his wife's body on his shoulder. In order to end this, the other gods entered Sati's body and tore off pieces, which fell to the earth. Among the 108 places listed in the *Matsya Purana* (chapter 13) are Vishalakhi in Kashi and Lalita in Prayaga. For followers of the Goddess (*shaktas*) and Tantrists, these places are particularly sacred places for performing austerities.

Maps

Today, pilgrims arrive in Varanasi and Allahabad by train, bus, even plane. A thousand years ago, it was mostly by foot or ox-cart. The *mahatmyas* urged pilgrims to avoid comforts and displays of wealth—spiritual merit depended on modesty. But travelers—say from South India—could learn the locations of these two cities and could plan with some precision the duration of their journey. Of course, no actual maps—cartographic images on paper—older than the seventeenth century have been found in India. But loosely speaking, verbal maps of India and the cosmos, descriptions of continents, mountains, rivers, and states, including even directions and distances, did exist before the Gupta period. What form did those verbal maps take, and how were specific locations indicated?

The relation between a map and the territory it represents in a given culture (cosmography) reveals a great deal about the way both cartographer and travelers situate their physical environment in relation to imagination and thought. The same, of course can be said in relation to time. The way a historian locates a given king or dynasty within the grand span of history (cosmology) reveals the boundary (or overlap) between history and mythology. The *Matsya Purana* describes both space and time in painstaking detail, and its verbal cosmography and cosmology are expansive (fig. 9.1). The descriptions are not always internally consistent or exhaustive; competing versions may have entered into the same redaction. A historical geographer (e.g., Bimana Churn Law) would have to consult all the Puranas in order to get a more complete picture, but the competing versions remain.

The country of Bharatavarsha was divided into nine major regions, including Indradivpa, Kashera, and Nagadvipa. Also among these regions was apparently an island (*sagarasamvrita*), perhaps Sri Lanka. The extreme south of Bharatavarsha was Kumari (today Kanyakumari), and the land extended, in an ever-broadening pattern, 1,000 *yojanas* (8,000 miles) to the sources of the Ganges, on top of mountains standing 10,000 *yojanas* high! The *Markandeya Purana* (57.59) explains that the country looked like a stretched bow, with the Himalayas representing the taut string and the end of the peninsula in the south the arrow tip.

The overall outline was consistent with modern maps, which is hardly surprising. Indian merchants, sailors, tourists, pilgrims, soldiers, and administrators had been traveling the subcontinent for over a millennium, and there was no reason to get its shape wrong. The interior of Bharatavarsha was varied: there were seven major mountain ranges, including Mahendra, Malaya, and

FIGURE 9.1. Jain Mandala. Jain diagram of the universe, 'Jambudvipa', 1830. Rajasthan school. Circular design with concentric circles, showing the mythological Mount Meru, axis of the world. Stylized floral decoration in the corners. British Library, London, Great Britain. Photo Credit: HIP / Art Resource, NY

Vindhya, with thousands of smaller ranges and individual peaks. Hundreds of rivers were also known; the *Matsya Purana* lists several dozen, including the Ganges, Sindhu, Sarasvati, Sutlej. Numerous cities and states (*janapadas*) occupied the land, most of them historically significant: Panchala, Kuru, Shalva, Kashi, Avanti, and many others.

The authors knew their geography, but they were not gazetteers—the first of these was probably Alberuni in 1030 CE—so they added a touch of theology as well. They claimed that members of the four *varnas* lived in the center—the higher the *varna*, the closer to the center of Bharatavarsha. The *mlecchas* (foreigners), on the other hand, lived on the boundaries: Yavanas (Indo-Greeks) in the west and Kiratas (tribals) in the east. Ethics and theology (dharma) also found a place in this geography: the authors insisted that in Bharatavarsha, residents pursued the *varna-dharma* and *ashrama-dharma* meticulously (114.13) and, above all, this was the best place to attain heaven, *moksha,* or an intermediate state between the two.

Like the verbal map of India (the description of Bharatavarsha), the verbal maps of the cosmos reflect a number of views. In the *Matsya Purana,* for instance, there is a seven-part map of the world (113.7–42) followed by a four-part map (113.43). Both maps share one center, where an immense mountain— Mt. Meru (or Maha Meru, Great Meru)—stands either 84,000 or 100,000 *yojanas* high. The barren mountain is four-sided, and each side is a different color that corresponds to a different *varna,* with white, red, yellow, and black representing the descending order from the Brahmins. The continents encircle the mountain in seven concentric circles, separated by mountain ranges; or four semicircular petals extend out from Mt. Meru in the second map. In both maps, a vast ocean encircles the entire cosmos. And in both, the Indian subcontinent (Jambudvipa in the seven-part map, Bharatavarsha in the four-part one) stands to the south of the center. It seems clear that the Himalayas were the approximate location of Mt. Meru.

Like the map of India, this map, too, adds human detail, including matters of ethics, religion, and even health. For example, the residents of Bhadravarsha, the eastern continent, were said to be always happy; they were white and their women were beautiful. They lived to ten thousand years and remained youthful throughout their long life by drinking the juice of the black mango fruit.

The Puranic maps were not entirely original, of course. Older maps (geographical descriptions) or fragments of maps could be found in Buddhist, Jain, and earlier Hindu works (*Mahabharata*). But here, as in the earlier sources, questions for historians of science arise. Where does empirical geography end and mythology begin, if such a distinction could be made at all? Are the vast numbers (distances, heights, life spans) factual errors, hyperbole, or symbolic representations of some hidden cultural value? The narrator (*suta*) of this vast cosmography was both a realist and a rationalist. He prefaced his geography lesson with a reminder to his audience that the true divisions (*dvipa*) of the world added up, in fact, to thousands, and that both his seven- and four-part schemes were only simplifications. Only reason, he added, should be used to explain immensities or realities that extended beyond common experience. His maps, in short, were representations of something greater—mere facsimiles, however reasonable. He seemed to be urging restraint among his listeners when they considered comparing what they heard in his narration to what was truly out there in the world. This is still good advice for modern readers of the Puranas, but it is not a definitive help in understanding the enormous scale.

Similar issues arise in reference to the history and cosmology of the Puranas. Here, in the temporal dimension, lists of historically known dynasties competed with astoundingly vast cosmological schemes. The *Matsya Purana* is replete with genealogies (*vamsha*), many of which can be examined independently. Though rarely regarded as accurate history, these lists have still been useful to historians, both in identifying individual Indian rulers and in dating pre-Puranic historical material. The *Matsya Purana* lists several historic dynasties (271–273), including the Ikshvakus in Madhya Desha (Ayodhya); the Pauravas, who transferred their capital from Hastinapura to Kaushambi; and the Barhadrathas, who ruled in Magadha. There were also Shishunagas, Nandas, Mauryas, Shungas, Andhras, and many others—most of them historic lineages. The name of each king and length of his rule are stated: Chandragupta (Maurya), 24 years; Vindusara, 25; Ashoka, 36; and so forth.

Other genealogies pertain to mythical dynasties, others yet to sages (*rishis*) or to forefathers (*pitris*). These lists are not even approximately historical. Both *rishis* and *pitris*, we are told, owed their origins to the emergence of breath (*prana*) from the "self-existent" (*svayambhuva*) in a complex metaphysical and cosmogonic process. The authors of the Purana were clearly interested here in more than simple history, though it is virtually impossible to separate, within the detailed lists of names, truly historic figures from mythical ones or even sort out the intent of the author for the purpose of distinguishing among them.

However, history most clearly meets myth in the doctrine of the four ages or eons (*yugas*), which I have already discussed in chapter 6. The *Matsya Purana* version reports that Vishnu was the one who created the universe. Then it was destroyed, dissolving back into the body of Vishnu, and repeatedly so, in a permanent cyclical pattern. During the cycle, the cosmos undergoes four eons (*yugas*) that represent a progressive decline in length as well as moral and physical qualities. While the dynasties in the Puranas stretch to tens or hundreds of years, the *yugas* consist of vast cosmic durations. The first age, Kritayuga, is four thousand divine years, along with four hundred each for its dawn and twilight. That adds up to 4,800 divine years. Each divine year equals 360 human years, so the total is 1,728,000 human years for the first cosmic age. The succeeding ages are Treta, Dvapara, and Kali, consisting of 3,600, 2,400 and 1,200 divine years, respectively, or 1,296,000, 864,000, and 432,000 human years. The total of the four *yugas* is 12,000 divine years, or 4,320,000 human years.

This conception is famous for its moral implications. The first age, named after the perfect unit (divisible by four) in the game of dice, was characterized by perfect dharma and enormous human longevity, health and happiness. The passage of time sees a gradual decline in all, until the age of Kali (in which we now live), which is characterized by deceit, egoism, and a short, unhappy life. But this is not all: 71 cycles of the four *yugas* make up an Age of Manu, or Manvantara. That means that a new Manu, whose story I will shortly tell, appears once in 71 cycles of four *yugas* or 366,720,000 years. Fourteen cycles of Manu make up a *kalpa,* or great eon, at the end of which a great dissolution (*maha pralaya*) takes place that lasts twice as long as the *kalpa* itself (*Matsya Purana* 142.37).

In light of these vast cosmologies, the great Maurya empire suddenly seems very short-lived and puny. Both our history and our geography shrink against the scales of duration and extension in the Purana's maps. Important as Prayaga and Varanasi are to bathers and pilgrims, they are mere dots on lines that extend to a nearly infinite horizon. Still, it is one and the same map.

The Puranic Agenda

The authors of the *Matsya Purana* framed their world in temporal and spatial maps because they wished to situate their salvific message within fundamental and recognized values. For them, mythical maps were the representation of a territory that was overflowing with such values. They collected encyclopedic amounts of material ranging from myths to rules of morality and law, architecture, and numerous other topics.

But the Purana was not an encyclopedia. It was a narrative with a coherent agenda: creation, destruction, and recreation; the arising of gods, celestial beings, and humans; the meaning of the Vedas and philosophies; the history of kingdoms and countries; correct rituals and rules of law; lists of other Puranas; and artistic standards. All of this was designed to give a rich picture of the universe we live in and to describe the paths we can take in order to attain a good life and the highest spiritual goals. The many old myths collected in the *Matsya Purana* and other Puranas must be examined, then, not only with the antiquarian's (even the Purana's own) fascination for exotica but as a set of tools in the hands of rational editors who are aiming at fairly concrete goals.

Matsya Purana, simply translated, means "ancient chronicle of Matsya,"— the first of Vishnu's ten incarnations. In Sanskrit, *matsya* means "fish" and refers to a fish that saved humanity in one of India's best-known myths. Like most Indian myths, this one, too, appears in several texts and numerous versions, representing of course a tiny fraction of all the ways the story could be told to a living audience. The *Matsya Purana* version (1.9–2.19), briefly told, is as follows. The first king of the Solar Dynasty, Manu, handed over his kingdom to his son and retired to perform austerities. Brahma (the creator) was so pleased that he gave the king the boon of being the one who would save creation at the time of *pralaya*, the dissolution of the world at the end of the cosmic age. One day, as the king was pouring water into his palm while offering ablutions to his ancestors, a small fish fell into his hand. In order to protect the tiny creature from the bigger fish, King Manu placed it in a water jar, but within 24 hours, the fish outgrew the container and begged to be removed. The king put it in a large pitcher, but the same thing happened. The king then moved the fish to a well, then a tank. When the fish grew to a full *yojana* (8 miles!) the king transported it to the Ganges, then finally to the ocean, where it kept growing to monumental proportions. It was then that the king recognized the fish as Vishnu, or Keshava.

Vishnu warned the king that following a scorching drought, the world would soon be destroyed in a cataclysmic flood. He explained that the *devas* had built a large ship that Manu was to occupy and save everything that needed to be saved: the moon, sun, Vishnu(!), Brahma, Shiva, Narmada River (a possible clue to the place where this version of the myth was composed), the sage Markandeya, the Vedas, the Puranas, and the ancillary sciences. Vishnu himself would guide the ship to safety after Manu tied it to the horn of the fish.

As Vishnu predicted, the world suffered the drought, and then the flood commenced. King Manu collected all living beings, as this portion of the text tells it, and put them on the ship. He tethered the ship to the fish and climbed aboard, paying honor to God.

The Politics of Interpretation

If mythical geography and history mean that some places and times are imbued with certain meanings, what does the enigmatic story of Manu and the fish communicate? It is, after all, about time. But it is also rich with apparently loaded and oblique symbols that seem to signify in a manner that goes beyond the mere mapping of space and time. What does the story mean, then? That depends on whom you ask, and when. First of all, there is no single story here, properly speaking. What one reads in the commonly used edition of the *Matsya Purana* is one frozen version of many actual tellings that somehow found their way into manuscript form. The recitations themselves were performed before different audiences during different periods in history and on different occasions. Such performances create distinct meanings. In the Gupta or Maurya court, a king might hear the story as telling him that royal dharma is the foundation of all existence. The fish, after all, was afraid of the "laws of the fish" (*matsya-nyaya*)—the moral jungle that prevails without royal dharma. In a pilgrimage place near a river, perhaps during the period of an Islamic ruler, bathers and pilgrims might take it as a narrative about the inadequacy of all worldly government. To that audience, the containers might suggest social or legal categories, perhaps *varnas*, that the king is unable to enforce. Who can say what the story means? Because we do not possess all versions of the myth, and because we cannot attend all actual tellings, it is impossible to speak of the narrative as possessing a single meaning. It might be more judicious to say that the myth more or less successfully refracts or channels the meanings assigned to it by listeners.

Just as important as this first problem is a more recent, political one. A deep abyss separates the communities who may take an interest in Hindu myths. Communities of believers will take myths, certainly during the centuries of so-called Puranic Hinduism, in notoriously sectarian ways. A follower of Shiva and a follower of Vishnu may have entirely different understandings of the significance and meaning of the fish, or Vishnu's cosmic role. But all sectarian communities share two basic axioms. First, the meaning of a religious narrative and symbol is a matter of conscious representation, or convention. Meaning derives from doctrine, cherished belief, or theology. These may be contested, naturally, but they remain transparent and proprietary: "it means what it means to me." Second, as is the case with maps, the conscious signification of a narrative is continuous with human existence. The myth is not just a symbol of extrahuman realities; it extends directly out of experience. The fish does not just symbolize God in an arbitrary manner. The mythical creature and events must also reflect the belief in God's presence within nature and history. Both representation and participation—economics, ecology, rituals—govern the ways myths are interpreted.

In contrast, academic communities since the nineteenth century have looked for mythical meanings the way a miner might look for precious metals underground. The mountain and the rock are nonessential, covering up the bonanza below. Max Muller started this type of gold-digging when he interpreted Vedic gods as linguistic phenomena: aberrations related to words for light. Historicist interpreters may look for defining events—say, river floods and urban destruction among river civilizations—behind the flood motifs that feature in numerous cultures. This interpretation remains unknown to the storytellers themselves. In a similar vein, Freudian and post-Freudian theorists have sifted through myths, disregarding cultural or theological contexts, in order to excavate "deeper" psychological meanings in the rather obvious doctrinal layers. These include sexuality, incest, guilt, fears, Oedipal and Electra complexes, and other hidden dynamics that drive the storyteller and enchant the audience. However one chooses to interpret a myth within academic settings, most scholars today tend to reject both singular and doctrinal readings.

In recent years, the two communities have clashed. One of the most recent flare-ups arose around Paul Courtright's psychoanalytical interpretation of Ganesha. The American scholar contrasted the limp trunk of the elephant-headed god with the erect phallus of Shiva's lingam, noting that Ganesha's head was the product of his father's rage at the son's attention to Parvati. The debates over the proper way to interpret Hindu material, self-righteous on one side and defensive on the other, continue to reflect both the power of religious symbols and the discursive quality of myths in relation to communities. Obviously, this extends to all religious traditions around the world; religious life is nothing if not the ongoing contest over acceptable discourse.

So what are we to make of the Genesis-like flood and the fish that grows so rapidly that nothing can contain it? What is water (the flood) and what is the scorching heat? The best policy about interpreting this or other myths is to decide why you wish to understand it. Do you wish to know what seventh-century North Indian intellectuals thought about dharma, or about the twin fundamental substances (water and fire; recall the ancient Soma and Agni from the late Vedic ritual and Tantra cosmology) of creation and recreation? Do you wish to uncover a barely hidden rivalry between Brahmins and Kshatriyas? Do you perhaps wish to understand the meaning of the fish symbol (as a substitute for Hiranyagarbha, the cosmogonic Golden Germ) in medieval Hindu theologies? All of these are possible but require that you cast your net as widely as possible in order to expose the widest web of symbolic relations of which the myth is a nexus. You may explore the themes of water, fire, fish, retired kings, or whatever interests you. But keep in mind that you are not explaining the myth but interpreting it—that is to say, rereading or paraphrasing it to suit your own interests. In a sense, as Levi-Strauss kept emphasizing, you are perpetuating the life of that myth, broadening its range of tellings.

Churning Mythology

In the narrative that makes up the frame of the *Matsya Purana,* the *rishis* ask the *suta* (storyteller) how the gods became immortal. He tells them the following story. During the same war between the *devas* and *asuras* that gets repeated so often and in so many versions, the *devas* suffered from a great disadvantage. The *asuras* possessed a mantra (called Sanjivani) that Shiva had given them that brought them back to life when they died in battle; and so the *devas* were threatened with certain defeat. Brahma counseled them to ask the *asuras* to join them and together seek the help of Vishnu in an effort to churn the ocean of milk and produce the nectar of immortality. Mount Meru would be the churning stick, the serpent Shesha (a form of Vishnu) would serve as the churning rope, and Kurma—Vishnu's tortoise incarnation—would serve as the base. The *devas* and *asuras* first approached the mountain, snake, and tortoise and won their help. However, extreme fatigue slowed down their work, and so they finally came to Vishnu for help. Using the following praise, they won his support:

> Salutations to the Lord of the three worlds, who shines with brilliant radiance. Salutations to Vishnu, salutations to Jishnu, to you— destroyer of the demon Kaitabha. Salutations to the creator of the world, protector of the universe. Salutations to the one who takes the shape of Rudra and Shiva, Destroyer of the world. Salutations to the one who carries Shiva's trident for the sake of enlightenment, to the destroyer of demons. (*Matsya Purana* 112.36–38; Sarma ed., my translation)

Vishnu then bolstered the sagging efforts of the churners. With his left hand he held Mt. Meru, while Bali—child of the demons—held the tail end of the snake. Because Vishnu covered the mouth of the poisonous Shesha, he turned blue, but the churning was successful, as the ocean of milk was turned into clarified butter through the mixing of the essential liquids. But the nectar itself had still not come out. Numerous poisonous creatures emerged instead, including mosquitoes, flies, centipedes, and finally the strongest poison of all, Kalakuta, which was dark and probably semi-solid in consistency. That flaming poison born of the churned ocean threatened to destroy both *devas* and *asuras*. Their only hope for salvation was to swallow it, or seek out Shiva. And so, this time, they approached Shiva and praised him with the following winning words:

> We salute you for destroying Kama and ruinous time. Honor and greetings to the forceful God of gods. Salutation to Shiva, Sarba, who has braided hair. To the Lord of Uma, the destroyer of the Tripura sacrifice. To the one who manifests in purity, intelligence, enlightenment, *moksha, kaivalya*. Whose form is the measurer of the three worlds and Varuna, Indra and Agni. Salutations to Rig, Yajus, Sama Veda, to Purusha and Ishvara. To the one who is supreme, fierce and wise, whose eyes are the Shruti we give salutations. (*Matsya Purana* 113.32–35; Sarma ed., my translation)

Shiva agreed to help and, using his left hand, held Kalakuta and poured it down his throat. The *devas* and *asuras* were impressed by the beauty of the dark venom in the throat of the white god, so Shiva withheld swallowing it. The churning of the ocean continued.

Several objects then emerged from the churned ocean, including the physician Dhanvantari, founder of Ayurveda, who was bearing the nectar of immortality in a cup. The *devas* and *asuras* began to fight for the precious fluid, but Vishnu assumed the form of a seductive woman, Mohini, and took hold of the cup. As the *devas* began to drink the nectar, an *asura*, Rahu, disguised as a *deva* took a gulp; but Vishnu beheaded him before he could swallow. The war between *devas* and *asuras* continued, but with Vishnu's weapons and with the help of Nara and Narayana, the *devas* defeated the *asuras*, who retreated to the sea.

The myth of the churning of the ocean is one of the best-known narratives in the Puranas. By the time the authors of the *Matsya Purana* collected it, the myth already had a long and diverse history. In different versions, in fragments or whole, it could be traced as far back as the *Rig-Veda* and was already fully developed in the *Mahabharata*. Like other narratives, this myth functioned as an intellectual and ideological tool in the hands of those who added it to their collections, with some details embellished or emphasized, while others were dropped. In a theological sense, it was bound to mean something different to an eighth-century chronicler from what it had meant to a Vedic ritual specialist fifteen centuries earlier.

For a student of India, it is important to keep in mind that the *Matsya Purana* version retained many of the layers countless retellings had added to the basic story. In the Purana, the myth looks almost like a miniature ency-clopedia of Hinduism. There are traces there of influences that predate the arrival of the Indo-Aryans in India, that is, the Persian themes of the conflict between the *devas* and *asuras* (light and darkness, good and evil). There may also be suggestions in the narrative of the encounter with indigenous populations during the Indo-Aryan arrival. The ancient Vedic ecology and economy is re-presented in the churning—turning milk into butter. The Vedic ritual under-lies the identification of *amrita* (the nectar of immortality) with the Vedic soma, which gave the gods their immortality but was also a psychogenic liquid hu-mans used. Vedic cosmology was represented in creation through water, the ritual identification of butter and the cosmogonic Hiranyagarbha (Golden Germ). There was also the late Vedic science of liquids and fire or Soma and Agni, the search for essences in sap (*rasa*) from plants, which in the *Ma-habharata* version of the myth is where the *amrita* originates. There are cosmic maps (Mt. Meru, the circles of oceans), Tantra thought (the interplay of ritual pairs in *mithuna*, water and heat, order and chaos), word games (Narayana is "the one who moves on water"). There are Ayurvedic medicine, poisons, astrology, and numerous other specific details or broad themes that suffuse the narrative, or extend beyond it, with a density that requires both ingenuity and expertise to decipher.

The modern reader's thirst for a single meaning defies the logic of the Puranic agenda, which was wide-ranging and polyvalent. For example, the author or authors of these chapters was clearly interested in exploding narrow sectarian loyalties and was using the narrative as a tool to that end. The recruitment of both Vishnu and Shiva, each as the sole god—the other being only a form of the true God—co-opts the language of sectarianism in the service of what might be called rotating monotheism. There is only one God, now it is Vishnu, next it will be Shiva. This task subordinates the elaborate myth with its vast history and range of meanings. The symbolic churning narrative becomes a signature or a seal in the hands of the Purana writer. He uses it to give authority to a tradition that encompasses the competing sectarian agendas of both Vishny and Shiva.

10

Shankara and Kumarila

Between Brahman and Dharma

Throughout the first millennium CE, but especially after the decline of the Guptas and the rise of *mleccha* (foreign) powers (such as Shakas, Yavanas, Hunas), Brahmins migrated from northern India to the south. But the political situation in peninsular India, south of the Vindhya Mountains, was hardly stable either. During the centuries after the fall of the Guptas, three roughly matched kingdoms competed for supremacy: the Chalukyas, Pallavas, and Pandyas. Members of these dynasties, and even lesser rulers, encouraged the migration and settlement of Brahmins, who established educational and monastic colleges (*ghatikas* and *mathas*) and were rewarded with lands for rural settlements (*agraharas*). These migrations helped Sanskrit become the formal language of royal communication and the mark of high culture in a region of Dravidian or non-Sanskritic languages. Vedic tradition, too, became a source of legitimacy for many of the kings who financed the rising Brahminical culture, including the construction of magnificent temples. The Kailasanatha in Kanchipuram, built by Narasimha-varman II and the model for the Mt. Kailasa rock temple in Ellora, is a prime example of this search for prestige.

But elite Brahminical culture did not operate in a religious vacuum. Dravidian-language cultures and literatures already had a long and rich history. During the seventh to tenth centuries, Bhagavata and Pashupata sects were already dominant, with their emphasis on devotional poetry (to Vishnu and Shiva, respectively); *puja* worship, with offerings of flowers and fruit, outranked Vedic sacrifices; and an openness to low-caste and women composers and teachers prevailed. The preferred languages were South Indian, such as Tamil, and the religious poets wrote of love and devotion to God as a path to spiritual liberation. These poet-saints were called Alvars (Shaivite) and Nayanars (Vaishnavite), and their songs resonated in extremely wide circles (*Manikkavasagar*; Kingsbury and Philips, p. 127):

> I had no virtue, penance, knowledge, self-control
> A doll to turn
> At other's will I danced, whistled, fell.
> But me He filled in every limb
> With love's mad longing, and that I might climb
> There whence there is no return.

At the same time, Buddhists and Jainas were still enjoying wide influence in the south, though their economic and political power was already in decline. The Buddhists had served as a successful institutional model for spreading knowledge, particularly through monasteries and universities. But their focus on intellectual centers, combined with a diminishing patronage, would eventually become their undoing. Still, they remained a direct and powerful intellectual threat to traditional Hindu ideas during these centuries.

The Legends of Shankara's Life

It was in the south of India, in the western coastal region of Kerala, that Shankara was born, perhaps around 788 CE. The sources of information about his life are more hagiography than biography; they dramatize what Indians have valued about this great philosopher rather than recording historical facts about his life. Two such sources, Madhava-Vidyarara's *Shankaradigvijaya* and the even later *Sankshepashankara-Vijaya,* were particularly influential in shaping the image of the great philosopher. They say that Shankara was born on the Malabar coast to a family of Brahmins. His parents, Shivaguru and Aryamba, had difficulty conceiving a child. One night Lord Shiva appeared to Shivaguru in a dream and offered him a choice: he would have a son who lived prosperously but without distinction, or his son would be a great teacher (*acharya*) but live a short life. In the morning, Shivaguru found out that his wife had had the same dream.

Shankara, whose father died a few years later, was a true prodigy. He learned to speak, read, and write Sanskrit by the age of one and entered the first stage of life (*ashrama*) at three. By age eight, Shankara completed his study of the Vedas. He decided to skip the stage of the householder and become a renouncer—against his mother's wishes. According to one of the best-known legends of Shankara's life, his mother finally agreed when Shankara was grabbed by a crocodile and dragged into the Purna River. Only when Aryamba agreed to release Shankara to become a *samnyasin* (renouncer) did the crocodile let go of the boy.

For some time, Shankara wandered in South India, looking for a teacher. Then he headed north. On the banks of the Narmada, the holy river so highly praised by the *Matsya Purana*, he met his guru, Govinda Bhagavatpada. Govinda himself had been a student of Gaudapada, the early Advaita (nondualist) Vedantist who had written an important commentary on the *Mandukya Upanishad*. From Govinda, Shankara received the four foundational teachings (*maha-vakya*) of early Advaita Vedanta:

1. Brahman is pure consciousness. ("Prajnanam brahman.")
2. I am Brahman. ("Aham brahmasmi.")
3. Thou art that. ("Tat tvam asi.")
4. The self is atman. ("Ayam atman brahman.")

These were ancient teachings—Yajnavalkya and Uddlaka Aruni had already taught them 1,400 years earlier. But great intellectual upheavals had taken place in the intervening years—not least the flowering of Buddhist philosophies—and Shankara's work spreading these ideas still lay ahead. After a number of years with Govinda, Shankara began to travel throughout northern India, looking for scholars to debate. The art and science of debating had not disappeared in India since the days of King Janaka. On the contrary, Brahmins, Buddhist, and Jain intellectuals traveled throughout the country taking on adversaries in intellectual contests that sometimes drew hundreds of spectators. The debates were elaborate affairs—they could take weeks—and the stakes were significant. The loser gave up his religious affiliation and became a follower of the winner.

Shankara's most famous debate—he was a renowned debater by then—involved Bharati, the wife of the Vedic expert Mandana Mishra. Shankara had already defeated Mishra by arguing that the Vedas consisted of both ritual sections (*karma-kanda*) and knowledge sections (*jnana-kanda*; the Upanishads). He also demonstrated convincingly that those (householders) who followed only the ritual sections were driven by ignorance. But Bharati now challenged the young renouncer to explain the art of making love. Of course, Shankara knew nothing at all about this subject. He requested a one-month recess, but how could he study the topic? Just then, according to the narrative, a king had died, and Shankara used a special esoteric technique to enter the man's body, while his disciples guarded his own body, which remained in deep trance. For a month he experienced the pleasures of sex, so much so that his students had a hard time recalling their teacher back to his own body. But Shankara won the debate, and both Mandana Mishra and Bharati became *samnyasis* and followers.

Mandana Mishra was a distinguished scholar of Purva-Mimamsa, the school that analyzed ritual language, but he was not preeminent. The most influential scholar in that school of Vedic interpretation during the second half of the seventh and the early years of the eighth century was Kumarila Bhatta. According to the hagiographers of Shankara, Kumarila Bhatta, along with his colleague and intellectual rival Prabhakara, was in Prayaga when Shankara arrived there looking to debate. Most scholars would dispute that a debate could possibly have taken place, given Kumarila's likely age, but the legends tell us that Shankara defeated the two great men. Of course, this is just another way of saying that Uttara (late) Mimamsa trumped Purva (early) Mimamsa, or that Advaita Vedanta put Vedic interpretation to better use.

According to the same sources, Kumarila was also a South Indian Brahmin who developed into a revered scholar, though he never became a renouncer. He owned several rice fields and over a thousand slaves. Like Shankara, he was a devotee of Shiva and a very successful teacher. Both Mandana Mishra and Bhavabhuti were among his many students. And again, like Shankara, he was deeply engaged in theoretical debates with Buddhists. According to conflicting traditions, either Kumarila once pretended to convert to Buddhism in order to research its philosophy for winning debates or his own school was penetrated by the Buddhist philosopher Dharmakirti, disguised as a Hindu follower, and Dharmakirti was subsequently defeated.

The reliability of Kumarila's sketchy biography is as doubtful as that of Shankara, from which in fact it came. The debate between the two is probably fiction. Even if the young Shankara met Kumarila shortly before his death, there is no way of knowing what was said. But the juxtaposition of the two great philosophical figures, and both of them with Buddhism, remains poignant. Both Purva Mimamsa and Uttara Mimamsa (Vedanta) consciously set out to defend the Vedic tradition against the compelling force of Buddhist ideas. At the most basic level, Buddhism rejected that tradition, both as a source of knowledge and a source of legal and moral authority. But on a more rarefied philosophical plane, some Buddhists (Madhyamikas) argued that reality is ultimately a metaphysical void (the Shunyavada school), while the school of Vijnanavada (also Buddhist) countered that reality was consciousness only. Upanishadic ideas such as atman and Brahman were rejected, as were the many metaphysical and epistemological claims of other Hindu schools (*darshanas*).

TABLE 10.1. The Two Sides of the Debate of the Great Hindu Philosophers

	Side 1	Side 2
Scripture	Veda	Veda
Section	karma-kanda	jnana-kanda
Source	Jaimini *Mimamsa Sutra*	Badarayana *Brahma Sutra*
Debater	Kumarila	Shankara

Ultimately, both Kumarila and Shankara were traditionalists for whom knowledge and truth emerged out of scripture. Thus, if a debate had taken place and could be reconstructed, even at its most passionate, it would still have taken place within the parameters of the Vedic worldview. The two scholastic and scriptural sides would look roughly as shown in table 10.1.

In order to clearly see the boundaries within which the philosophers worked, consider the following scenario. Imagine you are on top of the Empire State Building. You suddenly notice that something unusual is taking place on the streets below. The cars appear to be stuck in a chaotic pattern, and smoke is rising from the scene. It may be an accident, but the tiny objects you take to be cars do not seem to be burning. The pedestrians are too far away for you to see them individually, but you can make out a milling crowd in the area, or so it seems. What is happening? You are stuck on top of the building, but you must know. The telescopes do not tilt down far enough, and no one on the observation deck knows more than you do. This, in a very crude sense, is the task of metaphysics. Of course, its object is not so prosaic as a New York street. Instead, it seeks to fathom reality, essence, the relation between unity and multiplicity, among other questions. But how we come to know what is "out there"— epistemology—is a universal matter. Indian schools considered six main ways of knowing (*pramana*):

1. *Perception:* Look down closely and see the mayhem and the smoke. Can you hear a siren?
2. *Inference:* You're a logical person—where there is smoke, there must be fire. Something is burning.
3. *Comparison:* How do you know these are cars, anyway? You seem to be taking it for granted, despite the huge distance. But you've been this high before, so you know how distance distorts size.
4. *Postulation:* None of the cars seem to have collided, which conflicts with the presence of smoke. Is a shop on fire? Was there a terrorist attack?
5. *Noncognition:* You know your own limitations; you failed your LSAT three times before enrolling in law school in the Cayman Islands. Something is going on precisely because you have no knowledge of it!

6. *Verbal testimony:* You turn your head, and there's a newspaper stand. The *New York Times* Metro section reports that there's a rodeo in Madison Square Garden this weekend and sidewalk barbecues all over town. So avoid the area!

So this is what Kumarila and Shankara were after, what they would debate: how best to know. But while Kumarila was searching for dharma, Shankara pursued Brahman. Because both subjects are unusual—"transcendent," some might say—the philosophers would have set aside five ways of knowing and kept the sixth (verbal testimony). In a sense, they would be arguing over the pages of the *Times* while the cooking went on down below.

Jaimini's *Mimamsa Sutras*

The rise and spread of early Buddhism had largely been fueled by its attacks against the Vedic scriptures, Vedic rituals, and Brahminical social ethics (dharma). Various Hindu schools of thought and individual philosophers rose to this challenge, but the earliest surviving response was that of Jaimini. We know nothing of the man himself, but his work, the *Mimamsa Sutras*, is generally dated to the second century BCE. The work is divided into twelve chapters (*adhyayas*) consisting of eight sections (*padas*) each, for a total of 2,500 sutras. Due to its philosophical nature, the first section of the first chapter, called "Tarakapada," has attracted the greatest attention from commentators and modern scholars. The remaining sections focus more closely on the Vedic sacrifice and the rules for interpreting the Vedic texts. Jaimini was drawing, for his methodology, on the work of late Vedic authors (of the Shrauta Sutras), who had begun centuries earlier to sort out Vedic ritual rules into systems and devise a way of interpreting these that they called *mimamsa* (investigation).

As Jaimini's essential task was to defend dharma, he began his work by declaring this goal at the very start. He then defined dharma as that which has been commanded by the Vedas as leading to welfare. These first two sutras are followed by an epistemological reflection on how dharma may be known when one takes into account the ineffectiveness of the five usual ways of knowing, including perception, inference, and the rest. The only reliable way of knowing dharma, Jaimini concluded (sutra 5), is the revealed word of the Veda. He then explained that the portions of the Veda that revealed dharma were rules of conduct, and in the remainder of his very long work he laid down the principles and methods for correctly interpreting the appropriate Vedic sections.

Like other sutra texts I have already discussed, the *Mimamsa Sutras* were extremely condensed and enigmatic. Furthermore, the logic and organization of the ideas laid down by Jaimini was rarely transparent and had to be clarified. The first great commentary on the *Mimamsa Sutras* was written by Shabara-svamin, who may have lived in the first few centuries CE. His *Shabara Bhashya* (Commentary), as it came to be known, elucidated the text by dividing it into five analytical (hermeneutical) units called *adhikarana*. These performed the following functions:

1. Explaining the context that required the investigation of the topic under consideration (for instance, dharma)
2. Specifying a Vedic text that declared the subject matter at hand.
3. Providing the doubt or uncertainty that might complicate the investigation
4. Stating the prima facie (initial) view on the matter (*purvapaksha*); often based on the view of an opposing school
5. Giving the final and correct view (*siddhanta*).

Following on the heels of this influential early commentary by Shabara were numerous later commentaries that explained it in turn. The two most significant commentators were Kumarila Bhatta and Prabhakara Mishra. They were roughly contemporaries—Kumarila the older man, and perhaps the teacher—but they read Shabara differently. Their split produced two distinct approaches to Mimamsa interpretation.

A reading of Jaimini's defense of dharma against its detractors proceeds, then, from the initial enigmatic sutra ("athato dharma jijnasa," "next then comes the inquiry into dharma"; actually, *jijnasa* is a grammatical form called nominal desiderative. It is derived from the verbal stem "to know," so the meaning is literally "the desire to know" rather than "inquiry"). The analysis follows Shabara's fivefold procedure (the *adhikaranas*) and applies both to Jaimini and Shabara. Our own study deepens, and becomes more complicated, when we take into account such further elaborations by Kumarila and Prabhakara.

In brief, Shabara wished to know why Jaimini began his text with "next" (*atha*), which implies something that precedes the inquiry into dharma. Is it a study of the Veda? Does it come immediately after studying the Veda, or some time later? Shabara answered these questions by following his fivefold procedure:

1. The context is the completion of study of the Vedas by the student in the first of the four *ashramas*.
2. The Vedic text that touches on the subject matter at hand stated: "The Veda should be studied."

3. The doubt about this text: Does the foregoing quotation apply to the literal Veda text only or does it also apply to its interpretation (*mimamsa*)?

4. The initial view is that the quotation applies only to the literal text of the Veda.

5. The accepted conclusion is that the *mimamsa* investigation was included in the command (to study the Veda), and the broader implication was that the *mimamsa* study was an important source of knowledge about dharma.

This is where the *Shabara Bhashya* stops (on the first sutra of Jaimini's *Mimamsa Sutra*) and further commentaries begin. They applied the same fivefold scheme to set up their own (differing) interpretations, beginning with either an alternative Vedic text (to the one Shabara cited) or another interpretation of the context the text points to. Their analyses finally lead to conclusions that seem tangential to the main point (what does "next" mean?). Prabhakara concludes that only Brahmins can practice *mimamsa*, while Kumarila reasons that the top three *varnas* can do so. The two competing interpretations, following still the same procedure, would then proceed to the next sutra, with its definition of dharma. In such a way the commentaries move through the entire *Mimamsa Sutra* and *Shabara Bhashya*.

As a system of philosophy, this seems very odd indeed. In fact, it looks more like the Jewish Gemara (Mishna and Talmud) than Greek or European philosophy. Text plays a central role: Vedic text, sutra, interpretation, and counter-interpretation. The standards of evaluating a proper understanding of the text require strict adherence to logic, of course, but the primacy of scripture rules out abstract deductive speculations. But despite this commentarial procedure, the Purva Mimamsa developed coherent views about numerous philosophical and theological topics, including the soul, liberation, God, the world, heaven, epistemology, and others. The chief topic, however, remained dharma.

Badarayana's *Brahma Sutras*

Just as Jaimini was determined to save the authority of Veda and efficacy of dharma in the face of Buddhism, so was Badarayana. Badarayana began his text by closely imitating Jaimini's: "athato brahma jijnasa" ("next then comes the inquiry into Brahman"). But then he proceeded in another direction. The text continues in the next few sutras: "From which the origin etc. of this (existence and dissolution comes about). Because the source of this (knowledge) is scripture. That therefore (derives) from the agreement of scriptural statements" (*Vedanta Sutras* 2–5; Radhakrishnan).

Like Jaimini's, the aphorisms of Badarayana are elliptic, and the ideas they contain must be drawn out by means of commentary. What is clear, though, is that the subject of inquiry will be Brahman, that Brahman is the origin of reality as a whole, the method of knowing Brahman is scriptural and, like Mimamsa, is based on textual interpretation.

Shankara's interpretation on Badarayana's *Brahma Sutras* mirrored Shabara's (on Jaimini) in being the first and in following the *adhikarana* analytical-dialectical method. A brief summary of his commentary on the first two sutras illustrates both Shankara's method and his view on a number of central features of Advaita Vedanta. Following a brief discussion, Shankara concludes that the word "next" ("then" in some translations) implies that the inquiry into Brahman follows an antecedent on which it depends. And like the topic of dharma in Jaimini, here, too, that antecedent is the reading of Veda. But a doubt arises whether this must include dharma—religious duty—as well. Shankara's answer is no. The student who has read the Vedanta portions of the Vedas, that is, the Upanishads that cover the topic of Brahman, can do so before undertaking the study of dharma.

Dharma-study aims at religious fruit (*phala*)—for example heaven—that depends on dharma as its cause. Brahman-study, in contrast, leads to eternal bliss and does not depend on any action or cause. Shankara puts it in slightly more technical terms, of course: the effects of dharma-study do not exist at the time of study, while Brahman, the object of Brahman-study, is eternal: it already and always exists. What then, is the antecedent condition that precedes the study of Brahman? It includes a number of things: the discrimination (*viveka*) between the eternal and the transitory; the renunciation of desire for the fruits of action; tranquility; self-restraint; the desire for *moksha* (release). Only by meeting these conditions can one initiate the inquiry into Brahman.

Next Shankara introduces a serious doubt: Is Brahman known or unknown? If known, then what is the point of inquiry, and if unknown, it is impossible to undertake an inquiry to begin with because the antecedent condition does not apply. Answering his own question, Shankara claims that Brahman is already known. Because Brahman is the Self (atman) of every person, it is known in the way each of us is conscious of having a Self: "I am" or "I am conscious of being."

The challenge that now arises is sharper: If Brahman is already known in such an intuitive way as the Self, there is no room for inquiry! Not so, answers

Shankara in his final conclusion (*siddhanta*): Despite being known as the Self, there is room for error about the nature of that knowledge among the unlearned. Brahman may be confused with the intelligence, or with the internal organ, perhaps with a momentary idea, with emptiness, the transmigrating self, and other false notions. In other words, if other schools of philosophy can get the identity of Brahman so wrong—despite its intuitive transparency—it clearly must be inquired into. Only those who follow the teachings of Advaita Vedanta come to know Brahman correctly.

Now the philosopher could move to the next sutra, which said that Brahman was the source of the world, including its origin, subsistence, and dissolution. This was a formulaic way of covering everything, including even the differentiated world of names and forms, where agents (people who act) experience the fruits of actions through causal mechanisms that manifest in time and in space. In other words, the same apparent reality that deceives people about the true nature of Brahman, that is, *maya*, owes its existence to Brahman. And just as ordinary objects are known due to their own qualities, so, too, the knowledge of Brahman depends on Brahman itself and nothing else. But the difficulty arises that if Brahman is the object of correct knowledge through the traditional ways of knowing (perception, inference, and the others), then the study of Vedanta texts is unnecessary.

Shankara denies this. Brahman cannot be known by means of the senses; senses are designed to perceive external things, but not Brahman. In fact, if Brahman were perceived with the senses, it would be possible to see that the world was the effect of Brahman and that Brahman was the cause of the world. But because only the effect (world) is perceivable, the senses cannot inform us that Brahman is in fact the cause. Further, Shankara added, the sutra (of Badarayana) was not promoting inference either; inference ultimately depends on perception. Instead, the sutra indicated that a Vedanta text (Upanishad) was the source of knowledge about the nature of Brahman and its relation to the world. That Vedanta text was *Taittiriya Upanishad* 3.1–6:

> Bhrgu, the son of Varuna, once went up to his father Varuna and said: "Sir, teach me *brahman*." And Varuna told him this: "Food, lifebreath, sight, hearing, mind, speech." He further said: "That from which these beings are born; on which, once born, they live, and into which they pass upon death—seek to perceive that! That is *brahman*!"
>
> So Bhrgu practised austerities. After he had practised austerities, he perceived: "*Brahman* is food—for clearly, it is from food that these beings are born; on food, once born, do they live; and into food do they pass upon death."

> After he had perceived this he went up to his father Varuna once again and said: "Sir, teach me *brahman.*" Varuna said to him: "Seek to perceive *brahman* by means of austerity. *Brahman* is austerity."
>
> So Bhrgu practised austerities. After he had practised austerities, he perceived: "*Brahman* is the lifebreath—for, clearly, it is from the lifebreath that these beings are born; through the lifebreath, once born, do they live; and into the lifebreath do they pass upon death."
>
> After he had perceived this, he went up to his father Varuna once again and said: "Sir, teach me *brahman.*" Varnua told him: "Seek to perceive *brahman* by means of austerity. *Brahman* is austerity."

After food and lifebreath the text goes through sight, hearing, mind, and speech in turn. All are rejected by Varuna. The teacher then sends Bhrigu back to practice austerities until the boy learns the correct lesson.

> So Bhrgu practiced austerities. After he had practised austerities, he perceived: "*Brahman* is bliss—for, clearly, it is from bliss that these beings are born; through bliss, once born, do they live; and into bliss do they pass upon death." (*Taittiriya Upanishad* 3.1–3; 6; Olivelle)

The text itself was quite clear: The foundation of physical, psychological, and mental existence is Brahman, but none of these is in fact Brahman. Shankara does not quote the Upanishad in full or even explicitly. But he points to this text as the scriptural source of what he wishes to say about knowing Brahman and Brahman's relation to the world: Although Brahman is the origin of all there is, it cannot be identified with the world or be known through the world.

After these two sutras, Shankara goes on to say that it is the knowledge of Brahman that leads to the cessation of pain and that once the knowledge of unity (with Brahman) arises, the conception of duality (of Brahman and world) dissolves permanently. But the first two sutras of Badarayana appear to be primarily an argument on behalf of scripture and tradition as means of attaining knowledge about Brahman.

A Hypothetical Debate

Had Shankara and Kumarila met and debated, the affair would probably have lasted for weeks or even months. They would have known, of course, that they shared more and disagreed about less. But within the framework of consensus, their disagreement defined two separate pillars of Hindu thought.

The Purva Mimamsa promoted, as its central agenda, the primacy of dharma. Jaimini had defined it (sutra 2) as that which is indicated by the Vedic injunction (*codana*) as conducive to welfare. Kumarila then added that the Vedic injunction was the only means of knowing dharma. In other words, dharma is not ordinary morality or the visible results that follow good or bad acts. It is not the prudence that underscores good judgment either. Instead, dharma is an allusive, perhaps transcendent entity or value that somehow links ritual actions with supreme religious salvation. "Heaven" is only a metaphor for such a beatific state.

In contrast, the Uttara Mimamsa (Vedanta) offered Brahman as the highest good of the religious life. While Brahman, too, was known through the Veda, here it is the Vedanta portion, the Upanishad, not Vedic injunction, that provides foundational knowledge. More important, in no way could Brahman be placed as a link in a chain of cause and effect in the way heaven seems to be linked to dharma. Shankara quoted the *Katha Upanishad* (1.2.14), which had described *moksha* as different from merit or demerit, cause and effect, past and future. Unlike dharma, Shankara could claim, Brahman is eternal: it cannot come to be or cause something else to be.

The difference between these two elementary positions is the difference between a rigorously monistic metaphysic and a dualistic one in which both spiritual and ordinary realities coexist. Each of the two schools clearly identified and exploited the weakness of the other. Kumarila's weakness: Shankara's critique of the foundations of Purva Mimamsa is based on the concepts of *adhyasa* (superimposition) and *avidya* (ignorance). The Mimamsa metaphysic requires an acting agent who perceives a desired goal ("heaven"), who makes distinctions between good and bad acts, who identifies distinct Vedic texts with separate rules and prohibitions and follows this prudently. All of these distinctions are based, ultimately, on an error-inducing mental act. In the *Brahma Sutras* 3.3.9, Shankara defined this act (*adhyasa*) as the imposition of the idea of one thing on the idea of another thing when both are present in the mind. A man inside a temple looking at a statue of Vishnu confuses the object with the idea of the god Vishnu. Both the god and the statue are present in his consciousness, but the distinction is blurred, and the physical object is mistaken for the divine being.

The two most famous examples Shankara used for this type of mental error are the failure to distinguish between mother-of-pearl and silver and the failure to distinguish between a piece of rope and a snake. In all such cases, there is a failure to apprehend the differences between that which superimposes (the deluding idea) and that on which it is superimposed (correct idea). This leads to ignorance (*avidya*), on which the entire ethos of Vedic injunctions, actions, and goals is based. For example: the notion of a distinct person who chooses to act toward a distinct goal superimposes separation, ego, agency, intentions, and so forth on atman—the eternal Self that possesses none of those qualities in fact.

Hence the Mimamsa conclusion that dharma is something of true value is faulty.

The Mimamsaka Response: This criticism demonstrates the failure to understand the full scope of its argument. In the rules of the Veda, or more specifically, in the rules of sacrifice, Jaimini recognized a difference between those that function on the basis of ordinary cause and effect and those that function in an unusual way. The first type of consideration explained people's desire to act (to sacrifice) toward some concrete goal (such as cattle, health, heaven). Jaimini had called this type of ritual goal *purusha-artha*—a human goal. On this level of motivation, he identifies such entities as wealth, gods, or heaven as aspects (means or goals) of the ritual context. But there is another domain, called *kratu-artha* (*kratvartha* with the *sandhi* phonetic rule). Within this frame of reference, philosophers can argue that ritual actions are performed only for their own sake or, to be more precise, for the sake of the ritual itself. The purpose of such actions (for instance, facing in a given direction during the ritual) is the ritual as a whole, never some concrete and discernable goal outside the ritual. Such actions are "structural" (to use a modern term) rather than pragmatic; their value derives only from being indicated by Vedic injunction (*codana*), and their power is invisible and mysterious. In other words, the ritual order indicated by Mimamsa is not a pragmatic and causal calculation—it is a unique kind of ritual transcendence that promotes the intrinsic sanctity of ritual forms. That is the definition of dharma. It would be a complete misunderstanding to define dharma simply as acts that lead to heaven, prosperity, or any other goal.

Shankara's weakness: The monistic metaphysic of Shankara was extremely vulnerable to criticism, and Kumarila in his *Shlokavarttika* (84–86) repeated a point that many before him had made:

> Further, since [Brahman] itself is of pure nature and there exists nothing else [but Brahman], how could nescience (*avidya*) like a dream and so forth work on that [Brahman]?

> If one says that [Brahman] is invaded by something else, [his position] would become dualism. [In other words, since the two principles, Brahman and something else, have to be accepted, nondualism will be discarded.] On the other hand, if [one says that] nescience belongs to [Brahman] by nature, [which does not need another principle because of the function of nescience, we reply], nobody would be able to remove it. [And so no final release would be possible.] (*Shloka-vartikka*; Nakamura)

To simplify the text, if Brahman is the origin of everything, including ignorance, how could ignorance be removed? *Response:* There is no fully convincing answer to this critique of monistic (*advaita*, nondualistic) Vedanta. A number of attempts have suffered from the appearance of bootstrapping. For example, in his commentary on *Brahma Sutras* 1.1.5, Shankara compares the mistaken distinction between the transmigrating soul and Brahman to that of a jar and the space inside. There is only the jar, properly speaking—the space inside has no independent existence. Similarly, there is no transmigrating soul—only Brahman. In more abstract terms, there are two ways of talking about the change Brahman seems to undergo in order to become the world. One change is *parinama*, material substantive change. The other is *vivarta*, appearance. Molecules of oxygen and hydrogen become water in a substantive way. But silver only becomes ring in the sense that its appearance has changed—the ring is just another shape of the silver. Brahman does not change substantively; that would be conceptually impossible. Instead, the changes in Brahman that result in the world are mere appearance (*maya*); the world is still entirely Brahman. Unfortunately, this hardly resolves the problem: *avidya* (ignorance), which is defined as our inability to perceive that true reality is Brahman, persists in our continued error. And although from the perspective of the absolute, the error is also unreal, its existence is true as a matter of phenomenology: Like pain, it exists in as much as we experience it.

The World in a Book

To nonscholars, these distinctions may seem either trivial or obscure— especially because they are rooted in subtle interpretations of a shared scripture, the Vedas. Recall the commotion below the Empire State Building: It seems puzzling that philosophers would argue over the paragraphs of the *New York Times* while the smoke was hovering above the streets. But the topic now is not smoke, it is both Brahman and dharma in relation to the world. The reading of scripture produces two distinct and nontrivial worldviews here—the same two that run as the two main threads of this book. The Purva Mimamsa philosophy appears to uphold a commonsensical view of the world whereby people are actors with rational intentions and religion offers a predictable method of achieving personal salvation. Within this worldview, persons interact in social contexts according to enforceable rules, they fashion sciences and build civilizations. In contrast, the Advaita Vedanta philosophy appears to reject all world-building and personal salvation as a vast illusion—*maya*. This illusion arises from the failure to recognize that reality is only one, Brahman. Individual persons, with transmigrating souls occupying bodies whose needs must be met, are fiction. All that finally counts is the quiet practice of austerities in order to gain knowledge of Brahman and final release (*moksha*).

Over the last century, starting perhaps with Vivekananda's nineteenth-century visit to Chicago, Advaita Vedanta reigned as the most prestigious subject in Western scholarship of Hinduism. It was either the flower of Hindu "spirituality" or the clearest example of Indian "world negation." More recently, however, students of India have been more careful in assessing Advaita Vedanta. Francis X. Clooney, to give just one example, has demonstrated that the distinction between the two Mimamsas can be overplayed. In fact, he argues, both Badarayana and Shankara pegged their philosophy to scriptural interpretation for conventional reasons. They were defending the Vedic tradition from attacks by both Buddhists and materialists, using textual "intelligibility" (Clooney's term), or canon, as the primary method for propagating their own insights. Thus, despite his critique of ritual and morality (dharma), Shankara never regarded either as meaningless. Even ritual and moral actions play a role within the context of the world in preparing for the study of Brahman.

Still, when all is said and done, Shankara remains a forceful monist, some would even say a crypto-Buddhist. That is why, among other reasons, the two most prominent Vedantists who followed him, Ramanuja and Madhava, rejected monism.

According to the traditional accounts, Shankara only lived to the age of 32. He died, or attained *samadhi* (unity with Brahman), at Kedranatha in the Himalayas. But during his short life, he had been a prolific writer—over three hundred works have been attributed to him. His commentary on Badarayana's *Vedanta Sutras* (called *Brahmasutra Bhashya*) was the most important. Along with this one, two other commentaries, on the *Bhagavad Gita* and the Upanishads, make up the foundational trilogy of Advaita Vedanta texts. Although commentary on scripture was his method of exposition, Shankara also wrote works that stood alone—usually introductory synopses of his thought. Two such books are the *Viveka Chudamani* (Crest-jewel of discrimination) and *Upadesha Sahari* (One thousand teachings). There are also numerous collections of poetry and hymns.

Just as important as his literary and philosophical productivity was the founding of a system of monasteries (*mathas*) that emulated and rivaled the various Buddhist systems. The four most important monasteries, still existing and prospering today, were in Shringeri near Mysore in the south, Puri in the east, Badrinatha in the north, and Dvarka in the west, forming a diamond-shaped mandala of the entire subcontinent.

The intellectual legacy of Advaita (monistic) Vedanta is still strong. The scriptural sanctity of such texts as the *Chandogya Upanishad,* along with the intellectual prestige of Shankara, guarantee the legitimacy of the notion that all of reality is one nonmaterial being, namely Brahman. The reach of this Brahman-based idealistic metaphysic has extended beyond India and Shankara to European philosophy, American transcendentalism, and even the New Age/new science paradigms of many contemporary teachers, including Fritjof Capra and Deepak Chopra. Yet some of Shankara's own followers refused to accept the notion of a single reality.

Qualifying Monism

Shankara's uncompromising monism did not put an end to theology and devotion, but it reduced "God" to the master of a lesser world. In the second sutra of Badarayana's text, where Brahman was described as the origin of creation, existence, and dissolution—the paradigmatic role of the *trimurti*—the concept of divinity was essentially demoted. God, in Shankara's theology, became "Brahman with Qualities" (*saguna*), which is a relative aspect of the Absolute within the domain of *maya.* The true Brahman is *nirguna,* without qualities, beyond thought or anything that could be said. But for the critics of Advaita Vedanta, for example Ramanuja, it was not so much the theology as the psychology of Advaita that raised hackles.

Ramanuja was born in the south of India at Shri Parambattur, near Chennai. The most frequently cited date for his birth is 1017, about two centuries after Shankara. At that time, Shankara's monasteries were continuing to prosper, with numerous distinguished philosophers (and critics) following in the footsteps of the founder. Like Yamunacharya (d. 1036), who was one of the most prominent among these, Ramanuja belonged to the South Indian devotional Vaishnavite sect called Pancharatra. The sect dated to the first century BCE in Kashmir (in the far north) and asserted as its foundation that devotion to Vishnu was the supreme religious path. By the time of Ramanuja, Vishnu (God, Ishvara) had become identified with the Vedanta's Brahman and stood over and against the world as spirit to matter, or *purusha* to *prakriti.* Ramanuja accepted this, in line with the ancient dualistic metaphysics of Samkhya, already influential within the *Bhagavad Gita.* The world, on this metaphysic, consists of two coeternal principles—*purusha* and *prakriti.* Matter, or *prakriti,* is the dynamic interplay of three fundamental strands called *gunas* (*sattva, rajas,* and *tamas*). The agitation of matter, the constantly shifting balance of the strands, results in the psychophysical world of our experience and in the alienation from pure spirituality, or *purusha*.

Ramanuja wrote commentaries on many of the same works as Shankara, including Badarayana's *Brahma Sutras*, the Upanishads, and the *Bhagavad Gita*. But Ramanuja could not accept Shankara's way of identifying Being and consciousness. For Shankara, the awareness of the "I" that characterizes individual consciousness is an aspect of ego and is therefore false. Only absolute individual-transcending consciousness (atman) is identical with Being. For Ramanuja, in contrast, the I-consciousness of awareness is true and does not dissolve in the union with Brahman. In other words, the world contains many conscious selves that truly exist and are materially real, but these are all dependent for their existence on Brahman. This philosophy, in the briefest of sketches, has been called qualified nondualism—Vishishtadvaita Vedanta. The multiplicity of reality is real, but it exists as the attribute of Brahman, or God.

Other philosophers, especially Madhava (1197–1275), would go even further than Ramanuja's critique of Shankara. The *dvaita* (dualistic) view of Madhava would posit an outright break between Brahman and world, resonating more closely yet with Samkhya philosophy. It is important to keep in mind that while Indian philosophies and theologies have always accepted a whole spectrum of ideas, from radical materialism to radical monism and various shades of dualism in between, no single institution ever set out to establish a legally enforced orthodoxy. Dualistic philosophies tended to be more influential among the devotional sects of medieval India, but their dualism did not extend to the ethical domains of Manichean Christianity with its demonization of "evil," or the exclusiveness of the elect. In India, dualism described a gradation of being between two types of fundamental realities, not a fenced antinomy, guarded by the sword, between those who are virtuous and those who are sinful.

II

Devotion and Knowledge

The Indo-Muslim Centuries

For millennia, Indian thinkers exhibited both ingenuity and profundity in the ways they explained reality and the technologies they devised to improve life. Nonetheless, in the 1930s, Jacob Needham, a noted historian of science, raised the following question: Given their great scientific past, why had the great civilizations of Asia—both Chinese and Indian—not produced a modern science in the European mold? Why had the theories and technologies of India's ancient past failed to evolve into the same theoretical abstractions and great innovations seen in Europe after the Renaissance?

Indian scholars such as P. C. Ray and M. N. Saha have responded to this question by examining two types of explanation. First, outside of science itself there were caste and class hindrances, devotional sectarianism, Muslim and British exploitation, and similar limiting factors. Meanwhile, second, Indian thought also exhibited intrinsic characteristics of an antiscientific worldview. To give one example, the Vedanta system, which posits an ephemeral world (*maya*), could lead to the rejection of objective space and time. It might, in fact, undermine empirical investigations into observable phenomena. Defending scientific rationality in India, as Ray did, required a preference for extrinsic causes, with a strong focus on the sociology of science.

In the last few decades, the sharp separation between empirical observation and theoretical assumptions, or between science and metaphysics, has weakened. Historians of science in India, primarily Debiprasad Chattopadhyaya and A. Rahman, now closely link scientific with traditional modes of knowledge, and not just as a matter of social circumstances. Famously, the Ayurveda texts represented both sophisticated medicine and religious theory; astronomy and astrology were tightly interlocked, and mathematics was consistent with metaphysical philosophy. Still, for Indian historians of science, including Ray and Chattopadhyaya, the most abstract Vedantic ideas remain extremely difficult to reconcile with scientific rationality.

But science is not merely astronomy, medicine, or engineering. As much as the Indo-Islamic centuries in India produced in the scientific and technological fields (is there a more famous building than the Taj Mahal?), there are other, more socially oriented ideas to examine. This chapter will look at the general effects of devotion and Islamic culture on attitudes toward knowledge, with a special emphasis on social realities such as caste and national identity.

God and World: Different and Nondifferent

Long before Shankara's Advaita Vedanta, the Puranas drew maps that described both geographical and mythical locations. Varanasi, Gaya, and Vrindavana were real places on the North Indian landscape—anyone could travel to see them—but they all existed in mythical time and space. How might a philosopher explain the relation between the two domains—the mythical and the real? More broadly, what is "God" in relation to "world"? Would a historian of science like Jacob Needham be correct in claiming that mythology and "mystical" philosophy are so world-negating that they could only result in the abandonment of theoretical and practical knowledge as India moved from medieval to modern times?

The answer is more complex than either/or: myth or reality, God or world. The Vedanta philosopher might argue, for example, as the eminent South Indian philosopher Ramanuja certainly did, that God was different from the world but also not different. Brahman may be different (*bheda*) from *maya* but also not different (*abheda*). This strange idea, called "difference/nondifference" (*bhedabheda*), might mean that religious faith is not an obstacle to scientific and technological innovation. As it turns out, difference/nondifference proved to be decisive as a popular religious assumption during the medieval centuries in northern India. Poets, mystics, and immensely charismatic devotional leaders kept their gaze on God and the world at the same time, even to the point of turning God into a sort of craftsman. In the famous image of Kabir (quoted by Rahman 1999, p. 423):

The master weaver, whose skills are beyond our knowing,
Has stretched his warp through the world.
He has fastened his loom between earth and sky,
Where the shuttle cocks are the sun and the moon.
He fills the shuttle and weaves an endless pattern.
But, now says Kabir, the weaver! He breaks apart his loom
And tangles the thread in thread.

If you know weaving, you know the work of God, at least as a start. This may not be the Deists' Clockmaker of the European Enlightenment, but neither is it a world-negating abstraction. If God and world are related in the same way as the craftsman and his tool (or product), then a holy city can exist as geography and myth simultaneously. But if the divine craft (weaving) is a lowly one—Muslims in Varanasi specialized in it—then the creator is no standard Brahminical construction. During the early modern centuries, this idea struck roots within popular religion in northern India and found expression in the devotional songs of the poet-saints and among bhakti (devotional) groups. Many of the great poet-saints of the era, like Kabir, were low-caste craftsmen. Namdev was a tailor, Ravidas a cobbler, Dadu a corder, Sena a barber, and Tukaram a shopkeeper. The uncommon high-caste poet-saint (Rajput) was a woman: Mirabai.

Perhaps most compelling among the popular religious voices were incarnations of Vishnu: Ram and Krishna. The Krishna-oriented bhakti religion, in which the geographical Vrindavana dominated both as a dusty place of pilgrimage and as the divine home of God, was immensely influential. It took shape in the movement that centered on the person of Chaitanya:

> Radha is the manifested form of pure love for Krsna; she is his *hladini-sakti*. Because of this they had previously assumed different bodies on earth, although really one, but now they have become manifest under the name of Caitanya in order to attain to non-duality and oneness: I praise the true form of Krsna enveloped in the radiance of the bhava of Radha. (*Caitanya Caritamrta* 4.48, sloka 8; E. Dimock)

Who was this man, Chaitanya, described here in Krishnadasa Kaviraja's *Caitanya Caritamrta* (Immortal biography) as the manifestation of both Krishna and Radha? And what does "manifestation" mean, in the context of evaluating both a historic figure (the Bengali man) and the God of Vrindavana?

Born Vishvambara Mishra in Bengal in 1486, the great Vaishnava mystic became Krishnachaitanya when he renounced social life and became a *samnyasin*. Due to his enormous capacity for emotional and spiritual identification with God (Krishna), along with his charismatic external displays, Chaitanya became the most important Vaishnava figure of the sixteenth century. Not much of his own writing has survived, but numerous biographies, chief among them *Chaitanya Charitamrita*, have richly described his life and teachings. One of the best known and widely used aspects of Chaitanya theology was the juxtaposition of the earthly Vrindavana, where Krishna grew up and frolicked with the *gopis*, and the heavenly Vrindavana. The two were both different and identical in the same way God was both world and not-world.

The idea, later elaborated in more sophisticated terms by theologians including Rupa and Jiva Gosvamin, continued to resonate for centuries within Indian devotional theology. Adherents of "difference and nondifference" ran pitched battles with Advaita Vedanta (philosophical monism) for the prize of solving the most persistent issues of religious life: Is the sanctioned social structure of dharma inviolable and must one leave the world behind in order to submerge oneself in God? The resounding answer of numerous poets and mystics was that the world mattered but that caste and gender distinctions did not. The great fifteenth- and sixteenth- century saints seemed to agree that the world could not proceed with business as usual.

Obviously, Chaitanya and his direct followers were not scientists, but their religious worldviews appear to suggest two possible ways of organizing knowledge in medieval and early modern India. The first possibility, bifurcated knowledge, resembles the state of biology in the United States today: some of the finest laboratories and researchers operate in American universities, while a majority of Americans, according to polls, believe either in creationism or intelligent design—the idea that nature alone cannot account for the complexity of life forms. The second possibility, unified knowledge, is more consistent with what Jacob Needham (or Max Weber) had in mind when he explained why modern science developed in Protestant Europe. Unified knowledge implies that a religious worldview provides the ideological basis for an emerging scientific rationality—the intellectual curiosity and empirical methods of discovering the distant creator's natural laws.

The state of affairs in India, about four centuries before Chaitanya and Kabir, was probably bifurcated, if one is to accept the description of India's great medieval chronicler the Muslim Alberuni:

> The religious books of the Hindus and their codes of tradition, the
> Puranas, contain sentences about the shape of the world which
> stand in direct opposition to scientific truth as known to their
> astronomers.... [The] two theories, the vulgar and the scientific, have
> become intermingled in the course of time. (; Sachau 1971, p. 265)

Due to the complex calculations required by popular religious rituals, Alberuni explained, scientists gained enormous social prestige and became contented with the distortion of their science by sheer mythology. "Therefore, you mostly find that even the so-called scientific theorems of the Hindus are in a state of utter confusion, devoid of any logical order, and in the last instances always mixed up with the silly notions of the crowd" (quoted by Rahman 1999, p. 22)

But can Alberuni be trusted in his assessment of the state of science and religion in medieval India? Was he not, after all, part of an invading force? Alberuni was born in 973 CE in Khwarizm, in Central Asia, and grew up with an intense devotion to learning. His studies included the great languages of the era, including Arabic, Greek, and Sanskrit. He developed a special interest and competence in mathematics, physics, and astronomy but also studied geography, history, biology, and medicine and attained an immense knowledge of the medieval world. Oddly, his name became inextricably tied to that of Mahmud of Ghazna (998–1030), the Turk who invaded India, marauding through its northern regions and acquiring the undying reputation of a bloodthirsty "idol breaker," due to his religious fanaticism, plundering of Indian wealth, and destruction of places of worship and objects of art. However, Mahmud was also a patron of the arts in his own capital (Ghazna) and a generous employer of such scientists as Alberuni. It is inconceivable that Alberuni would have written his great work on India without the invader's support.

Alberuni tried to be as evenhanded as he could in his assessment of the Indian state of knowledge. This was simply an aspect of his own approach to data. As noted, he had studied Sanskrit in order discover what the ancient Indian texts actually said. He thought of himself as a dispassionate historian, bound to accurately describe India before denouncing it, and he favored empirical observation, measurement, and the testing of hypotheses as a way of discovering truth. Furthermore, he seemed to remain aware of the fact that even his own scientific knowledge, in physics, geography, cosmology, was grounded in a worldview that had religious implications. For instance, while it was in India that Alberuni made his famous calculation of the circumference of the Earth (24,778 miles), he also argued while in India that the geometrical principles that made his calculations possible reflected the intrinsic "harmony" of nature.

Islam in India

One might say that Alberuni was the earliest Muslim to hold up a mirror to India, the most prominent foreign chronicler since the two Buddhist pilgrim monks Fa Hsien and Hsuan Tsang and a more polished one. He was, after all interested in Indian sciences, technology, and humanities, not just the sacred history and geography of a holy land.

Between 711 and 1750, the formative years of Indo-Islamic cultures, Islam as a whole was both a dominant foreign civilization in India and a catalyst for vast modernizing influences on Hinduism. Islam in India, arriving on the heels of the military and political hegemony of prominent rulers (the Sultans, 1206–1526, and the Mughals, 1526–1759, were the most stable), took deep roots in a unique synthesis with Hinduism. Islam became a world religion by accommodating, appropriating, and assimilating (in the words of Richard Eaton) elements from local traditions, which in India included devotion, philosophy, and Yoga. In other words, one has to separate the military nature of political events, and certainly the fanaticism of a few rulers (e.g. Mahmud of Ghazna, Amir Timur, Sikander Lodi), from the largely peaceful process of cultural, scientific, and religious encounter.

True, one must acknowledge that even in the domain of arts and letters, the picture was not entirely serene. On the Muslim side, various narratives of conquest emerged, including Amir Khusrau's *Miftah al-futuh* or *Tugluq Nama*. On the Hindu side, epics of resistance were also written, especially within Rajput circles, where opposition to foreign (*mleccha*) invasions was paramount. Two examples noted by Aziz Ahmad are *Prithivi Raj Raso,* by Lal, and *Prithi-viraja Vijaya,* by the Kashmiri writer Jayanaka. Even Kabir, the Muslim weaver of Varanasi, a figure of supreme religious synthesis, in the act of articulating the unity of Islam and Hinduism gave voice to the tensions of coexistence (quoted in Zelliot 2005, p. 139):

> The goal is one; the ways of worship are different.
> Listen to the dialogue between these two:
> The Turk calls the Hindu "Kafir!"
> The Hindu answers, "I will be polluted—get away!"
> A quarrel broke out between the two;
> A great controversy began . . .

On another occasion, Kabir composed the following lines on the two communities (shabda 3; Hess and Singh):

> I've seen the pious Hindus, rule followers
> early morning bath-takers—
> killing souls, they worship rocks.
> They know nothing.

The Muslims did not fare much better with Kabir's tongue:

> I've seen plenty of Muslim teachers, holy men
> reading their holy books
> and teaching their pupils techniques.
> They know just as much.

And this is how he summed up what he saw of the two communities:

> The Hindu says Ram is the beloved
> the Turk says Rahim.
> Then they kill each other.

It may be inevitable that national self-identity emerges in the context of a cultural encounter, with its mixed bag of synthesis and confrontation. In India, it would be the Muslim who made "Hindu" a term that designated membership in a geographical and national group. This term first appears as a term of self-identity among Hindus in a fourteenth-century South Indian (Andhra) royal inscription.

Sheldon Pollock, who has spent decades researching and translating the *Ramayana*, has argued that the emergence of Rama as a leading god in northern India, with a rapidly spreading temple cult, was due to his heroic exploits against a "foreigner"—Ravana. The political and religious events surrounding the destruction of the Babri Masjid of Ayodhya in 1992, at the site of an old Rama temple, seem to bear out such observations, which equate Rama with political and religious self-identity: God himself is Hindu.

Still, when all is said and done, it would be both inaccurate from a historical point of view, and a culturally impoverished approach, to focus on the confrontational dimension of Hinduism's response to the mirror held before its face. The encounter with Islam resulted in a cultural and social introspection that was far more fecund than any confrontational model might suggest. Surprisingly, Rama and the *Ramayana* are a perfect place to see this. As national and religious self-identity emerged, the leading agendas were, in fact, usually internal: What is dharma and who speaks on behalf of true Hindu norms?

Tulsidas and the New Rama

Tulsidas (born 1532), a poor Varanasi Brahmin, was by his own account an abandoned child. He grew up to become an accomplished writer and poet, widely regarded as the most important writer of the Avadhi eastern dialect

Hindi. His great work the *Ramcaritmanas* was an enormous retelling of the *Ramayana*, the story of Rama's life, in Hindi. Tulsidas's changes to the original epic, very much a product of his own creative genius, also reflected the social and religious conditions in Varanasi in the second half of the sixteenth century. The new epic preserved the *Ramayana*'s emphasis on duty, moral virtues, and devotion to God. Tulsidas's hero was still the ideal man, the very embodiment of dharma. But at the same time, Tulsidas was keenly aware of the tensions recent history had exposed within the paradigm of dharma: How can intense devotion, so often disruptive to social life, be reconciled with the social morality of Rama?

The Hindi work, which remains enormously popular in stage performances—especially in Ramnagar, Varanasi—exposes the rift between devotion and social order but does not fully or consistently resolve it. Instead it is dramatically explored, even toyed with, in a number of plot relationships. In one of the best-loved scenes, as Philip Lutgendorf explains, the Kshatriya Ram demonstrates his superiority over a haughty Brahmin (Parashuram) by exposing his own true (divine) nature. The Brahmin, who did not respect the boundaries of appropriate behavior, had been on a murderous rampage against Kshatriyas, while the Kshatriya king (Ram) acted calmly and patiently—as a true Brahmin might. The reversal of roles and the humiliation of the Brahmin, when he realizes that Ram is an incarnation of Vishnu, never fail to delight the audiences. The play affirms order (dharma) but at the same time shows that devotion to God supersedes caste markers as the true foundation of society—at least in principle. In other words, dharma is not undermined, but it is invigorated with faith and devotion. Tulsidas places the following words in the mouth of Ram:

> I recognize only one relationship: devotion.
> Caste and lineage, virtue and status,
> wealth, power, family, merit, and intellect—
> a man possessing these, yet without devotion,
> resembles a cloud without water. (*Ramcaritmanas* 3.35.4–6;
> Lutgendorf 1991)

Tulsidas acknowledged the value of social order, unlike some of his famous earlier contemporaries (Kabir, Mirabai). But he also insisted on looking beyond the positive rules of dharma to the basic foundation of social morality.

In the process, Tulsidas had to address the problem of the identity of God. For if Kabir and others could deny that Ram (God) was an incarnation, what do we make of the hero of the *Ramayana* or of Krishna, or any of the other incarnations of Vishnu? What, in fact, is the reasoning behind the polytheistic theology that calls for a visible, even human, manifestation of the divine? The *Ramcaritmanas* provides a complex and equivocal response. In its final form, the epic is launched by Parvati's query to Shiva, asking him to explain why the Supreme Being would become a man who undergoes the trials Ram experienced during his exile. Shiva gives a rote answer but then acknowledges that the mystery is simply too deep.

But in another, much later episode, the matter is taken up more explicitly. A crow named Bhushundi tells Vishnu's bird Garud that he knew Ram when the hero was just an infant. The baby reached out and tried to touch the bird, but when Bhushundi retreated, Ram began to cry. The crow found it bewildering that the Supreme Lord would cry in such a way. As the baby kept lunging at the bird, it flew higher and higher, but Ram was always there, a mere inches from touching the bird. Just as Bhushundi began to feel that he might lose his mind, the baby suddenly opened his mouth and captured the bird. In Ram's mouth, Bhushundi saw all the worlds and all the eons of existence—an awesome revelation. When the baby finally spit him out, Bhushundi asked for the boon of faith. It could only be faith, or bhakti, that bridges the unfathomable gap between the Supreme Being in its transcendent reality (*nirguna*) and the incarnated manifestation (*saguna*), including even the infant Ram.

Tulsidas's *Ramcaritmanas* and his whole life work was a poetic articulation of the mystery and the faith that illuminates it. God and world were both the same and different at the same time, different yet not different. Like Chaitanya, Tulsidas denied neither world nor God but felt that bridging the two required faith above all else.

Against the Grain of Dharma

In the same city of Varanasi, a far more radical approach to God and world, and a more dramatic social upheaval, had emerged from the work of a lowly weaver who may perhaps be the most famous religious figure of the Indo-Islamic centuries.

A popular legend reports that Kabir and Sikander Lodi once met under extraordinary circumstances. Kabir was a low-caste weaver (*julaha*), a member of a caste of Muslim converts. He was despised both by Hindu Brahmins and Muslim leaders (*kazis*) for his unique form of devotion to Ram. They reported him to Sikander, saying that Kabir had abandoned the customs of the Muslims and broken the rules of the Hindus against untouchables. He had scorned the sacred bathing places and even the Vedas (*Kabir Parachai* 7.2). The sultan summoned the lowly weaver and demanded a show of respect, but Kabir refused to bow before him. Facing the charge that he had abandoned the traditional religion of both Hindus and Muslims, Kabir replied: "The Hindus and the Turks are the ones who will fall into hell. The kazis and the mullahs are clumsy fools. I have found salvation through *bhakti*. I have sung about the virtues of Ram through the guru's grace" (7.15; Lorenzen 1991). Thanks to the protection of Ram, he added, no one could kill him.

Both Hindus and Muslims were enraged by this blustery testimony. They demanded that the king stone the infidel, but instead Sikander had Kabir chained and thrown into the Ganges. Miraculously, the chains fell off as soon as Kabir hit the water, and he floated away to safety. Next the king threw the weaver into a burning house, but the flames became as cool as water. Finally, a wild elephant was set on Kabir, but God (Hari) took the form of a lion, who frightened the elephant. The sultan admitted defeat: "Kabir, your Ram is the true God. Just this once, please save my life. The kazis and the mullahs do not understand the inner truth. The Creator has accepted your word" (*Kabir Parachai* 9.3; Lorenzen 1991).

Indian historians such as Mohan Singh and Parashuram Chaturvedi have argued that the likely dates of Kabir and Sikander cannot possibly place the two together. The failed execution is simply Hindu hagiography, one of the central episodes in a theologically constructed narrative of the charismatic poet's life.

But even on this level, the story surprises. The weaver, who was a Muslim, found himself persecuted by Brahmins for violating the rules of caste and purity, defying the gods, and scorning all the sacred rituals of Hinduism. Why should they have cared, and who was Kabir, if legend claims that both Muslims and Hindus wanted him dead? What kind of a cultural niche was there in Varanasi in the fifteenth century in between the two major religions?

From where we stand today, Kabir's life is a patchwork of legends and bits of biographical information gleaned from his own songs. The scanty autobiographical clues can be gathered from such works as the Sikh scripture the *Adi Granth* (often called *Guru Granth*) or the *Bhaktamal* (Garland of saints) of Nabhaji. Most of the legends come from works that have been venerated by the followers of Kabir (Kabir Panthis), *Kabir-kasanti* and *Kabir-caritra*, or Anantadas's *Kabir Parachai*.

The core of Kabir's life is more or less simple. He was born to a family of *julahas*—a weaver caste whose members had converted wholesale to Islam and dominated sari-making in the region of Varanasi, as they still do today. He was probably born in Magahar, a ramshackle town occupied by members of the Dom tribe, as well as Buddhists and Muslims. It was close enough to Varanasi to be ridiculed as the antithesis of the holy city. Kabir spent most of his adult life in Varanasi, where he had a family, including at least one son, whose name was Kamal. The weavers were only nominally Islamicized, and Kabir was a Vaishnava who worshiped and wrote songs to God as Ram. He lived during the first half of the fifteenth century, when the Sharqi Sultans were ruling in Jaunpur and controlled Varanasi, although the local autonomous ruler was a Hindu raja named Virasimha Baghel. Kabir probably died back in his hometown of Magahar and may have been buried there, against the reigning Hindu values of Varanasi, where people went to die and be cremated on the banks of the Ganges. In Kabir's own sardonic words (*Guru Granth*, gauri 15.2; Vaudeville 1997):

My whole life I have wasted in Kashi
But, at the time of death, I have risen and come to Magahar.

The body of legends that grew around this man completely defies these modest facts. While the hagiography may bear some relationship to the writings and thoughts of Kabir, the overall trajectory of the confabulation reflects back on the people who told and enjoyed the stories and on their own times. For example, the story of Sikander's failed persecution of Kabir points to a time centuries later when a late Mughal ruler, Aurangzeb, persecuted Hindus. (Sikander was a descendant of Turks, a sultan, while the Mughals descended from Mongols.) It was then, in the eighteenth century, toward the very end of Islamic rule in India, that Vaishnava hagiography developed a strong anti-Muslim flavor. The mythically constructed life of the weaver is thus an exercise in wishful anachronism and a gold mine for cultural historians interested in the coexistence of Islam and devotional Hinduism.

The unifying theme of the legends is the story of an undistinguished low-caste man who repeatedly confronts superior adversaries such as a Muslim king, the narrow-minded Brahmins, or even a great Vaishnava guru who refused to teach him. Kabir overcomes the obstacles through cunning, magic, or the help of God—whatever works. The stories combine the mythical theme of the hero's journey (like Buddha's or Rama's) but spills into more modern lessons (and moods) about the irresistible power of stubbornness and the nobility of an iconoclastic personality.

The cycle of stories usually begins with the great Vaishnava teacher Ramananda, who refused to teach a lowly Muslim weaver. Kabir had received a vision from God, who told him to mark himself as a Vaishnava and seek out that teacher for initiation. Obeying the voice of God, Kabir lay down beneath a step in a dark alley where Ramananda was sure to pass on his way to an evening dip in the Ganges. When the great man tripped over Kabir in the dark he muttered "Ram," thus giving Kabir his initiatory mantra.

Several legends tell of mundane but vexing tests Kabir had to pass—a coterie of hungry Varanasi Brahmins congregating at the poor weaver's house and demanding to be fed, or falsely advertising a feast and attracting hundreds of hungry visitors. The stories usually depict Kabir running away and hiding somewhere in the city while God (Hari) supplies the food, disguised as the lowly host himself. The hagiographical accounts explain that as Kabir's fame grew throughout the city he looked for ways to regain his anonymity, even at the price of setting himself up for ridicule. One legend describes Kabir walking hand in hand with a known prostitute through the streets of Varanasi while holding a jar of water, which he pretended was liquor. Just as he had hoped, people immediately forgot their admiration for him as they responded with verbal abuse and insults. Even the local raja, who had been a great admirer, lost his respect for the weaver. But suddenly, the narrative continues, in the presence of the raja, Kabir poured the liquid from the jar onto his own feet, and explained to the surprised king that this was to save a priest in the Puri Jagannath temple hundreds of miles away from scalding his feet. Naturally, the raja sent men to inspect the matter, and indeed they discovered that the distant priest had, at that very moment, spilled boiling rice water on his feet but was miraculously saved from a severe burn.

The final and most famous legend of Kabir describes him choosing to die in Magahar. Popular tradition held that those who died in Kashi attained salvation, while those who died in Magahar were reborn as donkeys. As if to spite the belief, Kabir opted to die in the polluted town, singing:

> You say that he who dies at Magahar
> will become a donkey.
> Have you lost faith in Ram?
> If Ram dwells in my heart,
> What is Kashi? What is the barren
> ground of Magahar?
> If Kabir leaves this body in Kashi,
> What debt is owed to Ram? (*Kabir Bijak* 103; Lorenzen 1991)

Legends claimed that the Hindus and Muslims argued over Kabir's body, whether to cremate it in Varanasi or bury it in Magahar. But the body disappeared under 32 loads of flowers that had been placed over it. In heaven Shiva and Brahma themselves came to greet Kabir, and Indra even offered him the royal throne of the gods. Vishnu said: "Heaven is yours. Live here forever."

Cultural Background

Varanasi at the time of Kabir was a true microcosm of the North Indian religious scene. Despite the rule of Muslims, now more than two centuries old, the entire region was a dynamic mix of dozens of distinct religions, sectarian groups, and subgroups, both Hindu and Muslim. In Varanasi alone, one could see long-haired or shaved ascetics, naked or saffron-robed, ash-covered, bearded with matted hair, wearing the insignia of Vishnu or Shiva. Many were Tantra practitioners, Gorakhnathis, Kapalikas, Nagas, Nimbarkis, Madhvis, and many others. Amid all of these, the city was still dominated by Smartas, including the priests of the main temples (e.g. Vishvanatha), who followed the traditional *smriti*-based Hinduism of the dharma texts.

One of the most charismatic figures, who may or may not have been a true teacher to Kabir, was Ramanand, a high-caste Brahmin who had trained in the lineage of theologians going back to Ramanuja, the Vedanta critic of Shankara. Ramananda was a disciple of Raghavananda, the fourth teacher in the line, but he veered off and established own more liberal tradition. His followers rejected both the revelation of the central scriptures (Vedas, Puranas) and the sanctity of temple worship. In his own words:

> Wherever I go, I find but water and stones,
> But Thou art contained in full in everything (*Guru Granth*,
>   basant 1; Vaudeville 1997, p. 88)

God was worshiped as Ram, along with his wife, Sita, who represented *maya*—the manifest dynamic aspect of God in the world. Worship consisted mainly of a meditative, intentional repetition of God's name (*ramanama*) in a practice called *japa*: chanting of the divine syllables *ra-ma*. Ramanand was also a strict practitioner of Hatha Yoga.

Hatha Yoga as a systematic discipline owes its origin to Gorakhnath, a North Indian mystic who lived sometime between the ninth and twelfth centuries. Tradition places Gorakhnath as the third in the line of a new religion, usually called Nath Yoga. The first teacher (*nath*) was the god Shiva himself, and the second was Macchendra (or Matsyendra). But it was Gorakhnath who developed the systematic practice (called *sadhana*) that effectively translated esoteric Tantric techniques (of Mahayana Buddhist origins) into practices for popular and colloquial consumption. By the time of Kabir, the Naths or the "Jogis," as many of them were often called, were almost ubiquitous in Varanasi. They rejected the Hindu caste hierarchy and the ideology of dharma that justified the caste system, especially the rules of purity. Like the Ramanandis (followers of Ramananda), they rejected the revelation of Veda and Purana: their one God was Parama (Supreme) Shiva, and many of them were married men with families.

Still, the dominant ethos of Nath Yoga was rather puritanical, and most practitioners frowned on sexual activity even within marriage. They also abstained from eating meat and drinking alcohol, though the language of intoxication is a powerful symbolic tool in their religious writings. It usually refers to *amrita*, "the elixir," the ancient Tantric symbol of universal essence.

While the followers of Gorakhnath adopted from Tantra the veneration of the guru as the true spiritual guide, they maintained a complex attitude. On the popular level, gurus were worshiped in shrines as quasi-divine beings. But at more rarefied levels, it was the Sat-guru who was venerated. This term referred not to a human teacher but to Absolute Reality itself, the ground of all being, which resonated deeply within the practitioner's own consciousness. True instruction came from introspection, and the insight gained was often considered guru-less (*nir-guru*). The true adept could report hearing an inner sound (*shabda*), which was true revelation, without the stamp of authority tied to human transmission. This was an extraordinary development in the emergence of spiritual autonomy, religious introspection, even a sacred individualism.

These qualities were particularly evident in Kabir and the other Sants (roughly, "Saints") of northern India in the fifteenth and sixteenth centuries. The Sants were highly devotional lay mystics who often wrote poetry or sang to God in a nonsectarian manner. As noted, they were usually low-caste Hindus, though there were a few Muslims and women as well, and they never formed coherent religious organizations or doctrinal chains of authority based on the guru-disciple relationship. Namdev, Sena, Sadhan, Ravidas, and Pipa are some of the better-known low-caste Sants. The biographies of these and other Sants were recorded, with loving exaggeration, by writers who lived a short time later, including Nabhadas, Raghavdas, and Anandadas.

Finally, by the time Kabir was weaving saris in Varanasi, the entire region was inundated with both popular and elevated Islamic ideas and practices. Islam had been spreading for centuries in northern India. It took place by means not of the classical languages (Arabic, Persian on one side, Sanskrit on the other) but local vernacular languages such as Punjabi, Multani, Sindhi, Kachchi, and Gujarati and, in the Jaunpur region, Avadhi, Bhojpuri, and Hindustani or Hindi. On a popular level, the more effective exchange of ideas took place when central Hindu doctrines and myths were carried across into Islamic idioms. For instance, the last *avatara* (incarnation) of Vishnu, Kalki, was identified with Ali, who was the Shiite *imam*—the future messianic savior. Similarly, Shakti or Sarasvati was identified with Fatima, the daughter of

Muhammad. Much of this popular process depended on the efforts of Sufi masters (*shaykhs, pirs*), who were the recognized equivalents of Hindu gurus. Sufism was particularly influential in the way it combined monotheism and spiritual disciplines (chanting, meditations, songs), which resonated closely with Nath Yoga. Muslim vocabulary, in fact, was everywhere. Although the *julahas* (weavers) were only superficially Islamicized, they spoke of *kazis, hajj, pir* worship, *dhikr* chantings, and *khutab* (God) even as they worshiped Ram.

Knowledge and Identity

Kabir was an eclectic mystic who borrowed images, ideas, and probably even experiences from several Hindu traditions, from Islam and Buddhism (including the idea of Shunya of Nagarjuna). But his songs are finally simple, pointing to a personal experience of utter simplicity, which defies theological description. Like *moksha, kaivalya* (of Yoga), or *nirvana*, Kabir insisted, this experience was an unconditioned state that had to emerge spontaneously. He called it *sahaja*, referring to that which emerges together (*saha*)—the subject and object, transcendent and immanent reality—"I and Thou," if you will. One cannot bring it about; it is never the effect of some cause. In truth, even the name defies definition because of the reality behind it (*Kabir Granthavali* 16.1; Hawley and Juergensmeyer):

> The instrument is still,
> Its string snapped.
> What can the poor thing do?
> Its player's no longer there.

Still, the most profound significance of Kabir (or Ravidas) and other poets of this movement was the new prominence of caste- and class-consciousness, the emergence of individual identity as a social fact and moral problem. Paradoxically, this new form of awareness was also the source of the distortion that pitted Hinduism and Islam against each other as absolute and hostile categories. In fact, the same Sikander Lodi who is portrayed so villainously in the Kabir hagiography was a renowned sponsor of the sciences and a determined empiricist and rationalist. And the schools (*madrasas*) established by several Muslim rulers not only provided excellent scientific education but also acted as springboards for social mobility among the low castes of Hinduism. The Arab traveler and chronicler Ibn-Babuta recognized in his accounts of India a low-caste barber called Ratan who became a first-rate mathematician and was appointed by Mohammad bin Tughlaq as the *wali* (governor) of Sind.

Contemporary historians of Indian science are far more likely to focus on the mutually reinforcing influences of Indian and Islamic (and indirectly Greek) sciences than on political or theological tensions. Mathematics, grammar and language, logic came from the traditional Hindu sources. Newer sciences such as physics and optics, geography, geology, zoology, botany, and other empirical fields came from the West with Muslim scientists. Other fields, including medicine and astronomy, not to mention theology, were more equally distributed, producing deeper cultural syntheses.

Such a historiography has other heroes besides Kabir. For example, Amir Khusro (d. 1325), the fourteenth-century poet, riddler, and possible inventor of the sitar, was a Sufi practitioner—a committed Muslim—and an accomplished scientist in astronomy, mathematics, astrology, and history of science. His observations of Indian learning included the following: "Knowledge and learning of the Hindus, concealed wisdom, and learned ideas in India were beyond calculation. Greece was famous for its achievements in philosophy, but India was also not devoid of it. Here logic, astronomy and dogmatic theology could be learnt easily" (quoted in Rahman 1999, 27). Criticized by other Muslims for his admiration of Indian culture, Khusro wrote (quoted in Rahman 1999, 27):

> Rightly speaking I am an Indian bird
> Ask of me Hindvi [Hindi] that I may sing in it.

For writers like Khusro, in the light of scientific knowledge, the boundary between Hindu and Muslim dissolves, and what remains is simply India. Khusro remains influential today; in both India and Pakistan, his devotional Sufi songs (*qawwalis*) are enormously popular.

12

The Eternal Dharma

The end of Islamic rule in India led to a period of foreign domination—indisputably alien—by the British colonialists. No single date marks the exact transition, because British commercial and political influence had been growing over a period of decades under the patronage of local Muslim rulers. But the defeat of Siraj-ud-daulah in 1757 by a meager force led by Lieutenant Colonel Robert Clive did mark a notable turning point. Subsequently, the British East India Company transformed itself from a largely commercial enterprise into a governing one, first in northeast India (Bengal), then elsewhere. Over the next two centuries, until India's independence in 1947, the British rule became increasingly pervasive and deeply entrenched, until the relationship between colonizer and colony became virtually symbiotic—one body feeding off the other.

A century after Clive's victory, in 1857, the sepoys (the Indians serving in the colonial army) mutinied. They were crushed, and the British government responded by transferring official power from the Company to the throne. India became an administrative territory of imperial rule—the best one, the "jewel in the crown." In 1877, Queen Victoria was proclaimed empress of India.

The British rule (Raj), like earlier foreign hegemonies in India, presented a serious challenge for Hinduism, with consequences that persist today. Although the British seldom hounded those who refused to convert—they were in the business of making money, after all—still, colonialism in general exerted a pervasive and overwhelming pressure on traditional worldviews. The proliferation of missionary schools, the importation of legal concepts and institutions, the dissemination of English as the language of official India, the promotion of Western knowledge, taste, and manners as a condition for economic advancement were just some of the forces that worked against traditional Hindu beliefs and norms.

Since the early decades of the nineteenth century, numerous figures, deeply influenced by European ideas but working against British domination, have performed actions that have made them worthy of being considered founding fathers of modern India. Rammohun Roy, Debendranath Tagore and his even more famous son Rabindranath, Keshub Chandra Sen, Vivekananda, Aurobindo Ghose, Mohandas K. Gandhi, and Jawaharlal Nehru represent only a few of these men, who carried out their missions in a period of explosive creativity. This chapter will focus on three—Rammohun Roy, Mohandas K. Gandhi, and Aurobindo Ghose. Along with the political and intellectual achievements of these men came a profound loss that seldom receives attention: an increasing refusal to accept the pluralistic nature of Hinduism, its philosophies and theologies. The birth of a single political nation (before partition) seemed to require the flattening of an enormous world into a single, albeit eternal, dharma. This chapter will look at this development.

The Birth of National Hinduism

Under Lord Cornwallis's Permanent Settlement (1793), the British shifted the economic and property rights in Bengal in a way that established rent collection rights for rural landlords within Company administration. The idea of encouraging the growth of a strong moneyed middle class, or small gentry, resulted in strengthening the high castes that had previously depended on the local rajas and *zamindars* for support. This new class was set up to supply the British rulers in Bengal with Western-educated bureaucratic and midlevel government personnel. This class was also the economic backbone of a new intelligentsia within the more urban areas.

By the middle of the nineteenth century, the city of Calcutta was beginning to benefit from the injection of capital into institutions that focused on the collection and dissemination of scientific and cultural knowledge on behalf of the empire. During the middle decades of the nineteenth century, Calcutta saw the construction of the Indian Museum, with its collections of archaeology and natural history. On the same grounds soon followed the Geological Survey and a school of art, and the Asiatic Society—already a veteran institution—was situated nearby. All of these institutions of knowledge were built near the key colonial government buildings (Government House, the Treasury Building, the headquarters of the commissioner of police), closely allying colonial power with the newly emerging disciplines of colonial knowledge.

But the colonial government was not interested only in new economic, administrative, and intellectual initiatives. Among the more ambitious designs of that energetic age was a new missionary project as well. In 1835, Thomas Babington Macaulay, with the governmental aid of Governor General Lord Bentinct, ended the old style of doing missionary work in India—the so-called Orientalist approach. Macaulay's "Minute on Indian Education" advocated the universal use of English and a frontal assault on Hinduism. Though he was a secularist himself, the implication of Macaulay's statement was a comprehensive reevaluation of the cultural encounter between the West and India. The British Orientalist movement, which had previously sponsored the study and use of classical and regional Indian languages as a matter of intellectual interest and missionary strategy, now expired.

A new missionary triumphalism emerged, especially in the person of Alexander Duff (1806–78), a Scottish Presbyterian missionary who worked in Bengal for almost thirty years. Duff launched an aggressive and effective campaign to convert prominent Bengali intellectuals in a top-down approach to spreading Christianity. Among his most prominent converts were Michael Madhusudan Dutt, Krishna Mohun Banerji, and Mohesh Chandra Ghose.

In response to Duff's frontal assaults on Hinduism, including attacks on the rarefied philosophy of Vedanta, Bengali intellectuals began to speak out. The leading voices among them were Debendranath Tagore and later Keshub Chandra Sen. In the process, Hinduism began to take shape as a modern phenomenon with what appeared to be an essential core and a national flavor. Interestingly, both the missionary criticism and the Bengali responses resurrected the work of a man who had been nearly forgotten and now was suddenly hailed as the "Father" of modern India—Rammohun Roy.

Rammohun Roy was born in 1772 in Radhanagar (Bengal) to a gentry family that would later benefit from the Permanent Settlement and acquire very handsome land rents. He died in 1833, while visiting England (Bristol). During his relatively short life, he mastered several languages, including Persian, Arabic, Sanskrit, and English. He became deeply conversant in Islamic philosophy even before he began his studies of Vedanta. His first surviving work, *Tuhfat-ul-Muwahhiddin* (A gift to monotheists) was written in Persian and demonstrates a commitment to a universal and uncompromising Semitic-style monotheism. Roy's philosophical interests subsequently turned to the Upanishads—he translated several and wrote introductory commentaries on their monistic philosophy. He wrote several essays devoted to Shankara's

Advaita Vedanta. Roy's studies in European thought, including utilitarian ethics and Unitarian theology, began only after he moved to Calcutta and mastered English.

Although Roy is most often remembered in connection with his work on social reform, especially the abolition of Sati (widow burning) in the late 1820s, that was not the true source of his importance in shaping modern Hinduism. Nor was this the reason Debendranath Tagore resurrected Roy's name two decades later as the father of Hindu nationalism. Rather, it was the way he had combined skillful Vedanta interpretation with an emerging national consciousness in order to undermine Western religious and cultural hegemony. The corpus of writings he left behind, often written under a pseudonym, was split between sharply polemical and dispassionate essays. Both were intellectually impressive. The following samples illustrate Roy's approach to theological debates along with his unique style. The centerpiece of Roy's polemic was the idea that Hinduism spoke with a single voice, which was unambiguous and monotheistic:

> And also the Vedanta asserts, in the 1st text of 3d sec. of the 3d chap.: "The worship authorized by all the Veds is one, as the directions for the worship of the only Supreme Being are invariably found in the Ved, and the epithets of the Supreme and Omnipresent Being, &c. commonly imply God alone." ("A Defence of Hindoo Theism"; Robertson, p. 73)

The clearest statement of this monotheism can be found in the Upanishads that Roy had translated. The practical implications of monotheistic belief are also spelled out there:

> In the introduction of the *Cenopanishad*: "This work will, I trust by explaining to my countrymen the real spirit of the Hindoo scriptures, which is but the declaration of the unity of God, tend in a great degree to correct the erroneous conceptions which have prevailed with regard to the doctrines they inculcate;" and in the Preface of the *Ishopanished*: "Many learned Brahmins are perfectly aware of the absurdity of idol worship, and are well informed of the nature of the pure mode of divine worship." ("A Defence of Hindoo Theism"; Robertson, p. 70)

One would be hard pressed to deny that Hinduism gave the appearance of polytheism and the worship of images ("idol worship"), but Roy provided a reasonable explanation for this:

In that work, I admitted that the worship of these deities was directed by the Shastra; but, at the same time, I proved by their own authority, that this was merely a concession made to the limited faculties of the vulgar, with the view of remedying, in some degree, the misfortune of their being incapable of comprehending and adopting the spiritual worship of the true God. ("A Second Defence of the Monotheistical System of the Veds"; Robertson, p. 84)

Roy acknowledged that Christians were likely to ignore these social considerations behind Hindu theology and philosophy. But if Christians choose to ignore the best in Hindu thought, so might Hindus do the same regarding Christianity:

A Hindoo would also be justified in taking as standard of Christianity the system of religion which almost universally prevailed in Europe previous to the 15th Century . . . and which is still followed by the majority of Christians with all its idols, crucifixes, saints, miracle, pecuniary absolutions from sin, trinity, transubstantiation, relics, holy water, and other idolatrous machinery. ("A Reprint of a Controversy between Dr. Tytler and Ramdoss"; Kopf, p. 27)

But other Christian critics of Hinduism knew that Vedanta was the best of Hinduism and that this lofty philosophical tradition should be the proper target of attack. They argued that the metaphysics of the Upanishads and of Shankara resulted in a deep indifference to the ills of the world. Vedanta resulted in a kind of spiritual escapism; it was, in fact, amoral. Roy attacked such claims head-on:

In the abridgment of the Vedant, page 11th: "The Vedant shews that moral principle is a part of the adoration of God, viz. a command over passions and over the external senses of the body, and good acts are declared by the Ved to be indispensable in the mind's approximation to God." ("A Second Defence of the Monotheistical System of the Veds"; Robertson, p. 81–82)

In fact, in his famous response to Dr. Tytler's attacks on Hinduism, Roy argued that it was Christianity itself that was morally inferior:

The sin which mankind contracts against God by the Practice of wickedness is believed by us to be expiated by these penances, and not as supposed by the Queriest [Tytler], by the blood of a son of man or son of God, who never participated in our transgressions. ("A Reprint of a Controversy between Dr. Tytler and Ramdoss"; Kopf, p. 27)

Whether debating missionaries or writing learned commentaries on the Upanishads, Roy remained perfectly consistent. He crafted a charter for a new national Hinduism of near-Hebraic simplicity: God was one; worship of the one true God was essentially moral; polytheism and ritualistic idol worship were degenerate, though necessary, concessions to popular religious thought; the texts (Puranas and Shastras) that prescribed these forms of Hinduism took social realities into account, while ultimate scriptural truth had to be sought in the Vedanta. The charter of the Brahmo Samaj, Roy's institutional brainchild, insisted on these clearly articulated ideals:

> And that no graven image, statue, or sculpture, carving, painting, picture, portrait, or the likeness of anything, shall be admitted within said message, &c.; and that no sacrifice, offering, or oblation of any kind or thing shall ever be permitted therein and that no animal or living creature shall within, or on the said message, &c. be deprived of life, either for religious purposes or for food. ("The Trust Deed of the Brahma Samaj"; Robertson, p. 105)

These ideas and the institutions that developed and spread them in Bengal (Brahmo Samaj, Tattvabodhini Sabha) served Tagore and Keshub Chandra Sen extremely well in the war over minds in Bengal during the middle and later decades of the nineteenth century. Such ideas fostered the impression of a doctrinal unity within Hinduism that centered on the Vedanta. They also neutralized the polemical value to the missionaries of popular Hindu devotions. But these rarefied debates were confined to the press-reading Bengali intelligentsia. National Hinduism as a popular phenomenon would have to wait until Gandhi continued to popularize some of these ideas.

Gandhi's Life

Mohandas Karamchand Gandhi was born in Porbandar (Gujarat) in 1869 to a Vaishya family of Vishnu devotees. His father, Karamchand Gandhi, was a high-ranking local official, while his mother, Putlibai, was an extremely devout woman, a follower of Vallabhacharya. The boy was married off in 1883 to Kasturba, who was also thirteen years old at the time. The youthful marriage and the consuming sexual passion it triggered became one of the central concerns of Gandhi's later life, as he wrote an autobiography with which he sought to cleanse himself by means of merciless truthfulness.

In 1888, Gandhi began studying law in England, where he experimented both with the lifestyle of a Western gentleman and with a vegetarianism that became a consuming personal philosophy. His intellectual horizons in England far exceeded the study of law, as he opened up to a combination of Christian and Indian influences. He read and admired the New Testament and Tolstoy, but also the *Bhagavad Gita* (in the English translation of Sir Edwin Arnold), the life and teachings of Buddha, and the Gujarati poetry of Shamal Bhatt.

Gandhi's first position after becoming a barrister was in South Africa in 1893. By that time, he had already developed a strong sense of identity as an Indian gentleman, which landed him in almost immediate trouble. Gandhi had to leave a courtroom for refusing to remove his turban and, shortly after that, was thrown off the Durban-Pretoria train for taking a seat in a first-class car, reserved for whites only. He thus arrived at his first political and ideological campaign by realizing that he was not a white gentleman in racist South Africa. But personal insult soon gave way to early political struggles, which allowed him to refine a unique blend of political savvy and ironclad ethical principles. These eventually developed into his political strategy of "passive resistance" or *satyagraha* ("the seizing of truth").

In 1915, Gandhi returned to India, already famous for having developed an enormously successful and nonviolent political-social movement. He took his time before entering Indian politics and launching his campaign against the British colonial rule. As B. G. Tilak and Annie Besant dominated Indian politics, Gandhi concentrated his own efforts on social issues and on sustaining the ashram (religious community) he had established near Ahmedabad. Only in 1919, after the passage of the Rowlatt Bill (highly invasive "antisedition" laws) did Gandhi finally commence his *satyagraha* campaign in India.

The year 1919 is infamous in the annals of British colonial rule as the year of the Amritsar massacre. A force led by General Dyer gunned down four hundred men, women, and children, injuring over one thousand additional civilians, all unarmed. Gandhi organized an extremely broad coalition of participants in his insistently nonviolent campaign. He invited the Muslims of India to join it, securing their cooperation (for a while) through his own support of the Khilafat. Only a disciplined and effectively top-down approach could sustain the nonviolence of Gandhi's efforts. In time, his goals began to crystallize as a nonviolent noncooperation with the British-dominated economy and taxation system.

Over the next quarter century, after staking a position at the center of Indian resistance and politics in 1920, Gandhi experienced numerous triumphs and an equal number of disappointments. He spent years in British prisons, underwent a number of life-threatening fasts, and witnessed some of the worst communal riots in India's history. His most satisfying political moment may have been the salt march from Sabarmati to Dandi that protested the British salt tax in 1930. With its enormous publicity and effective nonviolent execution, the march exposed British economic exploitation and moral bankruptcy. And Gandhi's worst moment was undoubtedly the failure to maintain India's integrity when the British partitioned it and created Pakistan in 1947 as a new homeland for the substantial Indian Muslim minority.

On January 30, 1948, Gandhi was assassinated by a Hindu extremist from Poona, a member of a group who could not tolerate Gandhi's empathy for Muslims. He died with the name of God on his lips, as he had always wished.

Gandhi's Religious Thought

Gandhi always measured his own success not only by the expedience of his methods or his influence on the British or other Indian politicians but also by the purity and tenacity of his principles. Although he produced a voluminous corpus of writings—his collected works occupy a whole library shelf—his thinking reveals a surprising consistency about the basic ideas. And despite the fact that Gandhi addressed a large number of issues, including the politics of resistance, social injustice, family relationships, religion, work, even hygiene and diet, the underlying unity is not hard to detect. At the root of Gandhian thought was the philosophy and ethics of Advaita Vedanta.

I have already discussed Advaita Vedanta in the context of the texts of the Upanishads, the philosophy of Shankara, the poetry of Kabir, and the writings of Rammohun Roy. According to these sources, reality is ultimately one only— Brahman (or atman). It may have the appearance of multiplicity, but this is due to a perceptual error that owes its origins to mental habits formed by desire and aversion. Even the gods of the Vedic pantheon and the Puranas are mere appearances, the faces that cover the reality of One Being only.

As noted, Gandhi grew up in a household of Vishnu or, more precisely, Ram worshipers. Bhakti, or devotion, was the primary way of relating to the divine. This included emotional commitment, the chanting of the name of God (*ramanama*), offerings (*puja*), fasts (*vratas*) and other vows. But Gandhi professed to be a monist, like Shankara, for whom bhakti was only useful up to a point. Devotion ultimately rested on an intellectual failure to realize the true and utterly transcendent nature of ultimate reality:

> Brahma[n] alone is real; all else is non-existent. (Gandhi 1971, 14:97)

> Hindus, Muslims, Christians and others have employed innumerable epithets to describe God, but they are all products of our imagination.

God is without attributes and beyond all qualifications. (Gandhi 1971, 30:388)

But this was not only, or primarily, an intellectual problem. It led to moral failings, which for Gandhi were always most important. As a result, he did not shrink from leveling devastating critiques at the pervasive religious approach of devotion that dominated Hinduism:

> The popular notion of *bhakti* is soft-heartedness, telling beads and the like, and disdaining to do even a loving service, lest the telling of beads etc. might be interrupted. This *bhakti*, therefore, leaves the rosary only for eating, drinking and the like, never for grinding corn or nursing patients. (Gandhi 1971, 41:96)

Gandhi read the *Bhagavad Gita*, one of the earliest and probably the most sacred of bhakti texts, in a way that underemphasized devotion. Of the three disciplines or paths (*yogas*) the text promoted, bhakti was the least, he said. Karma, which he interpreted as social action (rather than the customary rituals) was higher than devotion, and *jnana*, or spiritual insight, was highest. It is insight that allows one to see that reality is ultimately one, and to develop the foundational principle of social ethics based on this insight, namely noninjury (*ahimsa*).

Gandhi is probably most famous in the West for his political philosophy and its reliance on nonviolent means. But Gandhi's concept of *ahimsa* was far broader than a political method. In other words, he was fully conscious of the difference between policy and what we might call creed, identifying the latter with Truth. Nonviolence depended on the recognition of the truth—he called it *sat* (Being)—of monistic philosophy; the political (and social) implications of nonviolence were merely derivative. He made this clear in his autobiography, to which he gave the subtitle "The Story of My Experiments with Truth":

> My uniform experience has convinced me that there is no other God than Truth. And if every page of these chapters does not proclaim to the reader that the only means for the realization of Truth is ahimsa, I shall deem all my labour in writing these chapters to have been in vain. . . . [A] perfect vision of Truth can only follow a complete realization of Ahimsa. To see the universal and all-pervading Spirit of Truth face to face, one must be able to love the meanest of creation as oneself. (Gandhi 1965, 39:401–402)

Clearly, Truth (*sat*) is an ontological concept, a synonym for Brahman, which is the unity of existence. This is not only an abstract metaphysical concept; it is an ethical one—the realization of the unity among all beings that precludes vio-lence as a means of acting in any context. The implications for the social hierarchy of the caste system are sweeping. Just as Kabir, whom Gandhi ad-mired and whose poetry he translated, rejected caste and sectarian distinctions, Gandhi also applied his religious convictions toward social equality: "In my opinion there is no such thing as inherited or acquired superiority. I believe in the rock-bottom doctrine of Advaita and my interpretation of Advaita excludes totally any idea of superiority at any stage whatsoever" (Gandhi 1971, 35:1). Gandhi's famous work on behalf of India's untouchables, whom he called Harijans (Children of God) and his empathy toward the Muslim minority derived from this monistic ethos. Gandhi paid the ultimate price for his con-victions in this area, but he also threw his own body into a battlefield in which metaphysics and social principles joined. His well-known fasts, some of them "unto death," represent perhaps the most reliable demonstration of the way Advaita philosophy acted as a moral tool.

Gandhi sometimes fasted for penitential reasons or for spiritual purifica-tion, as his mother had done throughout his childhood. But many of his fasts, for instance those in Bombay in 1921, Delhi in 1924, and in Calcutta 1947, were communal events. Such events were usually responses to violence or the loss of discipline within his community of followers and were designed to reimpose the higher values. In a sense, these fasts were highly refined acts of moral blackmail. "Nor is it against those of my countrymen who have no faith in me . . . but it is against those countless Indians . . . who believe that I represent a just cause. Above all it is intended to sting Hindu conscience into right religious action" (Tendulkar,1951–54 3:164). The concept of the fast, like the *vratas* of ancient and modern India, recognizes a bond that holds a community together. But while wives and sisters who perform *vratas* for their male relatives are engaging in a participative rationality (see chapter 8), Gandhi's reasoning re-flects a different principle. This is the moral co-dependence of a community based on the unity of *sat*, in which members care for each other and are shamed by their own failure to live up to their own standards. If Gandhi had not been a moral monist, he would not have expected his fasts to persuade.

A Second Perspective

In India, Gandhi has been known as much for his failures as for his success, for his opponents as much as his supporters. British colonialist detractors, in-cluding Winston Churchill, used racist epithets to describe his physical ap-pearance. Critics on the socialist side of the political spectrum, including

Ambedkar, criticized him for downplaying the crisis of untouchability while critics on the nationalist right attacked him for his sympathies to Muslims. It was the latter who finally took his life. Far less known outside of India was a sharp criticism that came from the very heart of the Hindu mainstream and that questioned both the philosophical core of Gandhi's thought and his political effectiveness. This was particularly true in Bengal, the intellectual home of Hindu nationalism and one of the places that suffered most from the partition of India. For instance, the renowned Bengali historian R. C. Majumdar reported an interview between P. B. Chakravarty and the British prime minister, Anthony Eden, in 1956, in which Eden confirmed that Gandhi's influence on the British decision to leave was minimal. In fact, the extremist Subhas Chandra Bose caused a far greater attrition of the British colonial resources and will in the aftermath of the exhausting world war.

But more interesting was the criticism that challenged the spiritual basis of Gandhi's central teaching, namely nonviolence, and it came from the sharp pen of Aurobindo Ghose:

> Gandhi's theories are like other mental theories built on a basis of one-sided reasoning and claiming for a limited truth (that of nonviolence and passive resistance) a universality which it cannot have. Such theories will always exist so long as the mind is the main instrument of human truth-seeking. (quoted in Coward, p. 88)

In other words, nonviolence as an intellectual ideal collapses the moral complexity of reality into a single dimension. Other aspects, such as justifiable violence, are equally valid in the context of a struggle for political freedom: "The attempt at self-government by self-help is absolutely necessary for our national salvation, whether we carry it to the end peacefully or not" (Heehs, p. 15).

What is surprising about Aurobindo's arguments against Gandhi's nonviolence is his insistence that Gandhi's failures were spiritual: a limited perspective in Yoga, a shallow level of meditative experience, and a mistaken interpretation of his own religious tradition, including a misreading of the *Bhagavad Gita*.

Aurobindo's Biography

Aurobindo Ghose, like Gandhi, lived his life as the subject of an alien empire. Born in 1872 in Calcutta, at age seven Aurobindo was shipped off by his father to England. The goal of preparing one's child for the life of a civil servant under the Crown required, in the mind of many upper-class urban Indians, the meticulous formation of a Western gentleman. Greek, Latin, Christian education, English literature—the whole of Western civilization (leading of course to its peak in England), had to be reprised in 10 intense years before the young Aurobindo could face his civil service exams. In 1893, having chosen to fail the horse-riding component of the examination, Aurobindo returned to India. At 21, he was an accomplished young scholar of classical and English subjects, but no civil servant.

The middle years of Aurobindo's life reveal why he could never have been a productive member of the Indian Civil Service. Although he accepted a position with the maharaja of Baroda, he moved from post to post with relative haste; he taught French and English, edited journals, ran (as principal) the Bengal National College, and held a series of other jobs. The frequent change was not so much a matter of a restless temperament as the product of political circumstances and Aurobindo's uncompromising—some would say headstrong—loyalty to a vigorous antiimperial stance. The publications to which he often contributed—*Indu Prakash, Bande Mataram, Karmayogin,* and others—put him at loggerheads not only with the British but with more influential Indian leaders who rejected what they considered his extremism. This was particularly true for the leaders of the Indian Congress, whom the young Aurobindo seems to have detested.

The events of Aurobindo's life, until his retirement, thus ranged widely from run-ins with the British police, incarceration, and being accused of an attempted assassination (he was acquitted) to an invitation in 1920 to preside over the Indian Congress, which he turned down. There was also a hurried escape from Bengal to Pondicherry in French South India, just ahead of the British constabulary. There, in Pondicherry, Aurobindo founded an ashram, to which he retired in 1926, renouncing all political and public activity. The brief but intense experiences he had had with Yoga throughout his public career now became his full occupation, along with correspondence with followers on the subject of Yoga and philosophy. The ashram eventually came to be known as Auroville and to be run by a French-born woman, Mother Mirra (Mirra Alfassa), who had by then become Aurobindo's great spiritual colleague. Aurobindo died in 1950, having seen his dream of a free India become a reality in 1947.

Politics and the Eternal Dharma

Aurobindo did not invent nationalistic criticisms of Congress; his political model was Bal Gangadhar Tilak, the charismatic politician and scholar from Poona whom the leaders of Congress had labeled an extremist. Aurobindo, too, would soon be identified with the extreme party; in fact his stand against the 1905 British plan to partition Bengal along Hindu/Muslim lines earned him the title of terrorist. But one cannot suppress some bemusement at what British colonialists and entrenched politicians considered extremism at this time. The so-called extremist party had laid out a four-part program as the ground of its political agenda. At a time when Gandhi was still in South Africa, it insisted on the following: (1) Swaraj (political independence, self-rule) must come first. (2) The economic life of India must be based on Swadeshi, locally manufactured goods. (3) British products were to be boycotted—they were flooding the Indian market with artificially set prices due to the wholesale looting of Indian raw material. (4) A national educational system must displace the missionary and foreign-sponsored systems dominating Indian education.

Indian nationalism, especially in its strong or aggressive form among leaders like Tilak or Aurobindo was an unusual colonial phenomenon. India was neither a nation in the sense that European countries were nor the amorphous collection of regional, tribal, or local organizations that characterized so many other colonized societies. Instead, the previous millennium had seen an immense civilization, combining regional governments with pan-Indian systems (for example the Mughal Empire) and developing a whole range of identities, from castes and villages to regional kingdoms and all the way to a national consciousness, captured by such nineteenth-century concepts as Hindutva. Surrounding this complex picture, at least in its dominant Hindu form, was a single frame: the concept of dharma.

The root of political ideology at the end of the nineteenth century was not simply an emulation of liberal political ideals—not as far as Aurobindo was concerned. Instead, politics was the expression of *sanatana-* (eternal) *dharma*, the normative foundation of corporate identity and action. And just as dharma in Indian history has always transcended the Western distinctions between religion, law, and ethics, Aurobindo's *sanatana-dharma* was a totalistic approach to life as well:

> We shall devote ourselves not to politics alone, not to social questions
> alone, nor to theology or philosophy, or literature or science by
> themselves, but we include all these in one entity which we believe to
> be all-important, the dharma, the national religion which we also
> believe to be universal. (Heehs, p. 43)

Aurobindo insisted that nation-building was not a mechanical process but a spiritual one. This may not have resonated with the liberal philosophy of political progressives or with the socialist values that other politicians, including M. G. Ranade, G. K. Gokhale, and Nehru, upheld. And, of course, the unfolding of historic events did not resonate with the dharma that framed Aurobindo's discourse.

But ultimately, Aurobindo was a mystic, and the philosophy of *sanatana-dharma* spilled into the domains of mysticism and spiritual evolution rather than a pragmatic social and political program. As Aurobindo grew older, he began to argue that *sanatana-dharma* was not a nationalistic force but a universal, world-embracing one: "This *sanatana dharma* has many scriptures, Veda, Vedanta, Gita, Upanishad, Darshana, Purana, Tantra, nor could it reject the Bible or the Koran; but its real, most authoritative scripture is in the heart in which the Eternal has His dwelling" (Heehs, p. 45). In other words, although Aurobindo began his public career as a spokesman for a strong nationalistic cause, he eventually moved on to a far broader agenda. Due to his experiences in Yoga, with which he began to experiment virtually full-time, politics in the narrow sense ceased to interest him. His new agenda proceeded along three major new lines:

- The primacy of knowledge derived from yogic experience
- The discovery of spiritual evolution in Hindu religious history
- The integration of religious life as its final goal

All of these can be taken as a single program broadly designated by Aurobindo as Integral Yoga.

Aurobindo's Thought

Aurobindo began to practice Yoga in 1905, but his practice deepened while he was spending a year in a British jail in 1908–9 awaiting trial on charges of terrorism. He became a dedicated and advanced adept at Hatha Yoga and reported a number of extraordinary experiences. Hatha Yoga owes its origins to the ancient system of Patanjali but was developed in its more technical and meditative aspects by Gorakhnath and his followers between the ninth and thirteenth centuries. The goal of Hatha Yoga (Yoga of Force) was *jivanmukti,* or the liberation of the embodied soul in the present life. The primary methods included a disciplined regimen of physical postures (*asanas*) and the control of breath (*pranayama*).

This practical and experimental meditative technique was based on phys-iological theories that have become the staples of both Yoga and Tantra ter-minology in Hinduism and that Aurobindo deeply respected. At the most basic level, the human body included, in addition to the gross anatomy, a subtle body (*sukshma sharira*). Along its central axis ran channels of energy (*prana-nadi*), from the base of the perineum (*mula-chakra*) up to the crown of the head. The purpose of meditation, according to many of the texts that prescribed various forms of Yoga, was to free up the energy (*prana*) that coursed through the channels, allowing it to "uncoil" and move through increasingly rarefied centers (chakras).

The physiological theories often relied on cosmological language. The most famous terms described the action of the goddess Kundalini as she moves up through the chakras until she unites with Shiva at the top of the head. In his writings, Aurobindo explicitly identified himself with the principle of *purusha*, the eternal complement of *prakriti*. Taken from the cosmology of Samkhya Yoga (see chapters 6 and 7) this idea acknowledged the unity of two fundamental coeternal principles as the true nature of reality. The Divine Mother and the Supreme Lord are the foundations; he remains passive: "I am the witness Purusha; I am silent, detached, not bound by any of these things" (Heehs, p. 334). The Divine Mother, in contrast, which Aurobindo identified with his female assistant, Mirra Alfassa, is active in service of the Lord and in relation to the world. She is a mediator, dynamic, active. Sometimes Aurobindo called her Shakti, at other times Maya.

Aurobindo was not a philosopher like Shankara or Kumarila, and his thinking was not primarily interpretive. In fact, he often expressed loathing for thinking as a source of knowledge. But he was an avid student of his own tradition, and his reading of Hinduism grounded his intuition that the human spirit was evolving. He recognized several major steps in that process, and analyzed these in terms of distinct Hindu literary traditions, as follows.

The Vedas

The idea and experience of the divine at this early stage comes to "physical man" through his "natural faith." The symbolic and ritual expressions of this religious phase represent a natural mediation between the human and the divine. But this system is esoteric: "For the Veda is full of words which, as the Rishis themselves express it, are secret words that give their inner meaning only to the seer" (Heehs, p. 73).

The Upanishads

Religious insight moves inward, from the natural symbols of the Vedas to a more direct spiritual truth. At the same time, this knowledge, namely of the One, opens up to a wider population, including members of all the upper castes.

The Puranas

The pantheon and mythology of the Puranas have often been characterized by Europeans as degraded forms of the earlier, lofty traditions. According to Aurobindo, this is a failure to understand that the new theology "expressed a deeper truth and a larger range of religious experience, an intenser feeling, a vaster idea" (Heehs, p. 81) That idea, readily accessible to those who are willing to observe, is the truth of the One in its many aspects. The trinity of the Puranic gods (Brahma, Vishnu, Shiva) is neither an amalgam of gods nor competing visions of God but a lesson in the pluralistic manifestation of one transcendent unity.

For Aurobindo, the lesson of the One and the many was not primarily theological, however. It was practical—one discipline and many techniques, or the three faces of a single Integral Yoga. The scriptural source of this idea was, of course, the *Bhagavad Gita*. The great achievement of that text was to recognize the compatibility of human engagement in the world with a deep commitment to spiritual goals. The *Gita* attempts "to reconcile and even effect a kind of unity between the inner spiritual truth in its most absolute and integral realization and the outer actualities of man's life and action (Heehs, p. 105).

Conclusion

Rammohun Roy, Mohandas Gandhi, and Aurobindo Ghose represent three distinct modernizing impulses, each responding to colonialism and nationalism in its own way. Roy and Gandhi advocated a universal philosophy and ethic based on Advaita Vedanta. Roy called his God Brahman, and Gandhi preferred the popular North Indian Ram. But both men shared a blind spot: they oversimplified Hinduism and internalized the dismissive and uninformed colonial (missionary) critique of India's pluralistic devotional and ritual traditions.

Aurobindo Ghose refused to collapse the entire tradition into a single presentable philosophy, like those men whom he called "fanatics of the absolute." His notion of spiritual evolution did not reject popular forms of worship as idolatry but accepted them as diverse forms of a hidden truth. Still, evolution implies a teleological judgment of India's religious history, and one cannot avoid the impression that the standard, the telos, toward which Aurobindo's evolution is conceived to move was the product of an India that was dominated by a foreign power.

Conclusion

I teach a seminar on pluralism with a focus on Hinduism at George-town University, which is located in Washington, D.C. Students—in one case, 22 Christians and one Jew—are required to visit the area's Hindu temples: Sri Siva Visnu Temple, Durga Temple, and others. None of these students has ever seen, let alone attended, Hindu services. Invariably they are struck by the rich sensory effects of the temples, by the rituals, even the by women's saris. The students introduce themselves and strike up conversations with Hindu visitors. They have read a number of excellent books on the Hindu diaspora (by Joanne Waghorne, Corrine Dempsey, Diana Eck, and others) and have interviewed a number of Hindu students at Georgetown. They write a final paper and report on their impressions in class. The Hinduism they describe encountering in the metropolitan D.C. area is vibrant and prosperous. It is also monotheistic and scientific.

They report that when they inquire about the identify of all those gods at the Sri Siva Visnu Temple—over one dozen—the answer they receive is usually quite sensible: The Vishnu and Shiva and Lakshmi and Parvati and all the rest, these are simply aspects of one true God—Brahman. Moreover, the elaborate rituals (*puja, arti, abhishekam,* and many others), the colors, the geometrical shapes, all of it is merely a traditional expression of an ancient system of knowledge that is perfectly harmonious with subatomic particle physics and quantum psychology. It turns out, almost as a matter of rule, that the students' guide is an engineer, physicist, or mathematician.

Occasionally he's a physician. Later, in class, students ask me which version of Hinduism is the correct one: the one they heard at the temple or the one they studied in class.

What they heard in class was not a single thing. After all, the *Rig-Veda* contains many accounts of creation, the tradition of Smriti had several codes of law, there were several sacred centers of pilgrimage, competing philosophies. There were even many different types of monotheism in what we now call "Hinduism." Indeed, it has been a very long time, well over two millennia, since someone in India (the authors of a few Upanishads) began to reduce the many religious views they were familiar with to one single truth. But this did not result in a single, unified tradition. Those ancient monists seldom wedded their discovery to the reigning political power of the day, so no machinery kicked into gear to eliminate "wrong" views. As a result, India's larger compendia—the *Mahabharata, Arthashastra, Brihat Samhita, Markandeya Purana,* and other texts—read more like encyclopedias or gazettes than sacred accounts of God's singular plan for the world. The philosopher's single view of reality continued to coexist along with the pluralistic one.

This openness began to change with the arrival of Islam and early modern administrations. Alberuni's splendid chronicle of India ridiculed the religion of the masses—he wrote his work under the auspices of the eleventh-century Muslim invader Mahmud of Ghazni, the "Idol Breaker" and enemy of heretics. Centuries later, British missionaries arrived in India, sponsored by colonial administrators and tax collectors. Monothematic and nationalistic Hinduism emerged not just in response to the theological derision of the missionaries but as the organic product of the newborn colonial administrative entity called India. This was true not only in trailblazing Bengal but throughout India. For example, the eminent Maharashtrian scholar-politicians— B. G. Tilak, M. G. Ranade, V. K. Rajwade, V. D. Savarkar, R. G. Bhandarkar—literally forged a sense of national identity (Aryan or Hindu, in both cases Brahmin) in the process of researching India's past.

There is a striking difference between the ancient monistic views of India and the early modern and contemporary versions of monothematic apology. The authors of the Upanishads, of the *Bhagavad Gita,* of the *Devi Mahatmya,* and even Shankara himself were creative monists and theologians. They were aware of other ways of understanding reality and of other gods. In response, they developed intellectual strategies to encompass, subsume, rename, identify, and underlie the other traditions within their own. Krishna *is* Maha Purusha, the supreme Vedic spirit, or *is* the Unmanifest, the transcendent Brahman. The others do not lose their existence but now reveal another dimension. Similarly, Devi *is*, in fact, the essence of all the other gods, their most subtle form, their light, their very being. The gods do not cease to exist, but we now acquire a loftier knowledge about them. Even Shankara, the ultimate monist, argued on the basis of scriptural interpretation; he accepted the (theistic) Vedic tradition as the foundation of ultimate knowledge.

Modern monists allowed Islam and Christianity, along with the political exigencies of empire, to turn them into reductionists. Roy and Gandhi both decried "idolatry" (polytheism and devotional rituals) or accepted it at best as a nod to the uneducated masses. So had Kabir centuries earlier. Had either of these men closely read Purva Mimamsa philosophy (or Tantric and Yoga psychologies) they might have changed their views. But Chaitanya, Tulsidas, and Aurobindo were not historians or professional philosophers either, and they refused to reduce all things to One or the world to Spirit. They kept alive the sense of mystery that cannot be dissipated by the logic of either/or: either God or world, either One or many, either me or you. Like Roy and Gandhi (or the Maharashtrian historians), their knowledge was also profoundly political, but it has a different, a mixed, flavor.

This politics of knowledge—postcolonialism is a dominant intellectual program today—persists in the Hinduism my students have encountered in suburban Washington, D.C. The difference is that nationalism and resistance have turned into matters of suburban prestige. In Fairfax County, Virginia, and Montgomery County, Maryland, the parents of Hindu public school students have demanded that the textbooks be changed to reflect more Indocentric views of the Aryan migration theory (that it had never happened), downplay the caste system, and so forth. The growing size of the suburban Indian community (overwhelmingly upper caste) calls for the same respect that the Christian and Jewish communities command. Such an American agenda generates a singular syllabus of India's history and religions.

In a different vein, the scientific understanding of temple rituals—Corinne Dempsey describes this in some detail at the temple in Rush, New York—has an extremely long pedigree. In fact, it connects the suburban engineer in the Washington, D.C., area with the Brahmins who performed or attended the Vedic rituals. It was they who invented elaborate verbal and mathematical codes to conceal the mysterious connections between the ritual and the cosmos. Ancient mathematics, geometry, astronomy (and astrology), grammar, and other scientific disciplines developed around the sacred rituals. These systems of knowledge, as this book has shown, linked in a rational manner the facts of the visible world with ultimate reality. This is the second of Vishnu's three strides: the scientific mesocosm.

In all likelihood, the engineer does not know this; it is not part of any curriculum. Instead, he sounds a bit like fundamentalist Christians and Jews for whom scripture and science are mutually reinforcing. But his is a different case, because here the science is so often particle physics, quantum mechanics, and advanced cosmological theory and converges with religion only as two lines that meet at the horizon—an abstract realm where matter and energy dissolve into each other or into "Brahman." There is no literal creationism here or a search for empirical evidence of God's miraculous handiwork in the Bible. (There are exceptions; the most frequently heard, perhaps, is the reference to satellite images of a sub-oceanic ridge between India and Lanka, which some Hindus describe as Rama's ancient causeway.) Instead, there is a synthesis, in a broad intellectual sense, between the ancient ritual and verbal formulas (mantras) and a cutting-edge understanding of the world. It is a modern *bandhu*. Some do it poorly, some well; some (Deepak Chopra, Fritjof Capra) make a lot of money at it, while others (Templeton Foundation) throw a lot of money at such projects.

Unfortunately, the result is both poor science and a limited scholarship of the tradition. Both science and Indology become teleological, each providing the other with a mutually reinforcing goal. My own personal belief, I tell the pluralism seminar students, is that the impressive diversity of India, local and pan-Indian, conceptual and social, has something valuable to teach us. I still do not fully know what that lesson is, but it can only emerge out of an open enquiry.

Bibliography

Agrawal, Ashvini. *Rise and Fall of the Imperial Guptas*. Delhi: Motilal Banarsidass, 1989.

Agrawala, Vasudeva. *Matsya Purana—A Study*. Varnasi: All India Kashiraj, 1963.

Ahaman, Aziz. *Studies in Islamic Culture in the Indian Environment*. New Delhi: Oxford University Press, 1999.

Ali, Daud, ed. *Invoking the Past: The Uses of History in South Asia*. New Delhi: Oxford University Press, 1999.

Alston, A. J. *The Devotional Poems of Mirabai*. Delhi: Motilal Banarsidass, 1980.

Amma, T. A. Sarasvati. *Geometry in Ancient and Medieval India*. Delhi: Motilal Banarsidass, 1979.

Asha, Vishnu. *Material Life of Northern India Based on an Archaeological Study*. New Delhi: Mittal, 1993.

Bailey, Gregory. "The Puranas: A Study in the Development of Hinduism." In *The Study of Hinduism*, ed. Arvind Sharma, 137–68. Columbia: University of South Carolina Press, 2003.

Bakshi, S. R. *Gandhi and Hindu-Muslim Unity*. New Delhi: Deep and Deep, 1987.

Bhardwaj, Surindar Mohan. *Hindu Places of Pilgrimage in India*. Berkeley: University of California Press, 1973.

Bhat, G. K. *Bharata-Natya-Manjari: Bharata: On the Theory and Practice of Drama*. Poona: Bhandarkar Oriental Research Institute, 1975.

———. *Theatric Aspects of Sanskrit Drama*. Poona: Bhandarkar Oriental Research Institute, 1983.

Bhat, M. Ramakrishna, tr. *Varahamihira's Brhat-Samhita*. 3 pts. Delhi: Motilal Banarsidass, 1981.

Bhat, M. S. *Vedic Tantrism: A Study of Rgvidhana of Saunaka with Text and Translation*. Delhi: Motilal Banarsidass, 1987.

Bhattacharya, N. N. *History of the Tantric Religion*. New Delhi: Manoharlal, 1982.

———. *The Indian Mother Goddess*. New Delhi: Manohar, 1999.

Biswas, C. C. *Bengal's Response to Gandhi*. Kolkata: Minerva, 2004.

Bloomfield, Maurice. *Hymns of the Atharva-Veda*. New York: Greenwood Press, 1969.

Bosch, F. D. K. *The Golden Germ: An Introduction to Indian Symbolism*. Deventer, Holland: Moutaon, 1960.

Bryant, Edwin F., and Lauri L. Patton, eds. *The Indo-Aryan Controversy: Evidence and Inference in Indian history*. Oxon: Routledge, 2005.

Callewaert, Winand M. *The Hagiographies of Anantadas: The Bhakti Poets of North India*. Richmond, Surrey, England: Curzon Press, 2000.

Cardona, George. *Panini: His Work and Its Traditions*. Vol. 1. *Background and Introduction*. 2nd ed. Delhi: Motilal Banarsidass, 1997.

Chakrabarti, Dilip K. *A History of Indian Archaeology. New Classical and Mediaeval India*. Wiesbaden: Franz.

Chatterjee, Partha, ed. *Texts of Power: Emerging Disciplines in Colonial Bengal*. Minneapolis: University of Minnesota Press, 1995.

Chattopadhyaya, B. D. "Mathura from the Sunga to the Kusana Period: An Historical Outline." In Srinivasan, *Mathura*, 19–27.

Clooney, Francis. *Thinking Ritually: Rediscovering of The Purva Mimamsa of Jaimini*. Vienna: De Nobili, 1990.

———. *Theology after Vedanta: An Experiment in Comparative Theology*. Albany: State University of New York Press, 1993.

Coburn, Thomas B. *Encountering the Goddess: A Translation of the Devi Mahatmya and a Study of Its Interpretation*. Albany: State University of New York Press, 1991.

Coomaraswamy, Ananda K. *Yaksas: Essays in Water Cosmology*. New Delhi: Oxford University Press, 1993.

Coward, Harold, ed. *Indian Critiques of Gandhi*. Albany: State University of New York Press, 2003.

Cronk, George. *On Shankara*. Boston: Thomson Wadsworth, 2003.

Czuma, Stanislaw, J. *Kushan Sculpture: Images from Early India*. Cleveland: Cleveland Museum of Art, 1985.

Dar, Saifur Rahman. *Taxila and the Western World*. Lahore: Library and Information Management Academy, 1998.

Das, Kalyani. *Early Inscriptions of Mathura—A Study*. Calcutta: Punthi Pustak, 1980.

Deutsch, Eliot, and J. A. B. van Buitenen, eds. *A Source Book of Advaita Vedanta*. Honolulu: University of Hawaii Press, 1971.

Dhavalikar, M. K. *Masterpieces of Rashtrakuta Art: The Kailas*. Bombay: Taraparevala, 1983.

Dimock, Edward C., tr. *Caitanya Caritamrta of Krsnadasa Kaviraja*. Cambridge, Mass.: Harvard University Press, 1999.

Diwedi, R. C., ed. *Studies in Mimamsa: Dr. Mandan Mishra Felicitation Volume*. Delhi: Motilal Banarsidass, 1994.

Doniger, Wendy ed. *Purana Perennis: Reciprocity and Transformation in Hindu and Jaina Texts*. Albany: State University of New York Press, 1993.

Doniger, Wendy, and Brian K. Smith, trs. *The Laws of Manu*. London: Penguin Classics, 1991.

Dubey, D. P. *Prayaga: The Site of Kumbha Mela*. New Delhi: Aryan Books International, 2001.

Eaton, Richard M., ed. *India's Islamic Traditions 711– 1750*. New Delhi: Oxford University Press, 2003.

Eggeling, Julius, tr. *The Satapatha Brahmana According to The Text of The Madhyandina School*. Delhi: Motilal Banarsidass, 1963.

Elizarenkova, Tatyana, J. *Language and Style of the Vedic Rsis*. Albany: State University of New York Press, 1995.

Elliot, H. M., and Dowson, J. *History of India as Told by Its Own Historians*. 8 vols. Allahabad: Kitab Mahal, 1963.

Filliozat, Pierre-Sylvain. *The Sanskrit Language: An Overview*. Translated by T. K. Gopalan. Varanasi: Indica Books, 1992.

Fleet, John F. *Inscriptions of the Early Gupta Kings and Their Successors*. Varanasi: Indological Book House, 1970.

Fuchs, Stephen. *The Vedic Horse Sacrifice*. New Delhi: Inter-India, 1996.

Futehally, Shama. *In the Dark of the Heart: Songs of Meera*. Walnut Creek, Calif.: Alta Mira Press, 1994.

Gandhi, M. K. *Songs from Prison*. New York: Macmillan, 1934.

———. *An Autobiography: Story of My Experiments with Truth*. Boston: Beacon Press, 1965.

———. *The Collected Works of Mahatama Gandhi*. Delhi: Government of India, 1971.

Ganguly, D. K. *History and Historians in Ancient India*. New Delhi: Abhinav, 1984.

———. *Ancient India: History and Archaeology*. New Delhi: Abhinav, 1994.

Gerow, Edwin. *Indian Poetics*. Wiesbaden: Otto Harrassowitz, 1977.

Ghosh, Manomohun, tr. *The Natyasastra: Ascribed to Bharata- Muni*. 2nd ed. Calcutta: Manisha Granthalaya, 1967.

Ghosh, Nagendra Nath. *Early History of Kausambi*. Delhi: Durga, 1985.

Goetz, Hermann. *Studies in the History, Religion and Art of Classical and Mediaeval India*. Wiesbaden: Franz Steiner, 1974.

Gonda, J. *The Rgvidhana: English Translation with an Introduction and Notes*. Utrecht: N. V. A. Oosthoek's Uitgevers, 1951.

———. "Bandhu in the Brahmanas." *Adyar Library Bulletin* 29 (1965): 1–29.

———. *Aspects of Early Visnuism*. 2nd ed. Delhi: Motilal Banarsidass, 1969.

———. *Visnuism and Sivaism: A Comparison*. Jordan Lectures, 1969. London: Athlone Press, 1970.

———. *Prajapati's Rise to a Higher Rank*. Leiden: Brill, 1986.

Goyal, Shankar. *Aspects of Ancient Indian History and Historiography*. New Delhi: Harman, 1993.

———. *History of Writing of Early India: New Discoveries and Approaches*. Jodhpur: Kusumanjali Prakashan, 1996.

Habib, S. Irfan, and Dhruv Raina. *Situating the History of Science: Dialogues with Joseph Needham*. New Delhi: Oxford University Press, 1999.

Halbfass, Wilhelm, ed. *Philosophy and Confrontation: Paul Hacker on Traditional and Modern Vedanta*. Albany: State University of New York Press, 1995.

Hawley, John Stratton, and Mark Juergensmeyer. *Songs of the Saints of India*. New York: Oxford University Press, 1988.

Hazra, R. C. *Studies in the Puranic Records on Hindu Rites and Customs*. Delhi: Motilal Banarsidass, 1975.

Heehs, Peter, ed. *The Essential Writings of Sri Aurobindo*. Delhi: Oxford University Press, 1998.

Hein, Norvin. "Kalayavan: A Key to Mathura's Cultural Self- Perception." In Srinivasan, *Mathura*, 223–34.

Heesterman, J. C. *The Broken World of Sacrifice: An Essay in Ancient Indian Ritual*. Chicago: University of Chicago Press, 1993.

Hess, Linda, and Shukdev Singh. *The Bijak of Kabir*. San Francisco: North Point, 1983.

Hiltebeitel, Alf. "Krisna at Mathura." In Srinivasan, *Mathura*, 93–102.

Hultzsch, E. *Inscriptions of Asoka (Corpus Inscriptionum Indicarum)*. Delhi: Indological Book House, 1969.

Huntington, Susan L. *The Art of Ancient India: Buddhist, Hindu, Jain*. New York: Weatherhill, 1985.

Hutchins, Francis G. *Young Krishna: Translated from the Sanskrit Harivamsa*. West Franklin, N.H.: Amarta Press, 1980.

Inscriptions of Asoka (Translation and Glossary). Calcutta Sanskrit College research series no. 142. Calcutta: Sanskrit College, 1990.

Isayeva, Natalia. *Shankara and Indian Philosophy*. Albany: State University of New York Press, 1993.

Jain, Ramchandra, ed. *McCrindle's Ancient India as Described by Megasthenes and Arrian*. New Delhi: International Books, 1972.

Jaiswal, Suvira. *The Origin and Development of Vaisnavism*. Delhi: Munshiram Manoharlal, 1967.

Jayakar, Pupul. *The Earth Mother*. New Delhi: Penguin, 1989.

Jha, Ganganath. *Purva-Mimamsa in Its Sources*. Varanasi: Banaras Hindu University Press, 1964.

Johnson, Willard. *Poetry and Speculation of the Rg Veda*. Berkeley: University of California Press, 1980.

Joshi, V. C. *Rammohun Roy and the Process of Modernization in India*. Delhi: Vikas, 1975.

Kane, Pandurang Vama. *History of Dharmasastra*. 8 vols. Pune: BORI, 1970–79.

Kangle, R. P. *The Kautiliya Arthasastra*. 3 vols. Bombay: University of Bombay Press, 1965–71.

Khana, Amar Nath. *Archaeology of India: Retrospective and Prospect*. New Delhi: Clarion, 1981.

Kingsbury, F., and G. E. Philips. *Hymns of the Tamil Saivite Saints*. London: Oxford University Press, 1921.

Kinsley, David R. *The Divine Player (A Study of Krsna Lal)*. Delhi: Motilal Banarsidass, 1987.

Kopf, David. *The Brahmo Samaj and the Shaping of the Modern Indian Mind*. Princeton: Princeton University Press, 1979.

Kramrisch, Stella. *The Hindu Temple*. Vol. 1. Delhi: Motilal Banarsidass, 1976.

———. *Indian Sculpture*. Delhi: Motilal Banarsidass, 1981.

Kumar, Brajmohan. *Archaeology of Pataliputra and Nalanda*. Delhi: Ramanand Vidya Bhawan, 1987.

Lal, B. B. *The Earliest Civilization of South Asia*. New Delhi: Aryan Books International, 1997.

———. "Aryan Invasion of India: Perpetuation of a Myth." In Bryant and Patton, *Indo-Aryan Controversy*, 50–74.

Law, Bimala Churn. *Ancient Geography of India*. Delhi: Bharatiya, 1976.

———. *Historical Geography of Ancient India*. Delhi: ESS, 1976.

Lele, Jayant, ed. *Tradition and Modernity in Bhakti Movements*. Leiden: Brill, 1981.

Lorenzen, David N. *Kabir Legends and Ananta-Das's Kabir Parachai*, Albany: State University of New York Press, 1991.

———. *Tradition and the Rhetoric of Right*. Madison, N.J.: Fairleigh Dickinson University Press, 1999.

Lutgendorf, Philip. *The Life of a Text: Performing the Ramcaritmanas of Tulsidas*. Berkeley: University of California Press, 1991.

Mahony, William K. *The Artful Universe: An Introduction to the Vedic Religious Imagination*. Albany: State University of New York Press, 1998.

Maity, Sachindra Kumar. *Problems and Perspectives of Ancient Indian History and Culture*. Delhi: Abhinav, 1997.

Malkovsky, Bradley J., ed. *New Perspectives on Advaita Vedanta: Essays in Commemoration of Prof. Richard De Smet S.J.* Leiden: Brill, 2000.

McDaniel, June. *Making Virtuous Daughters and Wives*. Albany: State University of New York Press, 2003.

McDermott, Robert A., ed. *The Essential Aurobindo*. New York: Schocken Books, 1973.

Michaels, Axel. *Hinduism: Past and Present*. Princeton, N.J.: Princeton University Press, 2004.

Michell, George. *The Hindu Temple: An Introduction to Its Meaning and Forms*. Chicago: University of Chicago Press, 1988.

Miller, Barbara Stoller, ed. *Theater of Memory: The Plays of Kalidasa*. New York: Columbia University Press, 1984.

Miller, Daniel. *Artefacts as Categories: A Study of Ceramic Variability in Central India*. Cambridge: Cambridge University Press, 1985.

Minor, Robert N. *The Religious, the Spiritual and the Secular: Auroville and Secular India*. Albany: State University of New York Press, 1999.

Modak, B. R. *The Ancillary Literature of the Atharvaveda*. New Delhi: Rashtriya Veda Vidya Pratisthan, 1993.

Morinis, Alan E. *Pilgrimage in the Hindu Tradition: A Case Study of West Bengal*. Delhi: Oxford University Press, 1984.

Mukherjee, B. N. "Growth of Mathura and Its Society." In Srinivasan, *Mathura*, 61–68.

Mukta, Parita. *Upholding the Common Life: The Community of Mirabai*. Delhi: Oxford University Press, 1994.

Nakamura, Hajime. *A History of Early Vedanta Philosophy*. Pt. 1. Delhi: Motilal Banarsidass, 1983.

Nanda, B. R. *Gandhi: Pan-Islamism, Imperialism and Nationalism in India*. Bombay: Oxford University Press, 1989.

O'Flaherty, Wendy Doniger, tr. *The Rig-Veda: An Anthology*. Harmondsworth, England: Penguin, 1984.

Oldenberg, Hermann. *The Doctrine of the Upanishads and Early Buddhism*. Translated by Shridhar B. Shrotri. Delhi: Motilal Banarsidass, 1991.

Oldenberg, Hermann, tr. *The Grihya-sutras*. Delhi: Motilal, 1964.

Olivelle, Patrick, tr. *Upanisads*. New York: Oxford University Press, 1998.

———. *Dharmasutras: The Law Codes of Ancient India*. Oxford: Oxford World Classics, 1999.

Paddaya, K. *The New Archaeology and Aftermath: A View from Outside the Anglo-American World*. Pune: Ravish, 1990.

———. "Theoretical Perspectives in Indian Archaeology: An Historical Review." In *Theory in Archaeology: A World Perspective*, ed. Peter J. Ucko, 110–50. London: Routledge, 1995.

Pande, Anupa. *The Natyasastra Tradition and Ancient Indian Society*. Jodhpur: Kusumanjali Prakashan, 1993.

Pandit, M. D. *Zero in Panini*. Pune: University of Poona, 1990.

Pannikar, Raimundo. *The Vedic Experience: Mantramanjari*. Berkeley: University of California Press, 1977.

Patton, Laurie L. *Bringing the God to Mind: Mantra and Ritual in Early Indian Sacrifice*. Berkeley: University of California Press, 2005.

Phillips, Stephen H. *Classical Indian Metaphysics: Refutations of Realism and the Emergence of "New Logic."* Chicago: Open Court, 1995.

Piatigorsky, Alexandre. "The Philosophy of the Bhagavad Gita." In *The Bhagavad Gita*, tr. J. A. B. Van Buitenen, 3–12. Rockport, Mass.: Element Press, 1997.

Radhakrishnan, S., tr. *The Brahma Sutra: The Philosophy of Spiritual Life*. New York: Greenwood, 1968.

Rahman, A., ed. *History of Indian Science, Technology and Culture AD 1000–1800*. New Delhi: Oxford University Press, 1999.

Rajan, K. V. Sundaran. *Mechanics of City and Village in Ancient India*. Delhi: Sundeep Prakashan, 1986.

Ray, Priyadaranjan, and Hirendra Nath Gupta. *Charaka Samhita (A Scientific Synopsis)*. New Delhi: Indian National Science Academy, 1980.

Robertson, Bruce Carlisle, ed. *The Essential Writings of Raja Rammohan Ray*. Delhi: Oxford University Press, 1999.

Rocher, Ludo. *A History of Indian Literature: The Puranas*. Wiesbaden: Otto Harrasowitz, 1986.

Roer, Dr. E. *Brhadaranyaka-Upanisad*. Delhi: Bharatiya Kala Prakashan, 2000.

Sachau, Edward C., tr., *Alberuni's India*. Abr. ed. New York: Norton, 1971.

Sadaka, Akira. *Buddhist Cosmology: Philosophy and Origins*. Tokyo: Kosei, 1998.

Saeed, Mian Muhammad. *The Sharqi Sultanate of Jaunpur*. Karachi: University of Karachi Press, 1972.

Sankalia, H. D. *New Archaeology: Its Scope and Application to India*. Lucknow: Ethnographic and Folk Culture Society, 1977.

———. *Indian Archaeology Today*. Delhi: Ajanta, 1979.

Sarma, Sriram, ed. *Matsya Purana*. Bareli: Samskriti Samsthana, 1970.

Sarasvati, Svami Satya Prakash. *Geometry in Ancient India*. Delhi: Govindaram Hasanand, 1987.

Sastri, Mahendra, and K. Rangacarya, eds. *Taittiriya Samhita of the Black Yajurveda*. Delhi: Motilal Banarsidass, 1986.

Sen, S. N., R. Kumar, and D. P. Chattopadhyaya, eds. *Science, Philosophy and Culture in Historical Perspective*. New Delhi: Project of History of Indian Science, Philosophy and Culture, 1995.

Sethi, V. K. *Mira: The Divine Lover*. Punjab, India: Radha Soami Satsang Beas, 1988.

Sharma, G. R. *The Excavations at Kausambi (1957–59)*. Allahabad: Allahabad University Press, 1960.

———. *Excavations at Kausambi 1949–50*. Delhi: Manager of Publications, 1969.

Sharma, Peri Sarveswara, ed. *Anthology of Kumarilabhatta's Works*. Delhi: Motilal Banarsidass, 1980.

Sharma, R. K., and Bhagawan Dash. *Charaka Samhita*. 4 vols. Varanasi: Chowkamba, 1983.

Sharma, S. R. *The Crescent in India*. Delhi: Sanjay Prakashan, 1986.

Shende, N. J. *The Religion and Philosophy of the Atharvaveda*. Poona: BORI, 1985.

Sinha, B. P., and Lala Aditya Narain. *Pataliputra Excavation 1955–56*. Patna, Bihar: Directorate of Archeology and Museums, 1970.

Smith, Brian K. *Reflections on Resemblance, Ritual and Religion*. New York: Oxford University Press, 1989.

———. *Classifying the Universe: The Ancient Indian Varna System and the Origins of Caste*. New York: Oxford University Press, 1994.

Srinivasa Iyenger, K. R. *Sri Aurobindo: A Biography and a History*. Pondicherry: Sri Aurobindo International Center, 1972.

Srinivasan, Doris Meth. *Mathura: The Cultural Heritage*. New Delhi: American Institute of Indian Studies, 1989.

Srivastava, K. M. *New Era of Indian Archaeology*. Vol. 1. Delhi: Cosmo, 1982.

Srivastava, Kanhaiya Lall. *The Position of Hindus under the Delhi Sultanate 1206–1526*. New Delhi: Munshiram Manoharlal, 1980.

Staal, Frits. *Agni: The Vedic Ritual of the Fire Altar*. Berkeley: Asian Humanities Press, 1983.

Sutherland, Gail Hinich. *The Disguises of the Demon: The Development of the Yaksa in Hinduism and Buddhism*. Albany: State University of New York Press, 1991.

Taluqdar of Oudh, tr. *Matsya Purana*. New York: AMS Press, 1974.

Tendulkar, D. G. *Mahatma: Life of Mohandas Karamchand Gandhi*. 12 vols. Bombay: Ministry of Information, 1951–54.

Thapar, Romila. *Cultural Pasts: Essays in Early Indian History*. New Delhi: Oxford University Press, 2000.

———. *Early India: From the Origins to AD 1300*. Berkeley: University of California Press, 2003.

Thibaut, G. *Mathematics in the Making in Ancient India* Edited and translated by Debiprasad Chattopadhyaya. Calcutta: Baghchi, 1984. (Originally published as *On the Sulvasutras and Baudhayana Sulvasutra*)

Thomas, Julian. *Time, Culture and Identity: An Interpretive Archaeology*. London: Routledge, 1996.

Tripathi, Radha Vallabh. *Lectures on the Natya Sastra*. Pune: Centre of Advanced Study in Sanskrit, 1991.

Tripathi, Rishi Raj. *Master Pieces in the Allahabad Museum*. Allahabad: Allahabad Museum, 1984.

Van Buitenen, J. A. B., tr. *The Bhagavadgita*. Rockport, Mass.: Element, 1997.

Vaudeville, Charlotte. *Kabir*. Vol. 1. Oxford: Clarendon Press, 1974.

———. *A Weaver Named Kabir*. Delhi: Oxford University Press, 1997.

Volwahsen, Andreas. *Living Architecture: Indian*. New York: Grosset and Dunlap, 1969.

Watters, Thomas. *On Yuan Chwang's Travels in India 629–645 A.D.* 2 vols. London: Royal Asiatic Society, 1904.

Wheeler, Mortimer. *My Archaeological Mission to India and Pakistan*. London: Thames and Hudson, 1976.

White, David Gordon. *The Alchemical Body: Siddha Traditions in Medieval India*. Chicago: University of Chicago Press, 1996.

Williams, Joanna Gottfried. *The Art of Gupta India: Empire and Province*. Princeton, N.J.: Princeton University Press, 1982.

Witz, Klaus G. *The Supreme Wisdom of the Upanishads*. Delhi: Motilal Banarsidass, 1998.

Witzel, Michael. "Indocentrism: Autochtonous Visions of Ancient India." In Bryant and Patton, *Indo-Aryan Controversy*, 341–404.

Wujastyk, Dominik. *The Roots of Ayurveda*. New Delhi: Penguin Books, 1998.

Zelliot, Eleanor. *Untouchable Saints: An Indian Phenomenon*. Delhi: Manohar, 2005.

Index